Pleasures of the
GARDEN

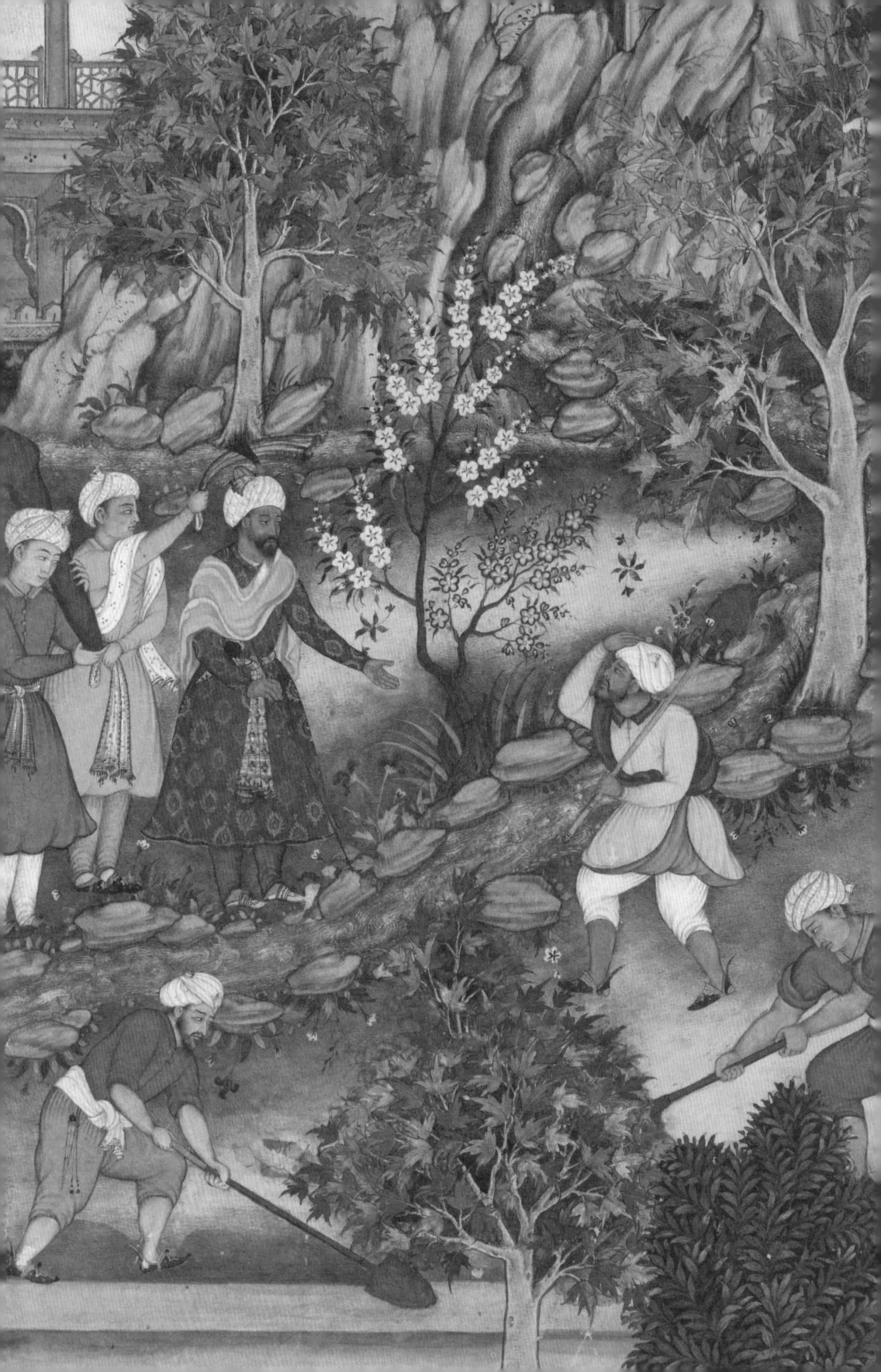

Pleasures of the
GARDEN

A LITERARY ANTHOLOGY

selected by
Christina Hardyment

The British Library

CONTENTS

3 Practical Gardening 111

4 Solace for Body and Soul 165

INTRODUCTION

Pleasure taken in gardens, whether in creation or recreation, has been recorded ever since storytelling began. Ancient Egyptians, Babylonian kings and Chinese sages all treasured their gardens. The Bible makes the Garden of Eden the first home of mankind, and the theme of the garden as an echo of Paradise recurs to the present day in Tim Smit's Eden Project, set in the old china clay quarries of Cornwall.

The wealthy cut themselves off from the world in their gardens; the poor and eco-minded sustain life in them. Herb gardens were the cradle of medicine, and John Gerard, author of the first great *Herbal*, was an Elizabethan doctor. The garden has been an escape from the frustrations of working life for centuries. 'The weary bird seeks its nest again,' exclaims a fourth-century Chinese official as he sips a glass of wine and contemplates his chrysanthemums. Gardening 'makes all our senses swim in pleasure, and that with infinite variety,' writes a sixteenth-century Yorkshire vicar. 'No occupation is so delightful to me as the culture of the earth, and no culture comparable to that of the garden,' notes the third American President, Thomas Jefferson.

The first printed book about gardening was Thomas Hyll's *A most brief and pleasant treatise teaching how to dress, sow and set a garden* (1558). Yet he was far from being the first horticultural author. In the first century AD, Pliny the Younger wrote long letters describing the elaborate layouts of the gardens around his many Italian villas. Walafrid Strabo offered still helpful practical tips on the layout of a ninth-century herb garden in his *Hortulus (The Little Garden)*; and the anonymous French author of *The Romance of the Rose* conjured up a thirteenth-century paradise in which his lovers wander.

There are four themes in this anthology. The first is love – not only the love of gardens expressed by men and women of all sorts (plantsmen such as John Gerard and the Reverend William Lawson; statesmen

from Sir Francis Bacon to Thomas Jefferson; novelists including Jane
Austen and Mary Russell Mitford) – but also love, both imaginary and
real, found and lost *in* gardens, recorded by writers as varied as Thomas
Malory, John Donne, Charlotte Brontë and W. B. Yeats.

The second theme is garden design – another activity older than
recorded history. This theme begins with the Hanging Gardens of
Babylon, opens a secret door into the private garden that Robert
Dudley, Earl of Leicester created for Elizabeth I at Kenilworth Castle,
hears Alexander Pope scoffing at topiary and glorifying grottoes, mean-
ders around the artfully natural landscapes of the eighteenth century,
includes a diatribe by William Morris on the 'carpet-gardening'
beloved of the Victorians, and ends with an inspiring plan by Gertrude
Jekyll for a scented garden that lasts all year round.

Next come practical considerations: a cornucopia of information
that remains useful today, beginning with an ancient Chinese poem
and moving on to the importance of the dung barrow and the watering
can. John Evelyn tells us exactly how best to root-prune orange trees
and refresh the soil around indoor plants; Thomas Jefferson notes the
progress of his plants on a daily basis, and begs rarities from plant-loving
friends. The poet William Cowper offers a recipe in purple prose for
a 'stercoraceous' heap of compost, ideal for growing cucumbers. We
salute too some outstandingly memorable professional gardeners: that
'finished grower of the plum' James Phillips of Erddig; Robert Louis
Stevenson's uncompromising Robert ('a Don Quixote who had come
through the training of the Covenant'); and the redoubtable bloomer-
clad women who worked at Kew Gardens in the 1890s.

Fourthly, we explore the ways in which gardening offers solace to
the soul. A garden teaches many things: patience, according to Bunyan;
philosophical resignation, according to Voltaire. In it a dejected bricklayer can reflect on unfulfilled youthful promise and a bishop can find
a lesson about gallantry in the face of death. The poet Swinburne
mourns lost roses and lovers in one forsaken garden; Frances Hodgson
Burnett finds hope for the future in another; and D. H. Lawrence
marvels at God 'cudgelling his mighty brain' to create the intensely
sensuous red geranium. The coda of the anthology celebrates how I
composed it – in a garden studying books about gardens – by praising
the delights of the garden as library.

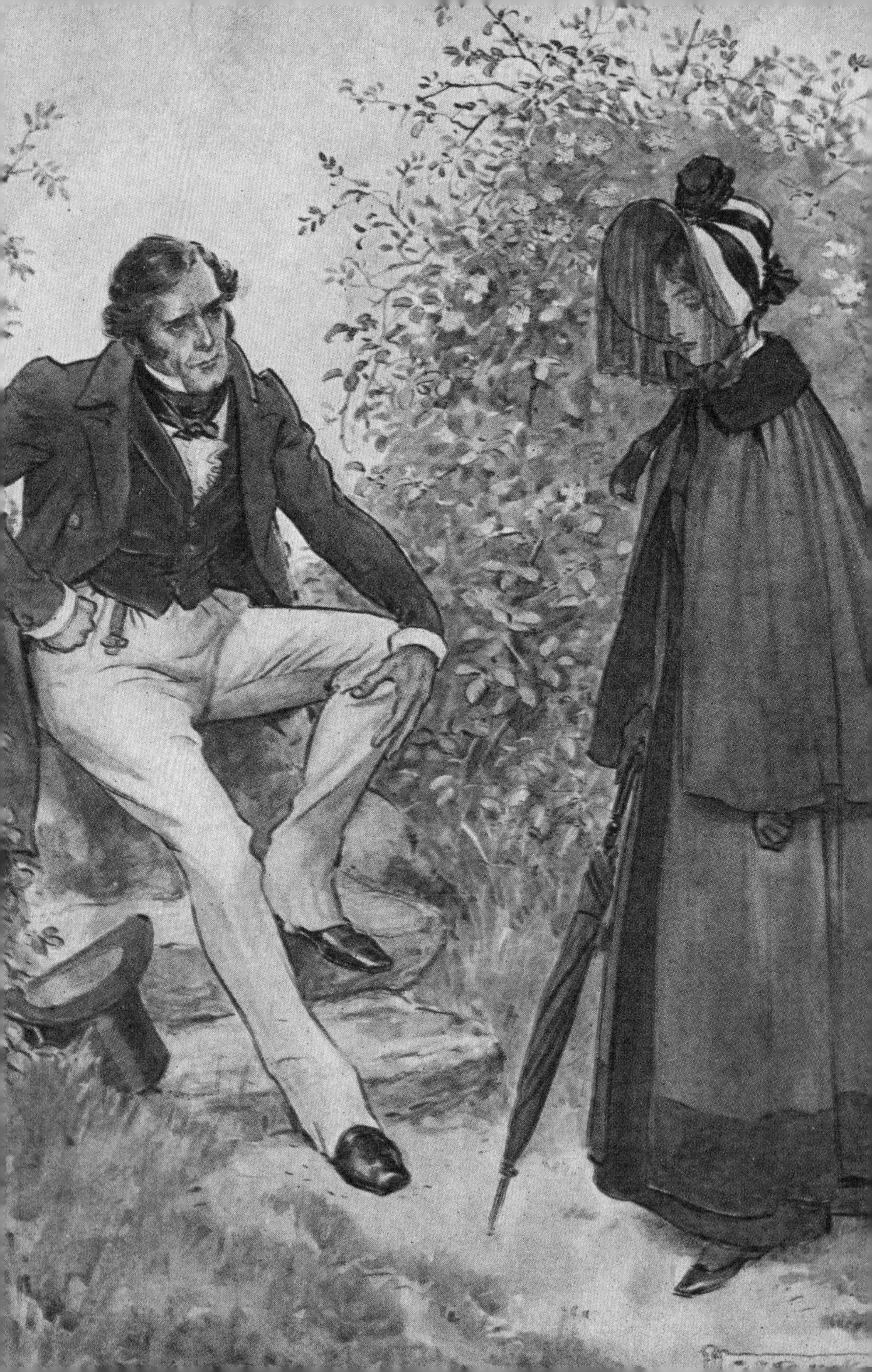

1 Lovers of Gardens and Lovers in Gardens

From ancient times to the present, gardens have been loved for the pleasure they provide; they have also made the perfect settings for romance. Philosophers and naturalists, poets and novelists unite in their praise.

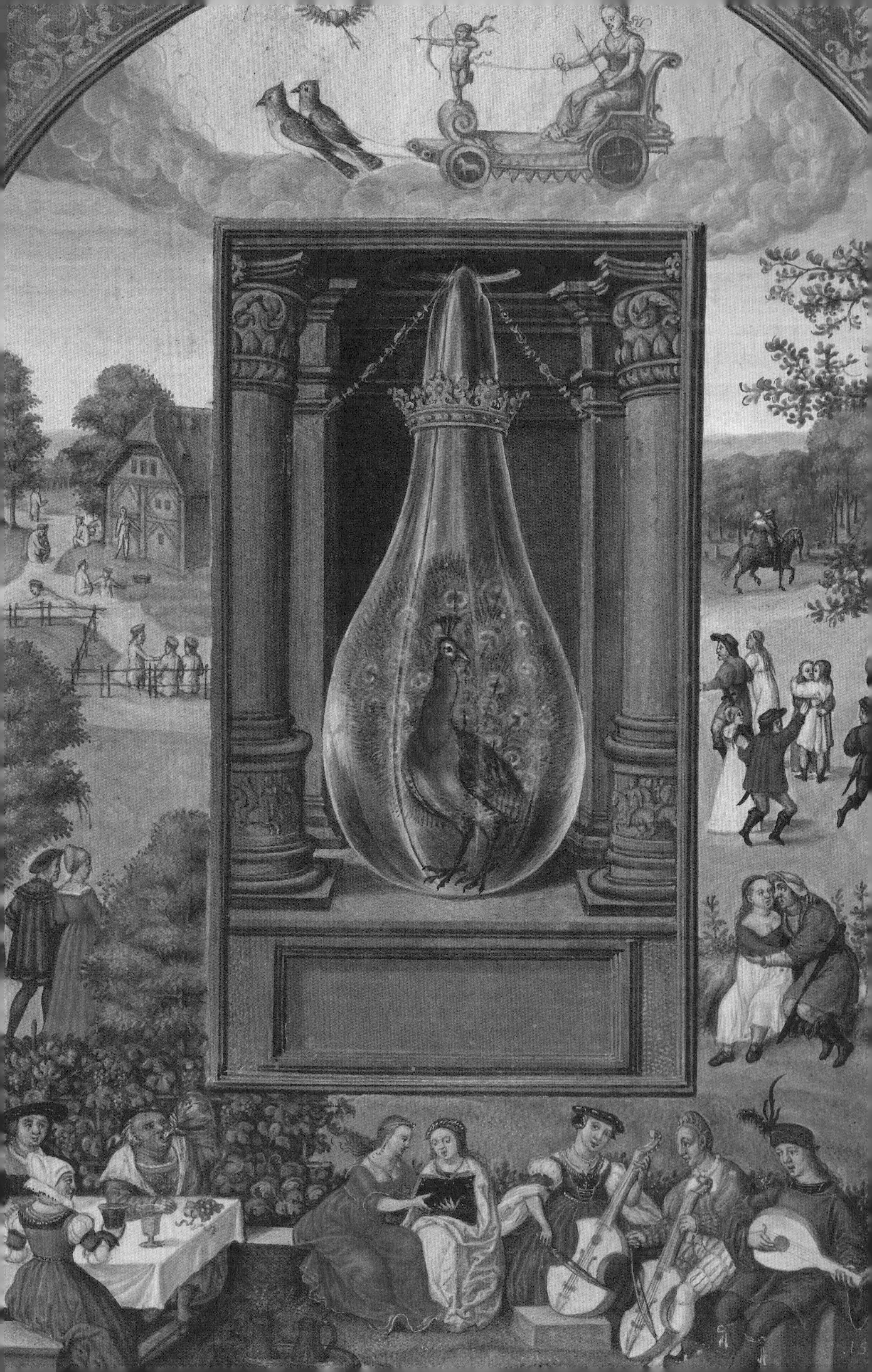

❧ Paradise Made

Then God said Let the earth produce fresh growth, let there be on earth plants bearing seed, fruit trees bearing fruit each with seed according to its kind.

Then the Lord God planted a garden in Eden away to the east, and there he put the man whom he had formed. The Lord God made trees spring from the ground, all trees pleasant to look at and good for food; and in the middle of the garden he set the tree of life and the tree of the knowledge of good and evil.

Genesis chapters 1, 2

The world can brag of no more ancient Monument than Paradise and the garden of Eden: and the fruits of the earth may contend for seniority, seeing their mother was the first Creature that conceived, and they themselves the first fruit she brought forth. Talk of perfect happiness or pleasure, and what place was so fit for that as the garden place where Adam was set to be the Herbarist? Whither did the Poets hunt for their sincere delights, but into the gardens of Alcinous, of Adonis, and the Orchards of Hesperides? Where did they dream that Heaven should be, but in the pleasant garden of Elysium? Whither do all men walk for their honest recreation, but thither where the earth hath most beneficially painted her face with flourishing colours? And what season of the year is more longed for than the Spring, whose gentle breath entices forth the kindly sweets, and makes them yield their fragrant smells? Who would therefore look dangerously up at Planets, that might safely look down at Plants?

John Gerard, The Herbalist, *1597*

❧ Homeward

Tao Yuan Ming was a fourth-century Chinese poet, who gave up the frustra-
tions of working for the government to live as a reclusive, self-sufficient farmer.
He called himself 'the Gentleman of the Five Willows'.

Homeward I bend my steps.
My fields, my gardens, are choked with weeds: should I not go?
My soul has led a bondsman's life; why should I remain to pine?
But I will waste no grief on the past.
I will devote my energies to the future.
I have not wandered far astray.
I feel that I am on the right track once again.

Lightly, lightly speeds my boat along,
My garments fluttering to the gentle breeze.
I inquire my route as I go. I grudge the slowness of the dawning day.
    From afar I see my old home, and joyfully press onwards in my
    haste. The servants rush forth to meet me:
My children cluster at the gate.

The place is a wilderness;
But there is the old pine-tree and my chrysanthemums.
Wine is brought in full bottles, and I pour it out in brimming cups.
I gaze out at my favourite branches.
I loll against the window in my new-found freedom.
I look at the sweet children on my knee.

And now I take my pleasure in my garden.
I lean on my staff as I wander about, or sit down to rest.
I raise my head and contemplate the lovely scene.
Sluggish clouds rise from the bottom of the hills:
The weary bird seeks its nest again.
Shadows vanish, but still I linger round my lonely pine.

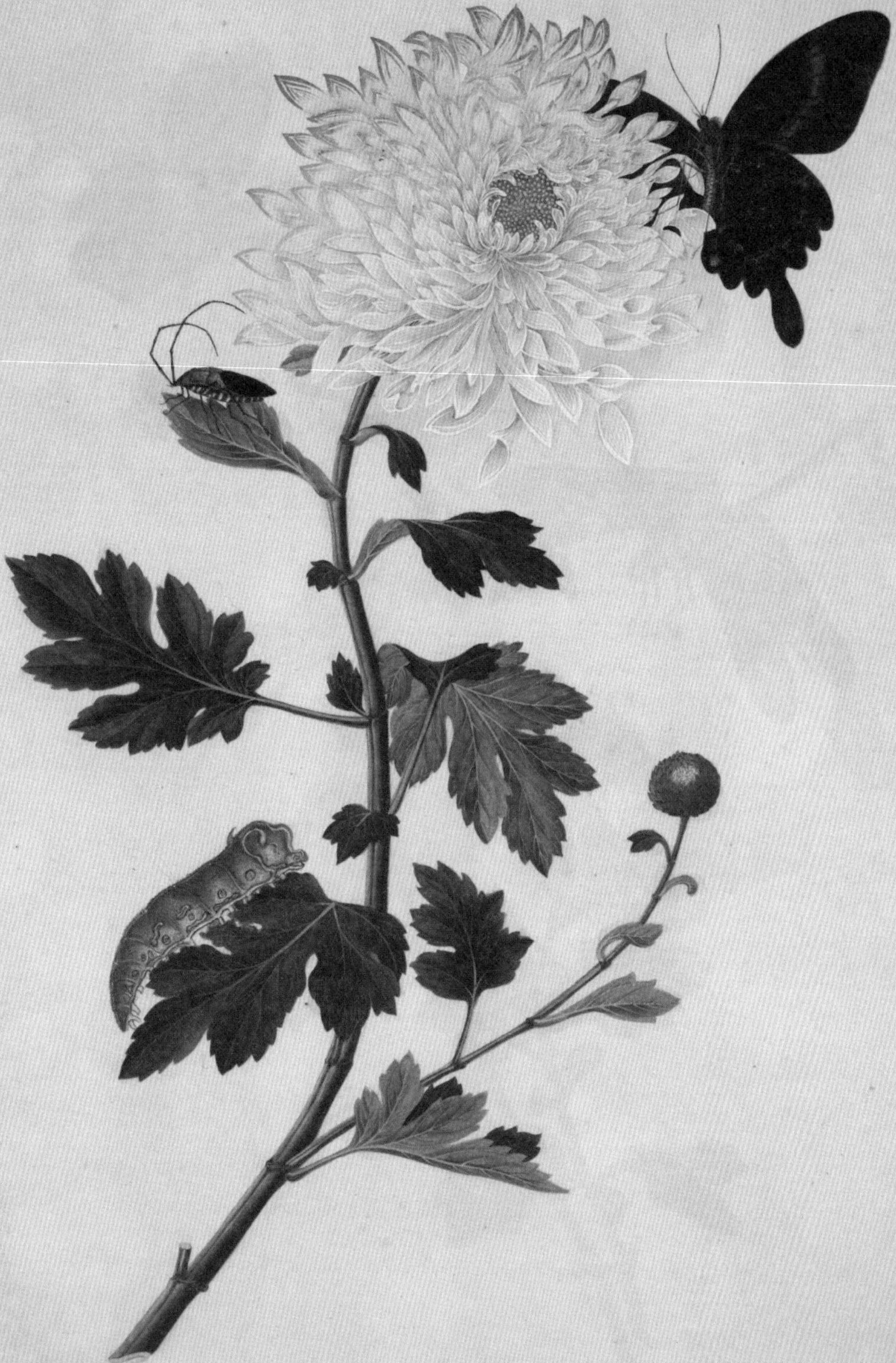

Home once more! I'll have no friendships to distract me hence.
The times are out of joint for me; and what have I to seek from men?
    In the pure enjoyment of the family circle I will pass my days,
Cheering my idle hours with lute and book.

My husbandmen will tell me when springtime is nigh
And when there will be work in the furrowed fields.
Thither I shall repair by cart or by boat,
Through the deep gorge, over the dizzy cliff,
Trees bursting merrily into leaf,
The streamlet swelling from its tiny source.

Glad is this renewal of life in due season:
But, for me, I rejoice that my journey is over.
Ah, how short a time it is that we are here!
Why then not set our hearts at rest,
Ceasing to trouble whether we remain or go?
What boots it to wear out the soul with anxious thoughts?

I want not wealth: I want not power: heaven is beyond my hopes.
Then let me stroll through the bright hours as they pass,
In my garden among my flowers; or I will mount the hill
And sing my song, or weave my verse beside the limpid brook.
Thus will I work out my allotted span,
Content with appointments of fate, my spirit free from care.

I pluck chrysanthemums by the eastern fence
And see the distant southern mountains.
The mountain air is fresh at dusk.
Flying birds return in flocks.
In these things there lies a great truth,
But when I try to express it, I cannot find the words.

❧ Bright Green and Lush

Whoever wrote the thirteenth-century Romance of the Rose *was evidently a garden lover, relishing the description of both plants and wildlife in the magical garden created by the goddess Mirth. I have adapted this from two early translations from the French.*

The garden was nigh broad as wide,
And every angle duly squared;
Of fruit had every tree its charge...
A cherry, pear and knotted quince,
Neath which a tender tooth will wince,
Brown medlars, plums both black and white,
Apples and chestnuts, peaches bright
There were, and that wot I full well,
Of pomegranates a full great deal,
That is a fruit full well to like,
Namely to folk when they be sick,
And trees there were in abundance,
That beareth nuts in their season,
And of almonds great plenty,
Figs, and many a date tree...
And many a spice delectable
To eat when men rise from table:
Cloves, cardamom and liquorice
Ginger, cinnamon and anise.
With many high laurels and pine ranged around
And olives and cypresses, of which nigh no plenty is.
There were elms great and strong
Maples, ash, oak, aspens and planes,
Fine yew, poplar and linden fair,
And other trees full many a pair...
And of squirrels full great plenty
From bough to bough always leaping.
Rabbits there were also playing,
Of sundry colours and manners

S sez y fery et
surtar·
Et maintesfois
le escoutay

Se te orroye seane mille anie
Le tauchet qui estoit de charine
Ille ouurit vne pucellette
Qui asse estoit cointe et nette
Elchaueir eut blonc come vng bassi
La chair plus tendre q̃ vng pouffin

front reluisant souraz voussi
Lentreoil si nestoit pas ver
Amefut assez trans y meffi
Le nez eut bien fait a droitu
Les yeulx eut vair come fauls
Pour faire enuie a tone sio
Doulce a faime eut et fauou
La face blanche et confou
La bouche petite et eftoffe
Et au menton vne foffe

And making many a tourneying
Upon the fresh grass springing.
Within the glades sprang fountains clear;
No frog or newt ever came near
Their waters, and beneath cooling shade
They gently sounded. Mirth had made
Therefrom small channelled brooks to fling
Their waves with pleasant murmuring
In tiny tides. Bright green and lush
Sprang up the grass, as thick set
And as soft as any velvet,
On which a man might his leman lay,
As on a featherbed to play...
The earth of flowers had plenty,
That both in summer and winter be.
The violet sweet in scent and hue,
The periwinkle's star of blue,
The golden kingcups burnished bright,
Mingled with pink-rimmed daisies white
Full gay was the ground, and quaint,
And powdered, as men had it paint,
With many a fresh and sundry flower
That casteth up full good savour.

❧ The Air of Paradise

Persian poets always seem to be ensconced in gardens as they compose their verses, for choice with a fine glass of vintage Shiraz wine in their hands. The coffin of the legendary fourteenth-century poet Hafez-e Shirāzi, who is to Persians what Dante is to the Italians, and Shakespeare to English speakers, is the centrepiece of an elaborate garden which is still constantly visited by pilgrims: they stand touching his coffin, intoning his verses aloud from memory. It is a vision predicted in his poem 'The Garden'.

The garden is breathing out the air of Paradise today,
Toward me, a friend with a sweet nature, and this wine.
It's all right for the beggar to brag that he is a King today.
His royal tent is a shadow thrown by a cloud; his throne room
   is a sown field.
This meadow is composing a tale of a spring day in May;
The serious man lets the future go and accepts the cash now.
Do you really believe your enemy will be faithful to you?
The candle the hermit lights goes out in the worldly church.
Make your soul strong then by feeding it the secret wine.
When we have turned to dust, this rotten world will press our dust
   into bricks.
My life is a black book. But don't rebuke me too much.
No person can ever read the words written on his own forehead.
When Hafez's coffin comes by, it'll be all right to follow behind.
Although he is a captive of sin, he is on his way to the Garden.

میان غرب و جنوب باغ حوض ده در دی سی است اطراف تمام

درختهای نارنج است درختهای انار هم هست کرد کرده حوض تمام

سبزه زار است جای عین باغ همین است در وقت زرد شدن

نارنجها بسیار خوب می نماید خیلی باغ خوبی طرح شده وطر ف

🌺 Purest of Human Pleasures

Sir Francis Bacon, scientist, philosopher and jurist, rose to political eminence as
Attorney General and Lord Chancellor of England in the first two decades of
the seventeenth century. He inherited Gorhambury, in Hertfordshire, in 1601,
and created elaborate water gardens that had as their central feature Verulam
House, a substantial summerhouse with galleries, dining rooms, bedrooms and
a library. In 1621 he fell into debt and had to retire, disgraced, to Gorhambury.
Verulam and its surrounding gardens were his greatest comfort. There he revised
his famous Essays, *first published in 1597 and still in print. One of the best*
loved of them is 'On Gardens'. Here is the first part of it.

God Almighty first planted a garden. And indeed it is the purest of human pleasures. It is the greatest refreshment to the spirits of man; without which, buildings and palaces are but gross handiworks; and a man shall ever see, that when ages grow to civility and elegancy, men come to build stately sooner than to garden finely; as if gardening were the greater perfection.

I do hold it, in the royal ordering of gardens, there ought to be gardens for all the months in the year; in which severally things of beauty may be then in season. For December, and January, and the latter part of November, you must take such things as are green all winter: holly; ivy; bays; juniper; cypress-trees; yew; pine-apple-trees; fir-trees; rosemary; lavender; periwinkle, the white, the purple, and the blue; germander; flags; orange-trees; lemon-trees; and myrtles, if they be stoved; and sweet marjoram, warm set. There follows, for the latter part of January and February, the mezereon-tree, which then blossoms; crocus vernus, both the yellow and the grey; primroses, anemones; the early tulippa; hyacinthus orientalis; chamairis; fritillaria. For March, there come violets, specially the single blue, which are the earliest; the yellow daffodil; the daisy; the almond-tree in blossom; the peach-tree in blossom; the cornelian-tree in blossom; sweet-briar. In April follow the double white violet; the wallflower; the stock-gillyflower; the cowslip; irises, and lilies of all natures; rosemary-flowers; the tulippa; the double peony; the pale daffodil; the French honeysuckle; the cherry-tree in blossom; the damson and plum-trees in blossom; the white thorn in leaf; the lilac-tree. In May and June come pinks of all sorts, specially the blush-pink; roses of all kinds, except the musk, which comes later; honeysuckles; strawberries; bugloss; columbine; the French marigold, flos Africanus; cherry-tree in fruit; ribes; figs in fruit; rasps; vine-flowers; lavender in flowers; the sweet satyrian, with the white flower; herba muscaria; lilium convallium; the apple-tree in blossom. In July come gillyflowers of all varieties; musk roses; the lime-tree in blossom; early pears and plums in fruit; jennetings and codlins. In August come plums of all sorts in fruit; pears; apricot; berberries; filberts; musk-melons; monks-hoods, of all colours. In September come grapes; apples; poppies of all colours; peaches; melocotones; nectarines; cornelians; wardens; quinces. In October and the beginning of November come services; medlars; bullaces; roses cut or removed to come late; holly-hocks; and such like. These particulars are for the climate of London; but my meaning is perceived, that you may have *ver perpetuum*, as the place affords.

And because the breath of flowers is far sweeter in the air (where it comes and goes like the warbling of music) than in the hand, therefore nothing is more fit for that delight, than to know what be the flowers and plants that do best perfume the air. Roses, damask and red, are fast flowers of their smells; so that you may walk by a whole row of them, and find nothing of their sweetness; yea though it be in a morning's dew. Bays likewise yield no smell as they grow, rosemary little; nor sweet marjoram. That which above all others yields the sweetest smell in the air is the violet, specially the white double violet, which comes twice a year; about the middle of April, and about Bartholomew-tide. Next to that is the musk-rose. Then the strawberry-leaves dying, which yield a most excellent cordial smell. Then the flower of vines; it is a little dust, like the dust of a bent [rush], which grows upon the cluster in the first coming forth. Then sweetbriar. Then wallflowers, which are very delightful to be set under a parlour or lower chamber window. Then pinks and gillyflowers, especially the matted pink and clove gillyflower. Then the flowers of the lime-tree. Then the honeysuckles, so they be somewhat afar off. Of bean-flowers I speak not, because they are field flowers. But those which perfume the air most delightfully, not passed by as the rest, but being trodden upon and crushed, are three; that is, burnet, wild thyme, and water mints. Therefore you are to set whole alleys of them, to have the pleasure when you walk or tread.

❧ A Brood of Nightingales

The Reverend William Lawson, who died in 1635, was vicar of the Yorkshire parish of Ormesby. A keen hands-on gardener, he published his New Orchard and Garden *in 1618, which later earned him the sobriquet 'the Isaac Newton of Gardening'. In it he writes with relish of the joys of gardening at a time when growing fruit-bearing trees and bushes among flowers was taken for granted, and there was no hard and fast boundary between the two.*

Now pause with your self, and view the end of all your labours in an orchard. To declare the unspeakable pleasure thoroughly is past my skill: and I count it as if a man should attempt to add light to the sun with a candle, or number the stars... For it is not to be doubted: but as God hath given man things profitable, so hath he allowed him honest comfort, delight, and recreation in all the works of his hands. Nay, all his labours under the sun without this are troubles, and vexation of mind: for what is greedy gain, without delight, but moiling [working hard], and turmoiling in slavery? But comfortable delight, with content, is the good of every thing, and the pattern of heaven. A morsel of bread with comfort is better by much then a fat ox with unquietness.

The very work of and in an orchard and garden is better then the ease and rest of and from other labours. What was paradise but a garden and orchard of trees and herbs, full of pleasure, and nothing there but delights?

For whereas every other pleasure commonly fills some one of our senses, and that only, with delight, this makes all our senses swim in pleasure, and that with infinite variety, joined with no less commodity... What can your eye desire to see, your ears to hear, your mouth to taste, or your nose to smell, that is not to be had in an orchard, with abundance and variety? What more delightsome than an infinite variety of sweet smelling flowers decking with sundry colours the green mantle of the earth, the universal mother of us all... and sweetening every breath and spirit.

The rose red, damask, velvet, and double, the double province rose, the sweet musk rose double and single, the double and single white rose.

IV.
Rosa provincialis flore albo.

III.
Rosa Milesia flore rubro olens.

II.
Rosa alba flore simplici.

I.
Rosa flore albo pleno.

The fair and sweet-scenting woodbine, double and single. Rosemary and sweet eglantine are seemly ornaments about a door or window, and so is woodbine... Purple cowslips, and double cowslips, primrose double and single. The violet nothing behind the best for smelling sweetly. A thousand more will provoke your content.

And all these... so comely, and orderly placed in your borders and squares, and so intermingled, that none looking thereon, cannot but wonder, to see, what nature corrected by art can do... Large walks, broad and long, close and open, like the temple groves in Thessaly, raised with gravel and sand, having seats and banks of camomile, all this delights the mind, and brings health to the body.

View now with delight the works of your own hands, your fruit-trees of all sorts, laden with sweet blossoms, and fruit of all tastes, operations, and colours: your trees standing in comely order which way so ever you look.

Your borders on every side hanging and drooping with feberries, raspberries, barberries, currants, and the roots of your trees powdered with strawberries, red, white, and green, what a pleasure is this? Your gardener can frame your lesser wood to the shape of men armed in the field, ready to give battle: or swift running greyhounds... Well-framed mazes a man's height, may perhaps make your friend wander in gathering of berries, till he cannot recover himself without your help. To exercise within your orchard, it shall be a pleasure to have a bowling alley, or rather (which is more manly, and more healthful) a pair of Butts, to stretch your arms.

If there were two or more conduits, it were not amiss. And in mine opinion, I could highly commend your orchard, if either through it, or hard by it there should run a pleasant river with silver streams; you might sit in your mount, and angle a speckled trout, or flighty eel, or some other dainty fish. Or moats, whereon you might row with a boat, and fish with nets.

Store of bees in a dry and warm bee-house, comely made of fir-boards, to sing, and sit, and feed upon your flowers and sprouts, make a pleasant noise and sight. For cleanly and innocent bees, of all other things, love and become, and thrive in an orchard...You need not fear their stings, for they hurt not whom they know, and they know their keeper and acquaintance... Some... use to make seats for them in the stone wall of their orchard, or garden, which is good, but wood is better. A vine over-shadowing a seat, is very comely, though her grapes with us ripe slowly.

One chief grace that adorns an orchard, I cannot let slip: a brood of nightingales, who with their several notes and tunes, with a strong delightsome voice out of a weak body will bear you company night and day. [They] will help you to cleanse your trees of caterpillars, and all noisome worms and flies. The gentle robin-red-breast will help [them], and in winter in the coldest storms will keep a part. Neither will the silly wren be behind in summer, with her distinct whistle (like a sweet recorder) to cheer your spirits. The black-bird and [thrush] sing loudly in a May morning and delight the ear much, and you need not want their company, if you have ripe cherries or berries, and would as gladly as the rest do you pleasure. But I had rather want their company than my fruit.

To conclude, what joy may you have, that you living to such an age, shall see the blessings of God on your labours while you live, and leave behind you to heirs or successors such a work, that many ages after your death shall record your love to their country?

🌺 Innocent Delights

Co-founder of The Spectator *magazine with Richard Steele, Joseph Addison was a Whig politician whose play about Cato, the Roman champion of freedom and republican virtues, was hugely popular in America in the years leading up to the War of Independence. Addison thoroughly enjoyed designing and spending time in his Warwickshire garden at Bilton Hall, where he lived from 1711 until his death in 1719.*

I look upon the pleasure which we take in a garden, as one of the most innocent delights in human life. A garden was the habitation of our first parents before the Fall. It is naturally apt to fill the mind with calmness and tranquillity, and to lay all its turbulent passions at rest. It gives us a great insight into the contrivance and wisdom of providence, and suggests innumerable subjects for meditation. I cannot but think the very complacency and satisfaction which a man takes in these works of nature, to be a laudable, if not a virtuous habit of mind.

I think there are as many kinds of gardening as of poetry: Your makers of parterres and flower-Gardens, are epigrammatists and sonneteers in this art: contrivers of bowers and grottoes, treillages and cascades, are romance writers. Henry Wise and George London are our heroick poets...

As for my self, you will find, by the Account which I have already given you, that my compositions in gardening are altogether after the Pindarick manner, and run into the beautiful wildness of nature, without affecting the nicer elegancies of art...But I have often wonder'd that those who are like myself, and love to live in gardens, have never thought of contriving a winter garden, which would consist of such trees only as never cast their leaves. We have very often little snatches of sunshine and fair weather in the most uncomfortable parts of the year; and have frequently several days in November and January that are as agreeable as any in the finest months.

At such times, therefore, I think there could not be a greater pleasure, than to walk in such a winter-garden as I have proposed. In the summer season the whole country blooms, and is a kind of garden, for which reason we are not so sensible of those beauties that at this

time may be every where met with; but when nature is in her desolation, and presents us with nothing but bleak and barren prospects,
there is something unspeakably cheerful in a spot of ground which is
covered with trees that smile amidst all the rigours of winter, and give
us a view of the most gay season in the midst of that which is the most
dead and melancholy.

I have so far indulged my self in this thought, that I have set apart
a whole acre of ground for the executing of it. The walls are covered
with ivy instead of vines. The laurel, the hornbeam, and the holly, with
many other trees and plants of the same nature, grow so thick in it, that
you cannot imagine a more lively scene. The glowing redness of the
berries, with which they are hung at this time, vies with the verdure of
their leaves, and are apt to inspire the heart of the beholder with vernal
delight. It is very pleasant to see the several kinds of birds retiring into
this little green spot, and enjoying themselves among the branches and
foliage, when my great garden, which I have before mentioned to you,
does not afford a single leaf for their shelter.

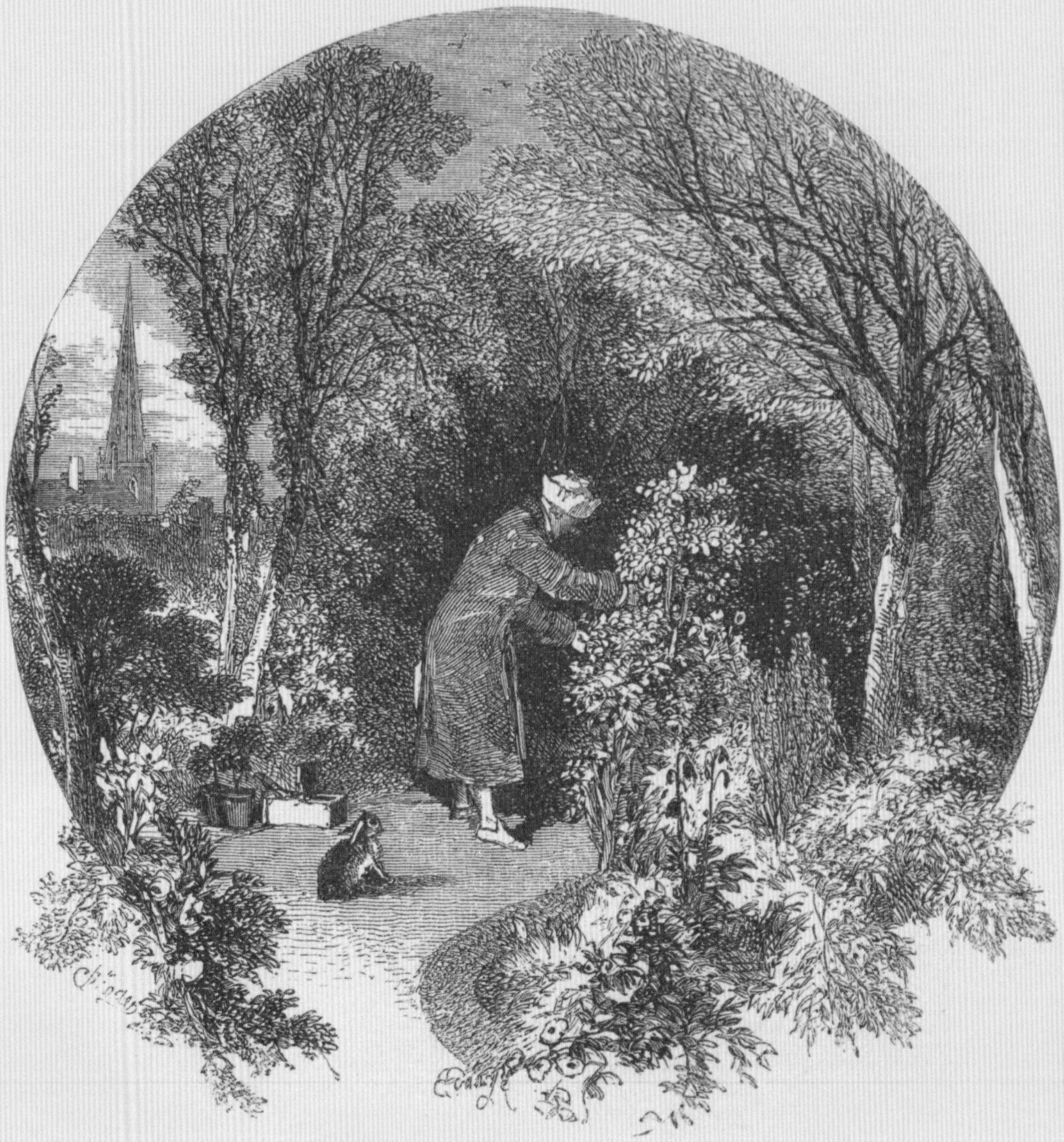

🏵 Syringa Ivory Pure

William Cowper was the most popular poet of the late eighteenth century. Both his letters and his marathon narrative poem The Task *sang the joys of rural retirement, domesticity and gardening. He wrote this letter to the Reverend John Newton in 1784.*

My greenhouse is never so pleasant as when we are just upon the point of being turned out of it. The gentleness of the autumnal suns, and the calmness of this latter season, make it a much more agreeable retreat than we ever find it in the summer; when the winds being generally brisk, we cannot cool it by admitting a sufficient quantity of air, without being at the same time incommoded by it. But now I sit with all the windows and the door wide open, and am regaled with the scent of every flower, in a garden as full of flowers as I have known how to make it. We keep no bees, but if I lived in a hive, I should hardly hear more of their music. All the bees in the neighbour-hood resort to a bed of mignonette opposite to the window, and pay me for the honey they get out of it by a hum, which, though rather monotonous, is as agreeable to my ear as the whistling of my linnets. All the sounds that Nature utters are delightful, at least in this country.

One of the most memorable imaginative feasts in The Task *is 'The Winter Walk at Noon', which conjures up, from the bare-stemmed plants and trees, the summer pleasures to come.*

These naked shoots,
Barren as lances, among which the wind
Makes wintry music, sighing as it goes,
Shall put their graceful foliage on again,
And more aspiring and with ampler spread
Shall boast new charms... Laburnum rich
In streaming gold; syringa ivory pure;
The scented and the scentless rose; this red
And of a humbler growth, the other tall,
And throwing up into the darkest gloom

Of neighbouring cypress, or more sable yew
Her silver globes, light as the foamy surf
That the wind severs from the broken wave.
The lilac various in array, now white,
Now sanguine, and her beauteous head now set
With purple spikes pyramidal, as if
Studious of ornament, yet unresolved
Which hue she most approved, she chose them all;
Copious of flowers the woodbine, pale and wan,
But well compensating their sickly looks
With never-cloying odours, early and late;
Hypericum all bloom, so thick a swarm
Of flowers like flies, clothing her slender rods,
That scarce a leaf appears... the broom,
Yellow and bright as bullion unalloyed
Her blossoms; and luxuriant above all
The jasmine, throwing wide her elegant sweets,
The deep dark green of whose unvarnished leaf
Makes more conspicuous, and illumines more
The bright profusion of her scattered stars.

❧ We Talk Also of a Laburnum

Jane Austen, who loved Cowper's verse, was also an enthusiast for gardens (if less hands-on among the weeds and compost heaps). In this letter to her sister Cassandra, she boasts of the garden of their new house in Southampton.

8 FEBRUARY 1807

Our garden is being put in order by a man who bears a remarkably good character, has a very fine complexion and asks something less than the first. The shrubs which border the gravel walk he says are only sweetbriar and roses, and the latter of an indifferent sort – we mean to get a few of the better kind, therefore, and at my own particular desire he procures us some syringas. I could not do without a syringa, for the sake of Cowper's line. We talk also of a laburnum. The border under the terrace wall is clearing away to receive currants and gooseberry bushes, and a spot is found very proper for raspberries… We hear that we are envied by many people and that the garden is the best in the town.

Jane's favourite garden was that of Chawton, the little Hampshire house which was her home from 1809 until her death, aged only 41, in 1817. Now the home of the Jane Austen Society, Chawton and its garden have been restored to the condition they were in when the Austens lived there. Jane's nephew James Leigh-Austen knew the place well, and described it in the memoir he wrote of his famous aunt.

A high wooden fence and hornbeam hedge shut out the Winchester road, which skirted the whole length of the little domain. Trees were planted each side to form a shrubbery walk, carried round the enclosure, which gave sufficient space for ladies' exercise. There was a pleasant irregular mixture of hedgerow and gravel walk and orchard and long grass for mowing, arising from two or three little enclosures having been thrown together. The house itself was quite as good as the generality of parsonage houses… and was capable of receiving other members of the family as frequent visitors. It was sufficiently well furnished; everything inside and out was kept in good repair, and it was altogether a ladylike establishment, although the means which supported it were not large.

After the Austens moved to Chawton in 1809, Jane's letters to Cassandra are full of domestic and horticultural detail.

WEDNESDAY 29 MAY 1811

The chickens are all alive and fit for the table, but we save them for something grand. Some of the flower seeds are coming up very well, but your mignonette makes a wretched appearance. Miss Benn has been equally unlucky as to hers. She has seed from four different people, and none of it comes up. Our young peony at the foot of the fir-tree has just blown and looks very handsome, and the whole of the shrubbery border will soon be very gay with pinks and sweet-williams, in addition to the columbines already in bloom.

The syringas, too, are coming out. We are likely to have a great crop of Orleans plums, but not many greengages – on the standard scarcely any, three or four dozen, perhaps, against the wall. I believe I told you differently when I first came home, but I can now judge better than I could then.

FRIDAY 31 MAY 1811

You cannot imagine – it is not in human nature to imagine – what a nice walk we have round the orchard. The row of beech look very well indeed, and so does the young quickset hedge in the garden. I hear today that an apricot has been detected on one of the trees. My mother is perfectly convinced now that she shall not be overpowered by her cleftwood [fencing], and I believe would rather have more than less... I will not say that your Mulberry trees are dead, but I am afraid that they are not alive.

THURSDAY, 6 JUNE, 1811

We began peas on Sunday, but our gatherings are small – not at all like the gatherings in *The Lady of the Lake*. Yesterday I had the agreeable surprise of finding several scarlet strawberries quite ripe; – had you been at home this would have been a pleasure lost. There are more gooseberries and fewer currants than I thought at first. We must buy currants for our wine.

❧ The Pride of My Heart

Mary Russell Mitford is best known for her affectionately domestic novel Our
Village, *a thinly veiled account of her own life with her spendthrift father
in Shenstone, near Reading. She painted a vivid picture of her garden in
'Whitsun Eve', an article written in July 1827 for a popular weekly magazine,*
The Mirror of Literature, Amusement, and Instruction.

The pride of my heart and the delight of my eyes is my garden. Our
house, which is in dimensions very much like a bird-cage, and might,
with almost equal convenience, be laid on a shelf, or hung up in a tree,
would be utterly unbearable in warm weather, were it not that we
have a retreat out of doors – and a very pleasant retreat it is. To make
my readers fully comprehend it, I must describe our whole territories.

Fancy a small plot of ground, with a pretty low irregular cottage at
one end; a large granary, divided from the dwelling by a little court
running along one side; and a long thatched shed open towards the
garden, and supported by wooden pillars on the other. The bottom is
bounded, half by an old wall, and half by an old paling, over which
we see a pretty distance of woody hills. The house, granary, wall, and
paling, are covered with vines, cherry-trees, roses, honey-suckles, and
jessamines, with great clusters of tall hollyhocks running up between
them; a large elder overhanging the little gate, and a magnificent bay-
tree, such a tree as shall scarcely be matched in these parts, breaking
with its beautiful conical form the horizontal lines of the buildings.
This is my garden; and the long pillared shed, the sort of rustic arcade
which runs along one side, parted from the flowerbeds by a row of
rich geraniums, is our out-of-door drawing-room.

I know nothing so pleasant as to sit there on a summer afternoon,
with the western sun flickering through the great elder-tree, and
lighting up our gay parterres, where flowers and flowering shrubs are
set as thick as grass in a field, a wilderness of blossom, interwoven,
intertwined, wreathy, garlandy, profuse beyond all profusion, where we
may guess that there is such a thing as mould, but never see it. I know
nothing so pleasant as to sit in the shade of that dark bower, with the
eye resting on that bright piece of colour, lighted so gloriously by the

evening sun, now catching a glimpse of the little birds as they fly rapidly in and out of their nests – for there are always two or three birds' nests in the thick tapestry of cherry-trees, honey-suckles, and China roses, which cover our walls – now tracing the gay gambols of the common butterflies as they sport around the dahlias; now watching that rarer moth, which the country people, fertile in pretty names, call the bee-bird; that bird-like insect, which flutters in the hottest days over the sweetest flowers, inserting its long proboscis into the small tube of the jessamine, and hovering over the scarlet blossoms of the geranium, whose bright colour seems reflected on its own feathery breast; that insect which seems so thoroughly a creature of the air, never at rest; always, even when feeding, self-poised, and self-supported, and whose wings in their ceaseless motion, have a sound so deep, so full, so lulling, so musical.

Nothing so pleasant as to sit amid that mixture of the flower and the leaf, watching the bee-bird! Nothing so pretty to look at as my garden! It is quite a picture; only unluckily it resembles a picture in more qualities than one – it is fit for nothing but to look at. One might as well think of walking in a bit of framed canvas. There are walks to be sure – tiny paths of smooth gravel, by courtesy called such – but they are so overhung by roses and lilies and such gay encroachers, so over-run by convolvulus, and heart's-ease, and mignonette and other sweet stragglers, that, except to edge through them occasionally, for the purpose of planting, or weeding, or watering, there might as well be no paths at all. Nobody thinks of walking in my garden. Even May glides along with a delicate and trackless step, like a swan through the wafer; and we, its two-footed denizens, are fain to treat it as if it were really a saloon, and go out for a walk towards sunset, just as if we had not been sitting in the open air all day.

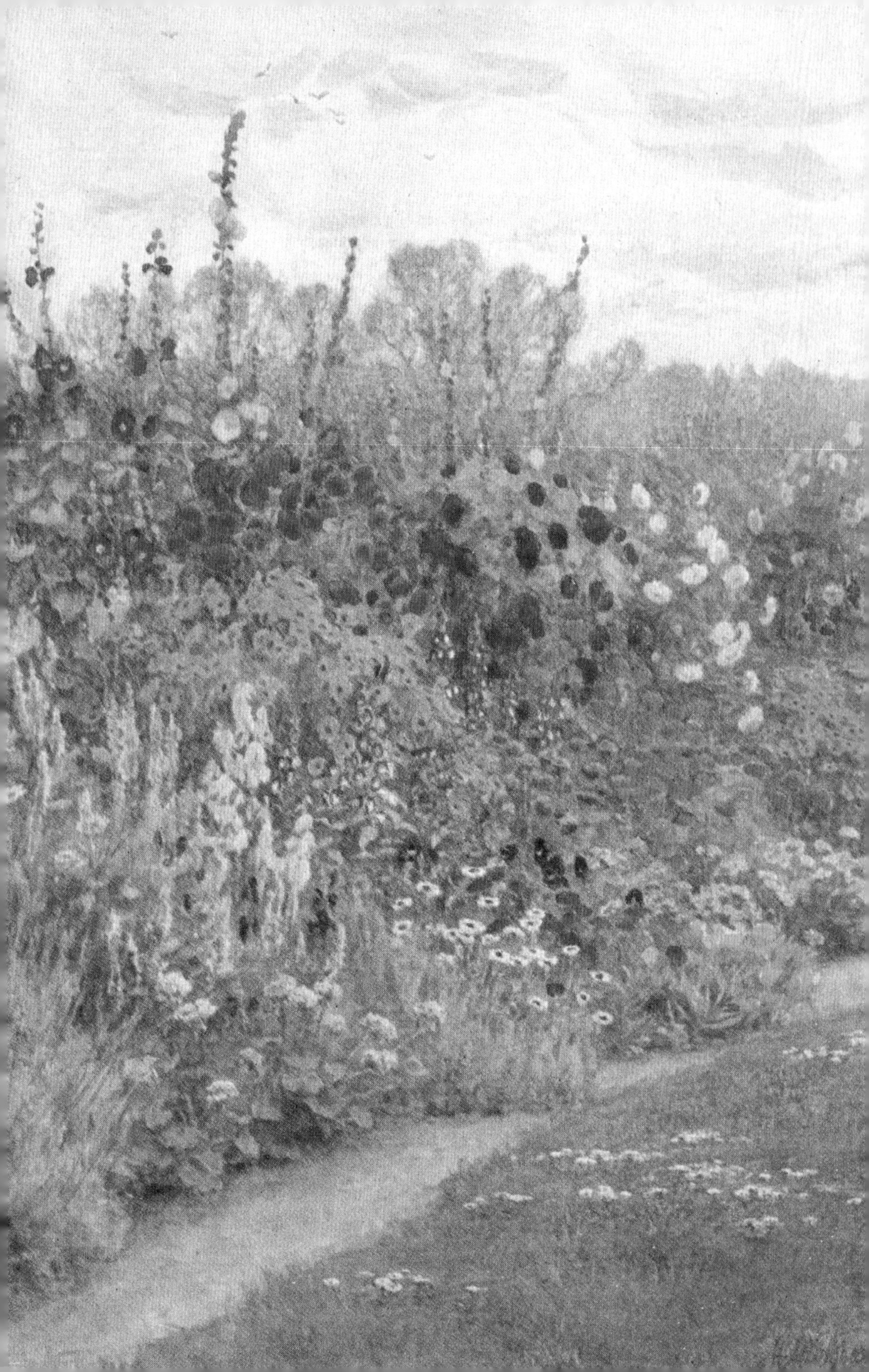

❧ How Little One Wants

The great gardens of the Edwardian Arts and Crafts houses are synonymous with the name of Gertrude Jekyll, who created more than 400 gardens for clients, many in partnership with the architect Edwin Lutyens. A talented artist and a friend of John Ruskin, Jekyll was renowned as a painterly gardener, massing colour to create effects inspired by J. M. W. Turner. Although she was a lover of plants and gardens all her life, Jekyll only turned to gardening as a profession in her mid-fifties, when her failing eyesight made it impossible to continue her career as a painter. But her other senses, as the next passages show, became ever more acute.

If it were possible to simplify life to the utmost, how little one really wants!...Throughout my life I have found that one of the things most worth doing was to cultivate the habit of close observation. Like all else, the more it is exercised the easier it becomes, till it is so much a part of oneself that one may observe almost critically and hardly be aware of it. A habit so acquired stands one in good stead in all garden matters, so that in an exhibition of flowers or in a botanic garden one can judge of the merits of a plant hitherto unknown to one, and at once see in what way it is good, and why, and how it differs from those of the same class that one may have at home. And I know from my own case that the will and the power to observe do not depend on the possession of keen sight. For I have sight that is both painful and inadequate; short sight of the severest kind, and always progressive (my natural focus is two inches); but the little I have I try to make the most of, and often find that I have observed things that have escaped strong and long-sighted people.

As if by way of compensation I have very keen hearing, and when I hear a little rustling rush in the grass and heath, or in the dead leaves under the trees, I can tell whether it is snake or lizard, mouse or bird. Many birds I am aware of only by the sound of their flight. I can nearly always tell what trees I am near by the sound of the wind in their leaves, though in the same tree it differs much from spring to autumn, as the leaves become of a harder and drier texture. The birches have a small, quick, high-pitched sound; so near that of falling rain that I am often deceived into thinking it really is rain, when it is only their own leaves hitting each other with a small rain-like patter. The voice of oak leaves is also rather high-pitched, though lower than that of birch. Chestnut leaves in a mild breeze sound much more deliberate; a sort of slow slither. Nearly all trees in gentle wind have a pleasant sound, but I confess to a distinct dislike to the noise of all the poplars, feeling it to be painfully fussy, unrestful, and disturbing. On the other hand, how soothing and delightful is the murmur of Scotch firs both near and far. And what pleasant muffled music is that of a wind-waved field of corn, and especially of ripe barley. The giant grasses, reeds, and bamboo sound curiously dry. The great reed, *Arundo donax*, makes more noise in a moderate breeze than when the wind blows a gale, for then the long ribbon-like leaves are blown straight out and play much less against each other; the Arabs say, 'It whispers in the breeze and is silent in the storm.'

❧ Enjoy Thyself a Day

But what of lovers in gardens? In the beginning, of course, there was Eve tempting Adam, but Eve has always struck me as a practical rather than romantic sort of woman and Adam as a somewhat hen-pecked man (and a sneak). There is a much more convincing seductress in a garden in an Egyptian story that is possibly almost as old as Genesis, the Nineteenth-Dynasty 'Tale of the Garden of Flowers', written around 1290 BC.

She led me, hand in hand, and we went into her garden to converse together. There she made me taste of excellent honey. The rushes of the garden were verdant, and all its bushes flourishing. There were currant trees and cherries redder than the ruby. The ripe peaches of the garden resembled bronze, and the groves had the lustre of the almond. Cocoanuts they brought to us, the shade was fresh and airy, and soft for the repose of love.

'Come to me,' she called unto me, 'and enjoy thyself a day in the room of a young girl who belongs to me. The garden is to-day in its glory; there is a terrace and a parlour.'

🦋 A Garden Enclosed

*By far the most famous ancient description of love in a garden is this passage
in the* Song of Solomon *from around 1,000 BC – although there is still
much debate as to whether it was written by or for Solomon, and whether its
impassioned words were meant to celebrate the consummation of a marriage or
God's relationship with Israel. Judge for yourself from the conversation between
bride and groom in these extracts from the* King James *version of the* Old
Testament *(1611).*

BRIDE'S VOICE
I am the rose of Sharon, and the lily of the valleys. As the lily among
thorns, so is my love among the daughters. As the apple-tree among
the trees of the wood, so is my beloved among the sons.

I sat down under his shadow with great delight, and his fruit was
sweet to my taste. He brought me with him to the banqueting house,
and his banner over me was love.

Stay me with flagons, comfort me with apples, for I am sick for
love...

BRIDEGROOM'S VOICE
A garden enclosed is my sister, my spouse; a spring shut up, a fountain
sealed.

Thy plants are an orchard of pomegranates, with pleasant fruits;
camphor, spikenard and saffron; calamus and cinnamon, with all trees
of frankincense; myrrh and aloes, with all the chief spices:

A fountain of gardens, a well of living waters, and streams from
Lebanon.

BRIDE'S VOICE
Awake, O north wind; and come, thou south; blow upon my garden,
that the spices thereof may flow out. Let my beloved come into his
garden, and eat his pleasant fruits...

For the winter is past, the rain is over and gone;

The flowers appear on the earth, the time of singing has come, and
the voice of the turtledove is heard in our land.

Apres q̃ deux out adam fet. E eue de soue coute tret. Seu̓ z vie ꝑ les dona.
Eꝛ paradis tereestre ꝑ les amena. E dit deu̓: ici te soꝛ meistre. De car̅
be tu veys eu vironn tereestre. Veke le fruit de coo poiner. Car ke tu ne
le voys tucher. De tur les fruiz q̃ tu ici veys. Ieo voᷓl q̃ tu meistre leys.
Ore see tren cu̅ ieo te du̓. E ne tuche pas le fruit ici. E si tu bꝛises mon
comandement. Tot iras uereiement. Deu̓ ne eistoit q̃ un tou al
lee. Ke le defens deu̓ ne fu bꝛisee. Mon gꝛit toꝛ adu̅ il fesoit. Saunt en tribuil

The fig tree puts forth its fruit, and the vines are in blossom; they give forth fragrance.

BRIDEGROOM'S VOICE
Arise my fair one, and come away...

I am come into my garden, my sister, my spouse: I have gathered my myrrh with my spice; I have eaten my honeycomb with my honey; I have drunk my wine with my milk; drink, yea, drink abundantly, O beloved.

BRIDE'S VOICE
I sleep, but my heart waketh: it is the voice of my beloved that knocketh, saying, Open to me, my sister, my love, my dove, my undefiled: for my head is filled with dew, and my locks with the drops of the night...

My beloved is gone down into his garden, to the beds of spices, to feed in the gardens, and to gather lilies.

I am my beloved's, and my beloved is mine: he feedeth among the lilies.

BRIDEGROOM'S VOICE
I went down into the garden of nuts to see the fruits of the valley, and to see whether the vine flourished, and the pomegranates budded.

Come, my beloved, let us go forth into the field; let us lodge in the villages.

Let us get up early to the vineyards; let us see if the vine flourish, whether the tender grape appear, and the pomegranates bud forth: there will I give thee my loves.

The mandrakes are strongly scented, and at our gates are all manner of pleasant fruits, new and old, which I have laid up for thee, O my beloved.

My vineyard, which is mine, is before me: Make haste, my beloved, and be thou like to a roe or to a young hart upon the mountains of spices.

❧ The Lusty Month of May

Medieval romances abounded in amorous episodes in gardens. The most graceful and dignified reflection on Maytide love in gardens is by Sir Thomas Malory, in his Life and Acts of King Arthur, *which dates from the 1460s. Caxton printed it as* Le Morte Darthur *in 1485.*

And thus it passed on from Candlemas until after Easter, that the month of May was come, when every lusty heart begins to blossom, and to bring forth fruit; for like as herbs and trees bring forth fruit and flourish in May, in like wise every lusty heart that is in any manner a lover, springs and flourishes in lusty deeds. For it gives unto all lovers courage, that lusty month of May, in something to constrain him to some manner of thing more in that month than in any other month, for divers causes. For then all herbs and trees renew a man and woman, and likewise lovers call again to their mind old gentleness and old service, and many kind deeds that were forgotten by negligence.

For like as winter rasure does always erase and deface green summer, so fares it by unstable love in man and woman. For in many persons there is no stability; for we may see all day, for a little blast of winter's rasure, anon we shall deface and lay apart true love for little or nought, that cost much thing; this is no wisdom nor stability, but it is feebleness of nature and great disworship, whosoever uses this. Therefore, like as May month flowers and flourishes in many gardens, so in like wise let every man of worship flourish his heart in this world, first unto God, and next unto the joy of them that he promised his faith unto; for there was never worshipful man or worshipful woman, but they loved one better than another; and worship in arms may never be foiled, but first reserve the honour to God, and secondly the quarrel must come of thy lady: and such love I call virtuous love.

❧ A Garden Fair by Music's Tower

Stephen Hawes, who wrote yards of high-flown verse, was a gentleman usher
to King Henry VII. This memorable picture of a forlorn lover seeking out his
lady, la belle Pucelle, in her aromatic and delightful garden comes from his poem
The Pastime of Pleasure.

When the little birds sweetly did sing tunes
With tunes musical, in the fair morning.
Then forth so went Good Council and I
At six clock, unto a garden fair
By Music's tower, walled most goodly
Where la belle Pucelle used to repair
In the sweet morning, for to take the air
Among the flowers, of aromatic fume.

And at the gate, we met the porteress
That was right gentle, and called Courtesy
Who saluted us, with words of meekness
And asked us, the very cause and why
Of our coming, to the garden sothell
Truly said we, for nothing but well
A little to speak, with la belle Pucelle.

'Truly', said she, 'in the garden green
Of many a sweet and sundry flower
She makes a garland that is very shene
With trueloves wrought, with many a colour
Replete with sweetness, and dulcet odour
And all alone, withouten company
Amidst an arbour, she sitteth pleasantly.

'Now stand you still, for a little space;
I will let her of you have knowledging.'
And right anon, she went to her grace,
Telling her then, how we were coming

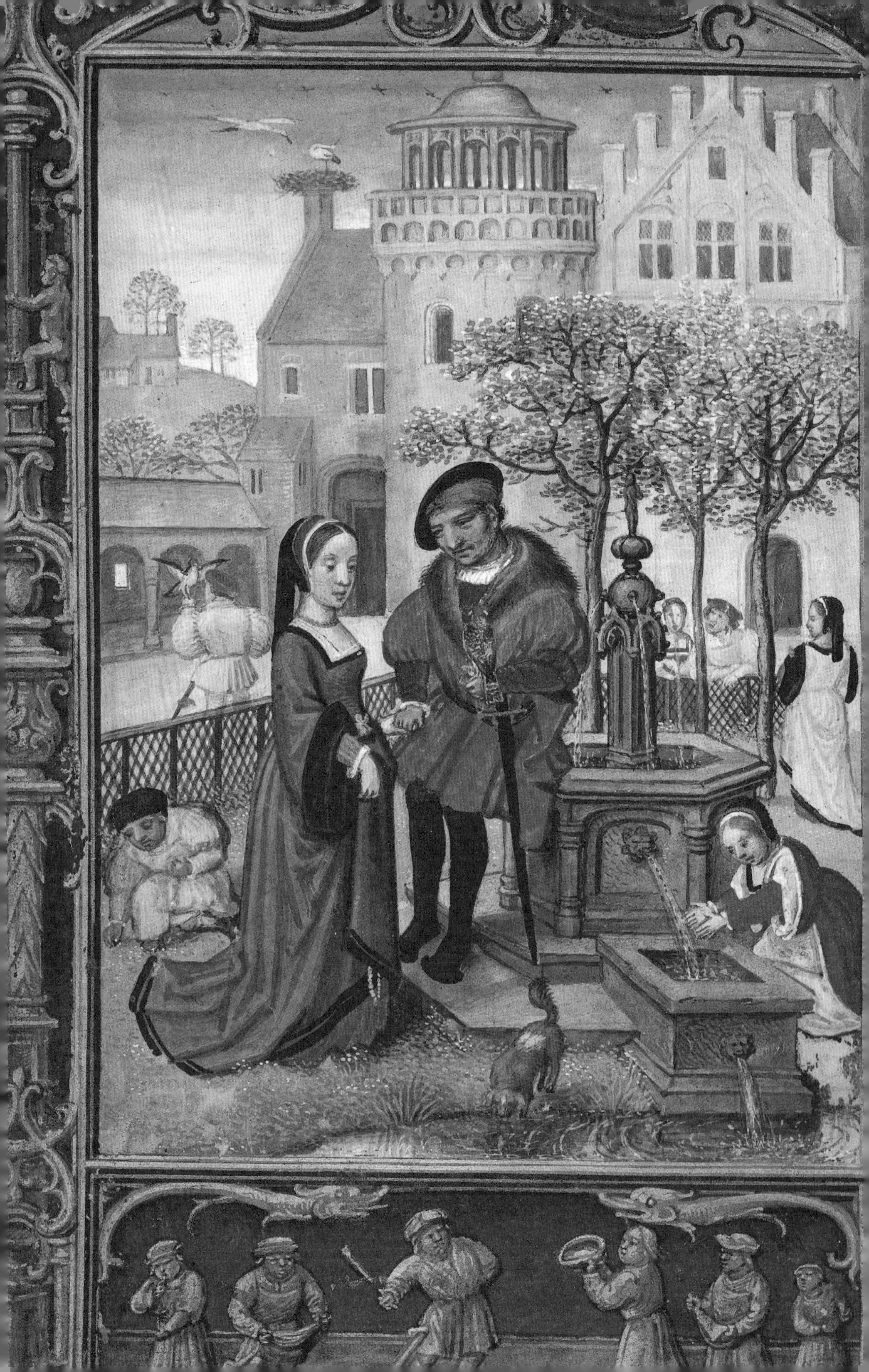

To speak with her greatly desiring.
'Truly', she said, 'I am right well content
Of their coming, to know their whole intent.

Then good Courtesy, without tarrying
Came unto us, with all her diligence
Praying us to take our entering
And come unto the lady's presence
To tell our errand to her excellence.
Then in we went, to the garden glorious
Like to a place, of pleasure most solacious
With Flora painted and wrought curiously
In divers knots of marvellous greatness
Rampant lions stood up wonderfully
Made all of herbs with dulcet sweetness,
With many dragons of marvellous likeness
Of divers flowers made, full craftily
By Flora coloured, with colours sundry

Amidst the garden so much delectable
There was an arbour, fair and quadrant
To Paradise right well comparable,
Set all about with flowers fragrant,
And in the middle, there was resplendisant
A dulcet spring, and marvellous fountain
Of gold and azure, made all certain.

In wonderful and curious similitude
There stood a dragon, of fine gold so pure
Upon his tail, of mighty fortitude
Wreathed and scaled, all with azure
Having three heads, diverse in figure
Which in a basin of silver great
Spouted the water, that was so dulcet

Beside which fountain, the most fair lady
La belle Pucelle, was gaily sitting

Of many flowers, fair and royally
A goodly chaplet, she was in making
Her hair was down, so clearly shining,
Like to the gold, late purified with fire
Her hair was bright as the drawn wire.

Like to a lady, for to be right true
She wore a fair and goodly garment
Of most fine velvet, all of indigo blue,
With ermines powdered bordered at the vent,
On her fair hands, as was convenient
A pair of gloves, right slender and soft
In approaching near, I did behold her oft.

And when that I came into her presence
Unto the ground, I did kneel adown
Saying, O Lady, most fair of excellence,
O star so clear, of virtuous renown...
Please it, your grace, for to give audience
Unto my woeful and piteous complaint.

❧ Make Me a Mandrake

Not everybody found happiness in gardens. In his poem 'Twickenham Garden'
(c. 1590s), John Donne bewails his mistress's failure to come up to scratch.

Blasted with sighs, and surrounded with tears,
Hither I come to seek the spring,
And at mine eyes, and at mine ears,
Receive such balms as else cure every thing.
But O! self-traitor, I do bring
The spider Love, which transubstantiates all,
And can convert manna to gall;
And that this place may thoroughly be thought
True paradise, I have the serpent brought.

'Twere wholesomer for me that winter did
Benight the glory of this place,
And that a grave frost did forbid
These trees to laugh and mock me to my face;
But that I may not this disgrace
Endure, nor yet leave loving, Love, let me
Some senseless piece of this place be;
Make me a mandrake, so I may grow here,
Or a stone fountain weeping out my year.

Hither with crystal phials, lovers, come,
And take my tears, which are love's wine,
And try your mistress' tears at home,
For all are false, that taste not just like mine.
Alas! Hearts do not in eyes shine,
Nor can you more judge women's thoughts by tears,
Than by her shadow what she wears.
O perverse sex, where none is true but she,
Who's therefore true, because her truth kills me.

🌿 No Nook More Eden-Like

In Jane Eyre *(1847) Charlotte Brontë establishes the most romantic horticultural atmosphere possible for Mr Rochester's perversely presented and doom-laden proposal of marriage to Jane.*

A splendid Midsummer shone over England: skies so pure, suns so radiant as were then seen in long succession, seldom favour even singly, our wave-girt land. It was as if a band of Italian days had come from the South, like a flock of glorious passenger birds, and lighted to rest them on the cliffs of Albion. The hay was all got in; the fields round Thornfield were green and shorn; the roads white and baked; the trees were in their dark prime; hedge and wood, full-leaved and deeply tinted, contrasted well with the sunny hue of the cleared meadows between.

On Midsummer Eve, Adele, weary with gathering wild strawberries in Hay Lane half the day, had gone to bed with the sun. I watched her drop asleep, and when I left her, I sought the garden.

It was now the sweetest hour of the twenty-four. 'Day its fervid fires had wasted' [a misquote from Thomas Campbell's 'The Turkish Lady'], and dew fell cool on panting plain and scorched summit. Where the sun had gone down in simple state – pure of the pomp of clouds – spread a solemn purple, burning with the light of red jewel and furnace flame at one point, on one hill-peak, and extending high and wide, soft and still softer, over half heaven. The east had its own charm or fine deep blue, and its own modest gem, a casino and solitary star: soon it would boast the moon; but she was yet beneath the horizon.

I walked a while on the pavement; but a subtle, well-known scent – that of a cigar – stole from some window; I saw the library casement open a handbreadth; I knew I might be watched thence; so I went apart into the orchard. No nook in the grounds more sheltered and more Eden-like; it was full of trees, it bloomed with flowers: a very high wall shut it out from the court, on one side; on the other, a beech avenue screened it from the lawn. At the bottom was a sunk fence; its sole separation from lonely fields: a winding walk, bordered with laurels and terminating in a giant horse-chestnut, circled at the base by a seat, led down to the fence. Here one could wander unseen. While

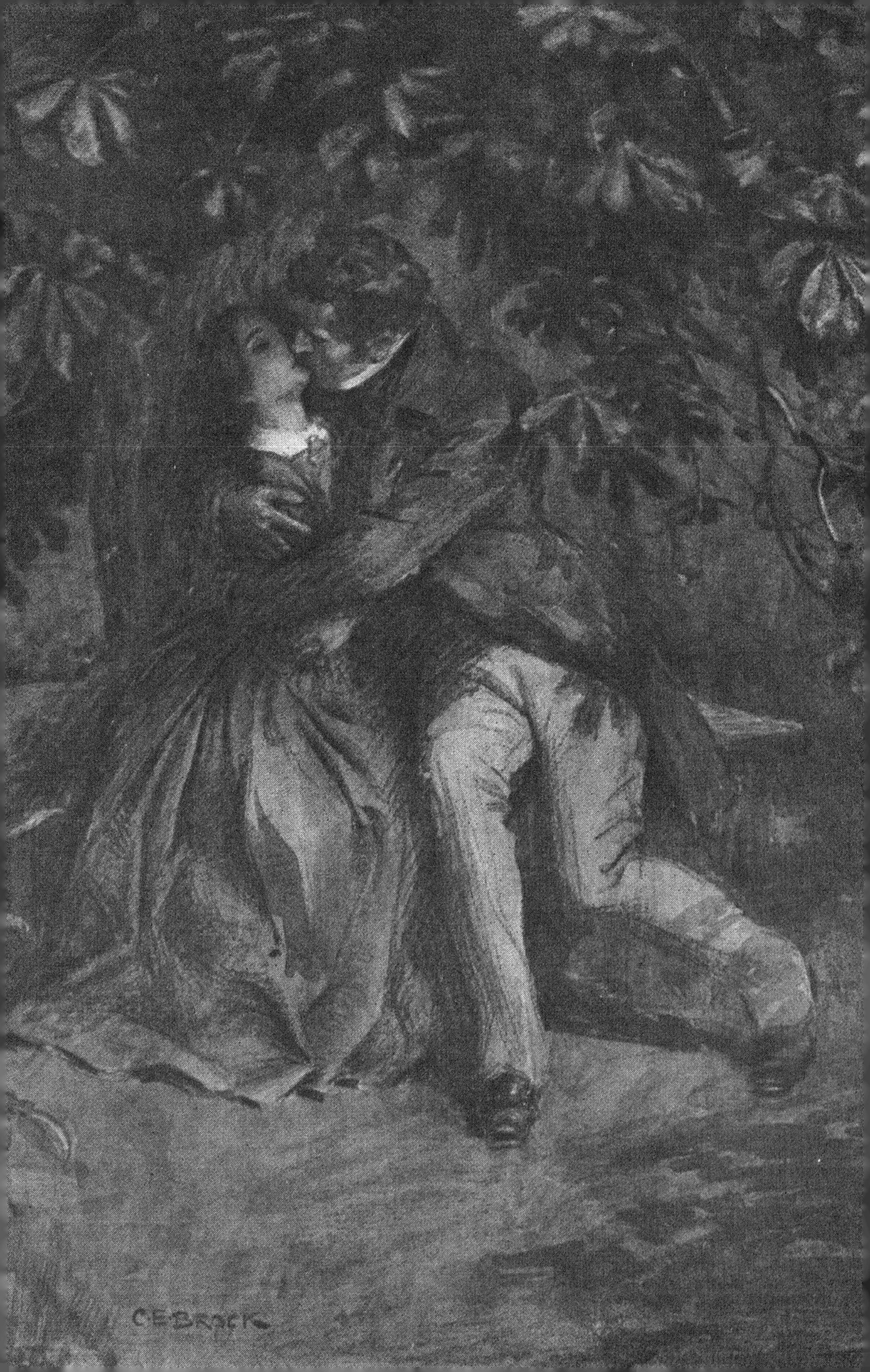
C.E.BROCK

such honey-dew fell, such silence reigned, such gloaming gathered, I felt as if I could haunt such shade for ever; but in threading the flower and fruit parterres at the upper part of the enclosure, enticed there by the light the now rising moon cast on this more open quarter, my step is stayed – not by sound, not by sight, but once more by a warning fragrance.

Sweet-briar and southernwood, jasmine, pink, and rose have long been yielding their evening sacrifice of incense: this new scent is neither of shrub nor flower; it is – I know it well – it is Mr. Rochester's cigar. I look round and I listen. I see trees laden with ripening fruit. I hear a nightingale warbling in a wood half a mile off; no moving form is visible, no coming step audible; but that perfume increases: I must flee. I make for the wicket leading to the shrubbery, and I see Mr. Rochester entering. I step aside into the ivy recess; he will not stay long: he will soon return whence he came, and if I sit still he will never see me.

But no – eventide is as pleasant to him as to me, and this antique garden as attractive; and he strolls on, now lifting the gooseberry-tree branches to look at the fruit, large as plums, with which they are laden; now taking a ripe cherry from the wall; now stooping towards a knot of flowers, either to inhale their fragrance or to admire the dew-beads on their petals. A great moth goes humming by me; it alights on a plant at Mr. Rochester's foot: he sees it, and bends to examine it. 'Now, he has his back towards me,' thought I, 'and he is occupied too; perhaps, if I walk softly, I can slip away unnoticed.'

I trod on an edging of turf that the crackle of the pebbly gravel might not betray me: he was standing among the beds at a yard or two distant from where I had to pass; the moth apparently engaged him. 'I shall get by very well,' I meditated. As I crossed his shadow, thrown long over the garden by the moon, not yet risen high, he said quietly, without turning – 'Jane, come and look at this fellow.'

I had made no noise: he had not eyes behind – could his shadow feel? I started at first, and then I approached him.

'Look at his wings,' said he, 'he reminds me rather of a West Indian insect; one does not often see so large and gay a night-rover in England; there! he is flown.'

The moth roamed away. I was sheepishly retreating also, but Mr. Rochester followed me, and when we reached the wicket, he said –

'Turn back: on so lovely a night it is a shame to sit in the house; and surely no one can wish to go to bed while sunset is thus at meeting with moonrise.'

It is one of my faults, that though my tongue is sometimes prompt enough at an answer, there are times when it sadly fails me in framing an excuse; and always the lapse occurs at some crisis, when a facile word or plausible pretext is specially wanted to get me out of painful embarrassment. I did not like to walk at this hour alone with Mr. Rochester in the shadowy orchard; but I could not find a reason to allege for leaving him. I followed with lagging step, and thoughts busily bent on discovering a means of extrication; but he himself looked so composed and so grave also, I became ashamed of feeling any confusion: the evil – if evil existent or prospective there was – seemed to lie with me only; his mind was unconscious and quiet.

'Jane,' he recommenced, as we entered the laurel walk, and slowly strayed down in the direction of the sunk fence and the horse chestnut, 'Thornfield is a pleasant place in summer, is it not?'

'Yes, sir.'

'You must have become in some degree attached to the house, – you, who have an eye for natural beauties, and a good deal of the organ of Adhesiveness?'

'I am attached to it, sir...'

'Pity!' he said, and sighed and paused.

'It's always the way of events in life,' he continued presently: 'no sooner have you got settled in a pleasant resting-place, than a voice calls out to you to rise and move on, for the hour of repose is expired.'

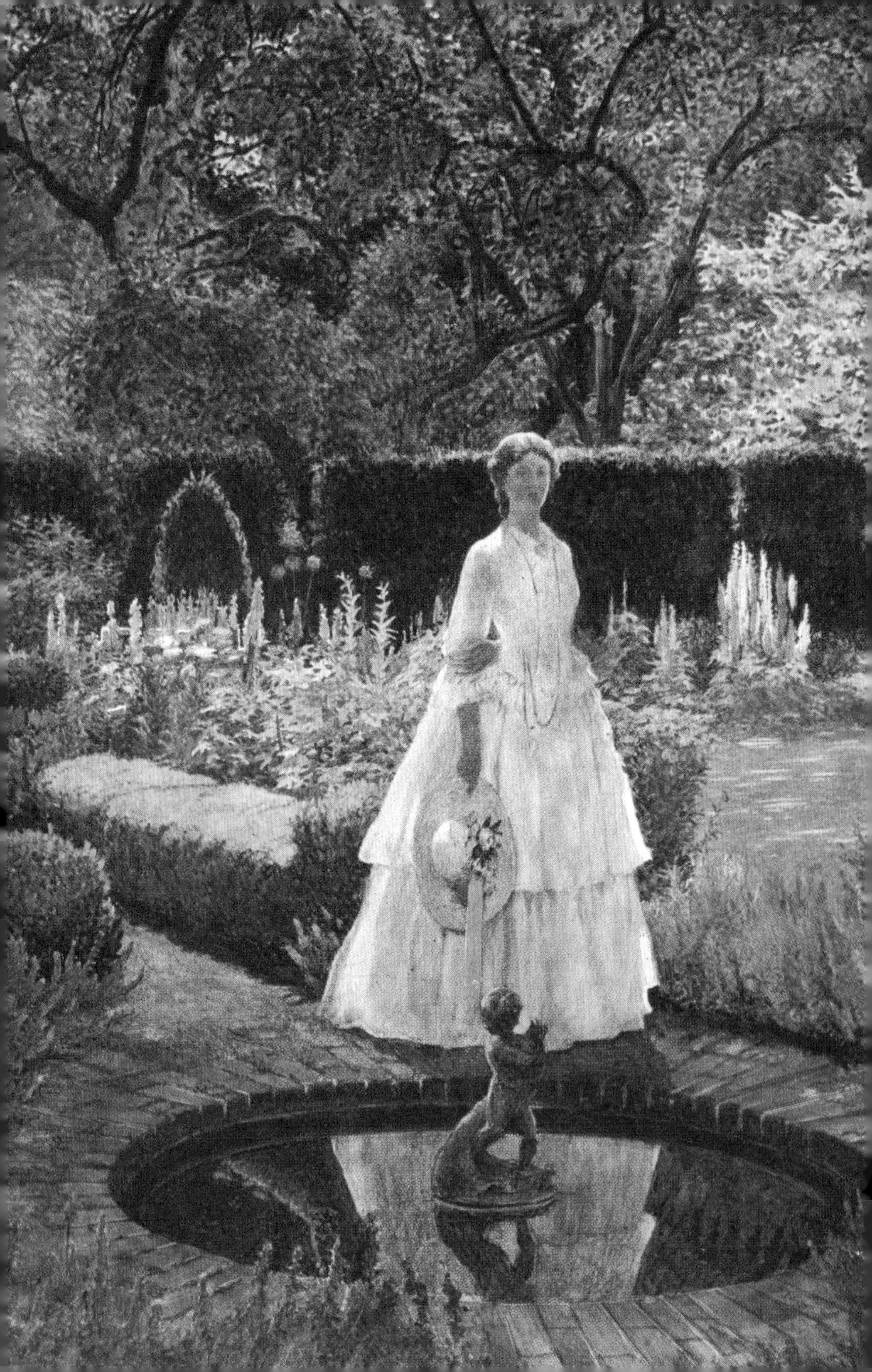

❧ The Planet of Love is on High

The most famous nineteenth-century verses about love in a garden are undoubt-edly these stanzas from Alfred Tennyson's Maud, *an interminably long poem published in 1855. Much loved by the Victorians, the verses have been set to music by several composers, most notably Balfe and Delius.*

Come into the garden, Maud,
For the black bat, Night, has flown,
Come into the garden, Maud,
I am here at the gate alone;
And the woodbine spices are wafted abroad,
And the musk of the roses blown.

For a breeze of morning moves,
And the planet of Love is on high,
Beginning to faint in the light that she loves
On a bed of daffodil sky,
To faint in the light of the sun she loves,
To faint in his light, and to die.

All night have the roses heard
The flute, violin, bassoon;
All night has the casement jessamine stirr'd
To the dancers dancing in tune;
Till a silence fell with the waking bird,
And a hush with the setting moon.

I said to the lily, 'There is but one
With whom she has heart to be gay.
When will the dancers leave her alone?
She is weary of dance and play.'
Now half to the setting moon are gone,
And half to the rising day;
Low on the sand and loud on the stone

The last wheel echoes away.
I said to the rose, 'The brief night goes
In babble and revel and wine.
O young lord-lover, what sighs are those
For one that will never be thine?
But mine, but mine,' so I swore to the rose,
'For ever and ever, mine.'

And the soul of the rose went into my blood,
As the music clashed in the hall;
And long by the garden lake I stood,
For I heard your rivulet fall
From the lake to the meadow and on to the wood,
Our wood, that is dearer than all;

From the meadow your walks have left so sweet
That whenever a March-wind sighs
He sets the jewel-print of your feet
In violets blue as your eyes,
To the woody hollows in which we meet
And the valleys of Paradise.

The slender acacia would not shake
One long milk-bloom on the tree;
The white lake-blossom fell into the lake,
As the pimpernel dozed on the lea;
But the rose was awake all night for your sake,
Knowing your promise to me;
The lilies and roses were all awake,
They sighed for the dawn and thee.

Queen rose of the rosebud garden of girls,
Come hither, the dances are done,
In gloss of satin and glimmer of pearls,
Queen lily and rose in one;
Shine out, little head, sunning over with curls.
To the flowers, and be their sun.

There has fallen a splendid tear
From the passion-flower at the gate.
She is coming, my dove, my dear;
She is coming, my life, my fate;
The red rose cries, 'She is near, she is near;'
And the white rose weeps, 'She is late;'
The larkspur listens, 'I hear, I hear;'
And the lily whispers, 'I wait.'

She is coming, my own, my sweet;
Were it ever so airy a tread,
My heart would hear her and beat,
Were it earth in an earthy bed;
My dust would hear her and beat,
Had I lain for a century dead;
Would start and tremble under her feet,
And blossom in purple and red.

❧ The Cap and Bells

Finally, of all the many depictions of lovers meeting or lamenting in gardens, the most beautiful and memorable is William Butler Yeats's 'The Cap and Bells' (1899).

The jester walked in the garden:
The garden had fallen still;
He bade his soul rise upward
And stand on her windowsill.

It rose in a straight blue garment,
When owls began to call:
It had grown wise-tongued by thinking
Of a quiet and light footfall;

But the young queen would not listen;
She rose in her pale night gown;
She drew in the heavy casement
And pushed the latches down.

He bade his heart go to her,
When the owls called out no more;
In a red and quivering garment
It sang to her through the door.

It had grown sweet-tongued by dreaming,
Of a flutter of flower-like hair;
But she took up her fan from the table
And waved it off on the air.

'I have cap and bells,' he pondered,
'I will send them to her and die';
And when the morning whitened
He left them where she went by.

She laid them upon her bosom,
Under a cloud of her hair,
And her red lips sang them a love-song:
Till stars grew out of the air.

She opened her door and her window,
And the heart and the soul came through,
To her right hand came the red one,
To her left hand came the blue.

They set up a noise like crickets,
A chattering wise and sweet,
And her hair was a folded flower
And the quiet of love in her feet.

EEN DER SCHOONSTE GESIGTE

'T VERMAARDE van PERK VAN SORGVL

Verklaringe der Cyfergetallen.

re Visryke Vyver. 19 Groote Vyver voor Vreemde en Inlandse Water-Vogelen. 20 Volieres of Vogelkooyen voor Vreemde en Inlandse Vogelen. 21 Fonteyn en groote Poort van latwerk. 22 Een groote
len. 28 Groote Waterkom met syn Fonteyn. 30 Somer plaats tot d'Orangerie en Vreemde gewassen. y. Groote Saal van d'Orangerie. 32 Winter plaats tot d'Orangerie etc. 17 Koets en Wagen

2 Grand Designs

'A garden must be looked into, and dressed as the body.' This nugget of folk wisdom was included by the metaphysical poet George Herbert in his collection of Outlandish Proverbs. *Visions of how bodies and gardens ought to be dressed have altered over the centuries. And until the early twentieth century, when the garden designer Avray Tipping could announce that 'We have become a nation of gardeners', gardens designed purely for pleasure were the preserve of the royal and the rich. The rest had gardens for thoroughly practical reasons.*

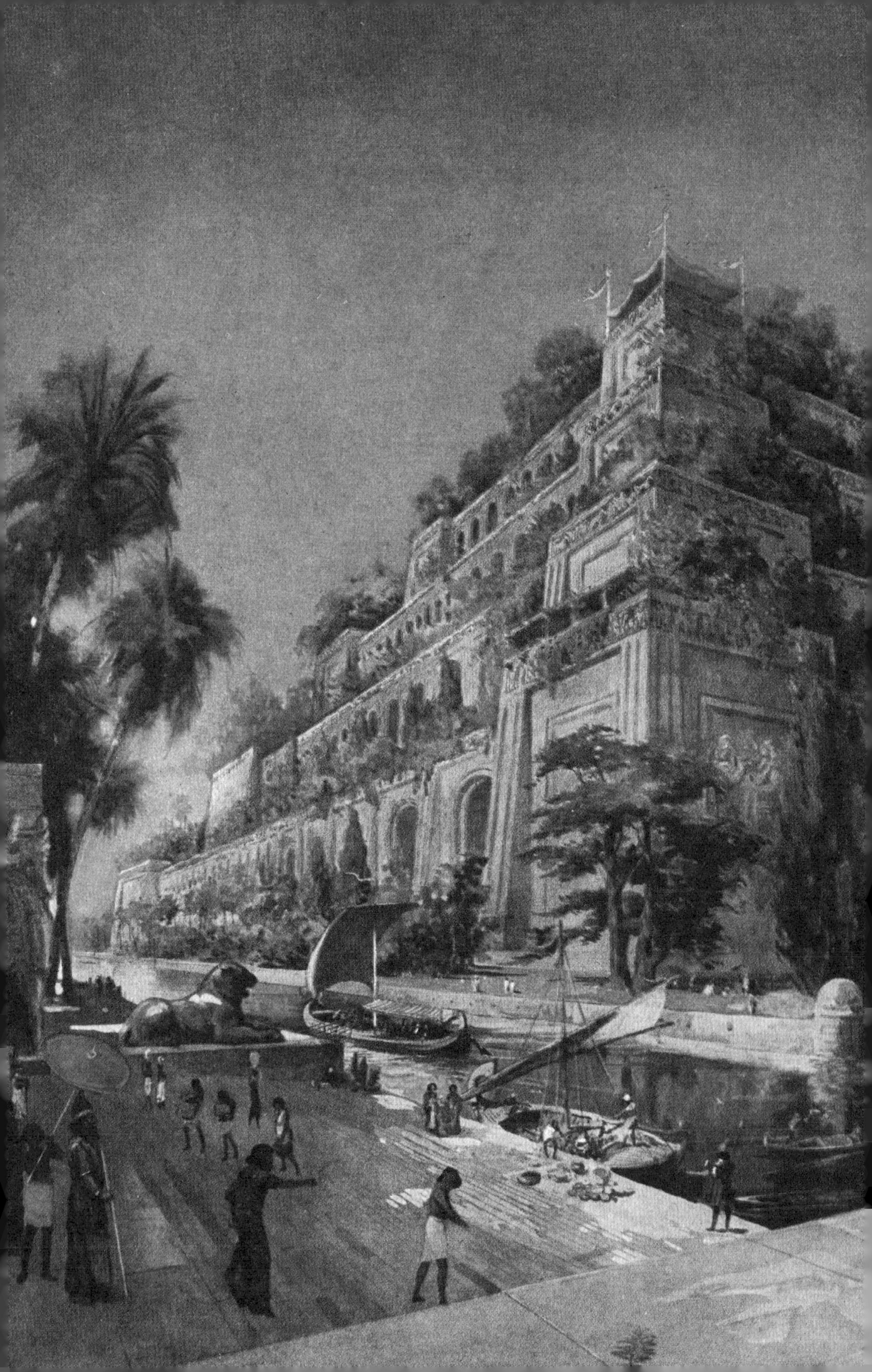

&s An Abundance of Brimstone

No one was more royal and rich than Nebuchadnezzar, who is said to have created the famous Hanging Gardens of Babylon for his wife. The result was rated by the Greeks as one of the Seven Wonders of the World. The first-century BC historian Diodorus Siculus looked behind its splendid plantings and explained its construction. The 'engines' he refers to were probably developed from Archimedes' screw. A cubit is half a yard; brimstone is similar to bitumen.

This garden was 400 feet square, and the ascent up to it was to the top of a mountain, and had buildings and apartments out of one into another, like a theatre. Under the steps to the ascent were built arches one above another, rising gently by degrees, which supported the whole plantation. The highest arch, upon which the platform of the garden was laid, was 50 cubits high, and the garden itself was surrounded with battlements and bulwarks. The walls were made very strong, built at no small charge and expense, being 22 feet thick, and every sally port [secure entrance] 10 feet wide.

Over the several storeys of this fabric were laid beams, and large massy stones, each 16 feet long and 4 broad. The roof over all these was first covered with reeds daubed with an abundance of brimstone, then upon them were laid double tiles, joined with a hard and durable mortar, and over them all were sheets of lead, so that the wet, which drained through the earth, might not rot the foundation. Upon all these was laid earth, of a convenient depth, sufficient for the growth of the greatest trees. When the soil was laid even and smooth, it was planted with all sorts of trees, which both for beauty and size might delight the spectators. The arches, which stood one above the other, had in them many stately rooms of all kinds, and for all purposes. There was one that had in it certain engines, which drew plenty of water out of the river Euphrates, through certain conduits hid from the spectators, and supplied it to the platform of the garden.

❧ The Blue Fig with Luscious Juice O'erflows

One of the lushest early accounts of elaborate gardens is Homer's description of the garden of Alcinous in The Odyssey. *Alcinous was the father of Nausicaa, who found the exhausted Odysseus washed up on their island home, Scheria (often identified with Corfu). Alcinous entertained Odysseus royally, before sending him home to Ithaca. This is Alexander Pope's translation from 1725.*

Close to the gates a spacious garden lies,
From storms defended and inclement skies.
Four acres was the allotted space of ground,
Fenced with a green enclosure all around.
Tall thriving trees confessed the fruitful mould:
The reddening apple ripens here to gold.
Here the blue fig with luscious juice o'erflows,
With deeper red the full pomegranate glows;
The branch here bends beneath the weighty pear,
And verdant olives flourish round the year,
The balmy spirit of the western gale
Eternal breathes on fruits, unthought to fail:
Each dropping pear a following pear supplies,
On apples, apples, figs on figs arise:
The same mild season gives the blooms to blow,
The buds to harden, and the fruits to grow.
Here ordered vines in equal ranks appear,
With all the united labours of the year;
Some to unload the fertile branches run,
Some dry the blackening clusters in the sun,
Others to tread the liquid harvest join:
The groaning presses foam with floods of wine.
Here are the vines in early flower descried,
Here grapes discoloured on the sunny side,
And there in autumn's richest purple dyed.
Beds of all various herbs, for ever green,
In beauteous order terminate the scene.

Two plenteous fountains the whole prospect crowned
This through the gardens leads its streams around
Visits each plant, and waters all the ground;
While that in pipes beneath the palace flows,
And thence its current on the town bestows:
To various use their various streams they bring,
The people one, and one supplies the king.
Such were the glories which the gods ordained,
To grace Alcinous, and his happy land.

❧ All is Calm and Composed

Gaius Plinius Caecilius Secundus, better known to us as Pliny the Younger, was an eminent Roman orator and lawyer who lived from AD 61 to 112. His uncle and mentor was the noted naturalist Pliny the Elder, who died in the fallout from Vesuvius' eruption in AD 79. Pliny the Younger is best known for his chatty and informative letters, several of which describe his various magnificent residences. Letter 52, to Domitius Apollinaris, describes Pliny's Tuscan villa, which was arranged overlooking his private hippodrome, a track for racing horses and chariots.

My house, although at the foot of a hill, commands as good a view as if it stood on its brow. Behind, but at a great distance, is the Apennine range. In the calmest days we get cool breezes from that quarter. The greater part of the house has a southern aspect, and seems to invite the afternoon sun into a broad and proportionately long portico, consisting of several rooms, particularly a court of antique fashion. In front of the portico is a sort of terrace, edged with box and shrubs cut into different shapes. You descend, from the terrace, by an easy slope adorned with the figures of animals in box, facing each other, to a lawn edged with the soft, I had almost said the liquid, Acanthus: this is surrounded by a walk enclosed with evergreens, shaped into a variety of forms. Beyond it is the promenade laid out in the form of a ring running round the multiform box-hedge and the dwarf-trees, which are cut quite close.

The whole is fenced in with a wall completely covered by box cut into steps all the way up to the top. On the outside of the wall lies a meadow that owes as many beauties to nature as all I have been describing within does to art.

The hippodrome lies entirely open in the middle of the grounds, so that the eye, upon your first entrance, takes it in entire in one view. It is set round with plane trees covered with ivy, so that, while their tops flourish with their own green, towards the roots their verdure is borrowed from the ivy that twines round the trunk and branches, spreads from tree to tree, and connects them together.

Between each plane tree are planted box-trees, and behind these stands a grove of laurels, which blend their shade with that of the

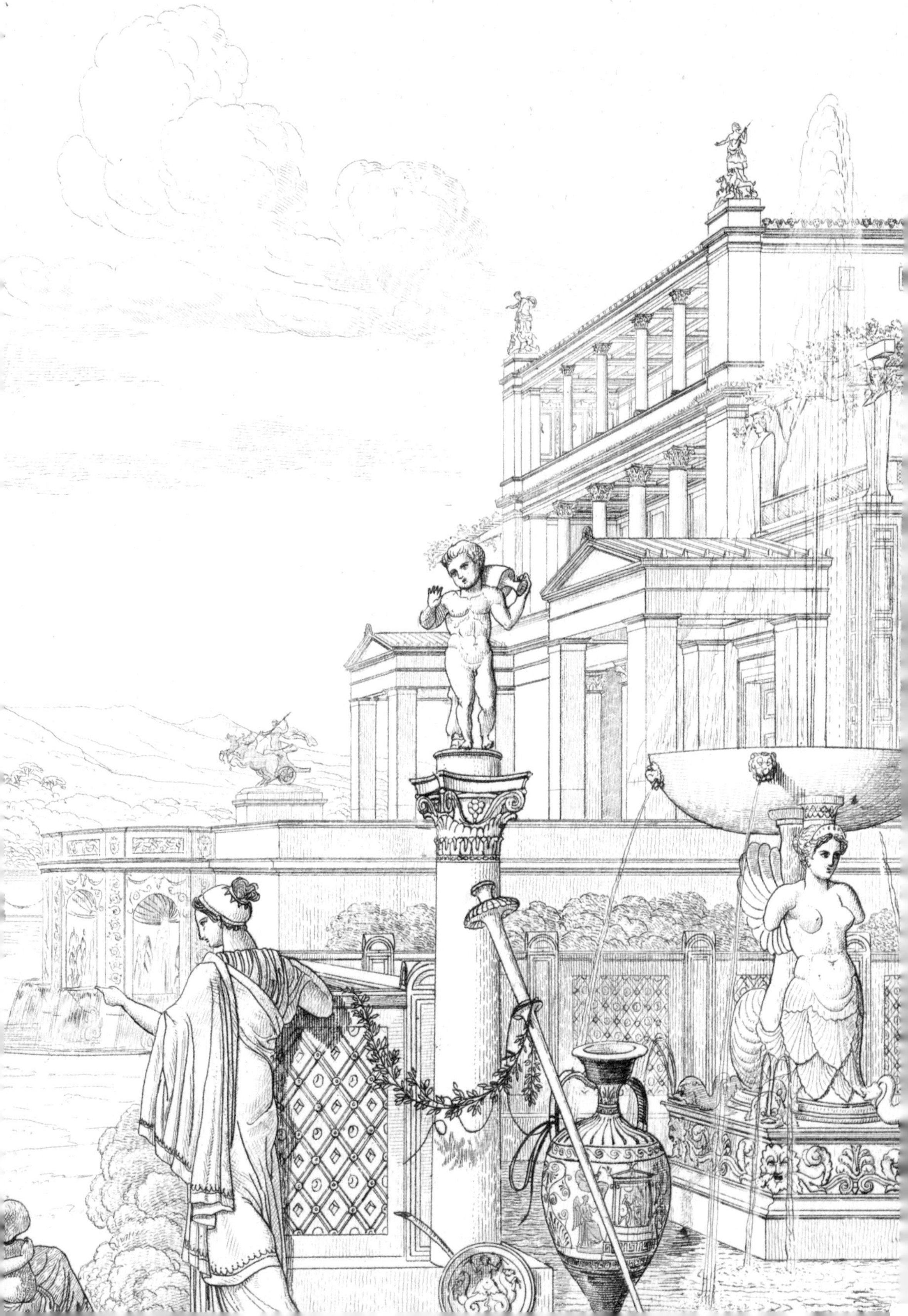

planes. This straight boundary to the hippodrome alters its shape at the farther end, bending into a semicircle, which is planted round, shut in with cypresses, and casts a deeper and gloomier shade, while the inner circular walks (for there are several), enjoying an open exposure, are filled with plenty of roses, and correct, by a very pleasant contrast, the coolness of the shade with the warmth of the sun. Having passed through these several winding alleys, you enter a straight walk, which breaks out into a variety of others, partitioned off by box-row hedges. In one place you have a little meadow, in another the box is cut in a thousand different forms, sometimes into letters, expressing the master's name, sometimes the artificer's, whilst here and there rise little obelisks with fruit-trees alternately intermixed, and then on a sudden, in the midst of this elegant regularity, you are surprised with an imitation of the negligent beauties of rural nature. In the centre of this lies a spot adorned with a knot of dwarf plane trees. Beyond these stands an acacia, smooth and bending in places, then again various other shapes and names. At the upper end is an alcove of white marble, shaded with vines and supported by four small Carystian columns. From this semicircular couch, the water, gushing up through several little pipes, as though pressed out by the weight of the persons who recline themselves upon it, falls into a stone cistern underneath, from whence it is received into a fine polished marble basin, so skilfully contrived that it is always full without ever overflowing.

When I sup here, this basin serves as a table, the larger sort of dishes being placed round the margin, while the smaller ones swim about in the form of vessels and waterfowl. Opposite this is a fountain which is incessantly emptying and filling, for the water which it throws up to a great height, falling back again into it, is by means of consecutive apertures returned as fast as it is received. Facing the alcove (and reflecting upon it as great an ornament as it borrows from it) stands a summer-house of exquisite marble, the doors of which project and open into a green enclosure, while from its upper and lower windows the eye falls upon a variety of different greens. Next to this is a little private closet (which, though it seems distinct, may form part of the same room), furnished with a couch, and notwithstanding it has windows on every side, yet it enjoys a very agreeable gloom, by means of a spreading vine which climbs to the top, and entirely overshadows it. Here you may lie and fancy yourself in a wood, with this only difference, that you are not exposed to the weather as you would be there. Here too a fountain rises and instantly disappears – several marble seats are set in different places, which are as pleasant as the summer-house itself after one is tired out with walking. Near each is a little fountain, and throughout the whole hippodrome several small rills run murmuring along through pipes, wherever the hand of art has thought proper to conduct them, watering here and there different plots of green, and sometimes all parts at once...

You see now the reasons why I prefer my Tuscan villa to those which I possess at Tusculum, Tiber, and Praeneste. Besides the advantages already mentioned, I enjoy here a cosier, more profound and undisturbed retirement than anywhere else, as I am at a greater distance from the business of the town and the interruption of troublesome clients. All is calm and composed; which circumstances contribute no less than its clear air and unclouded sky to that health of body and mind I particularly enjoy in this place, both of which I keep in full swing by study and hunting. And indeed there is no place which agrees better with my family, at least I am sure I have not yet lost one (touch wood!) of all those I brought here with me. And may the gods continue that happiness to me, and that honour to my villa. Farewell.

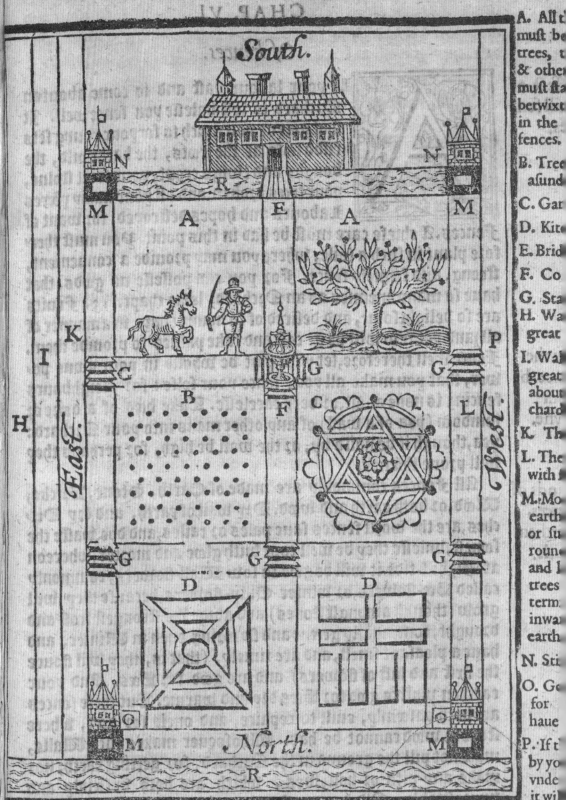

South.

N   N
M   E   M
A   A

K
I
H   East.   West.   P   L

B   F   C

D   D

M   O   O   M

North.

R

A. All t
must be
trees, t
& other
must sta
betwixt
in the
fences.

B. Tree
asund

C. Gar

D. Kite

E. Brid

F. Co

G. Sta

H. Wa
great

I. Wal
great
about
chard

K. Th

L. The
with

M. Mo
earth
or su
roun
and l
trees
term.
inwa
earth

N. Sti

O. Ge
for
haue

P. If t
by yo
vnde
it wi

❧ The Pleasant Whisking Wind

Robert Dudley, Earl of Leicester, created at Kenilworth Castle a fantastic private garden for Queen Elizabeth I's own use during her nine-day visit there in July 1575. It is to a trespasser that we owe a uniquely detailed description of it. Robert Laneham was 'beckoned in' by its keeper one day when the queen had gone out hunting. His accounts of its terrace, 15-foot obelisks and amazing bejewelled aviary are among the earliest mentions of such Italianate features in English gardens. The garden has been reconstructed at Kenilworth in recent times.

The Earl of Leicester's exquisitely appointed garden, an acre or more in quantity, lies on the north, whereon hard along by the castle wall is reared a pleasant terrace, ten feet high, and twelve feet broad, even under foot, and fresh of fine grass; as is also the side thereof towards the garden. In this, by sundry equal distances, with obelisks and spheres, and white bears, all of stone upon curious bases, in goodly show were set. At each end, two fine arbours made redolent with sweet trees and flowers the garden plot. Fair alleys, green by grass, even voided from the borders on both sides, and some (for change) with sand, not light, or too soft, or soily by dust, but smooth and firm, pleasant to walk on, as a sea-shore when the water is availed. Then, much gracified by due proportion of four even quarters; in the midst of each, upon a base of two feet square and high, seemly bordered of itself, a square pilaster rose pyramidically fifteen feet high. Each was symmetrically pierced through from a foot beneath to two feet from the top: and had, for a Capital, an orb of ten inches thick. Every one of these, with its base, from the ground to the top, was hewn out of one whole piece of hard porphyry, and with great art and heed thither conveyed and erected. Also by great cast and cost, there was sweetness and savour on all sides, made so respirant from the redolent plants, fragrant herbs and flowers, in form and colour so deliciously variant; and fruit-trees bedecked with apples, pears, and ripe cherries.

In the middle against the north wall of the terrace was a square cage sumptuously made, 20 feet high, 30 long and 14 broad. A grand framing was continued all about it, holding four great windows, each arched, supporting a comely cornice. A wire net of the finest knit was tightly overstretched over all. Under the cornice every part was beautified with great diamonds, emeralds, rubies and sapphires. This mansion was replenished with lively birds from England, France, Spain, the Canaries and Africa. Holes and caverns in orderly distance voided into the wall for roosts at night and refuge in weather.

In the centre was a goodly fountain, with two Athlants upholding a bowl three foot wide, from which sundry fine pipes cast sprays into the rest of the fountain; swimming round about were carp, tench, bream, perch and eel.

A garden then so appointed, as wherein aloft upon the shadowed walk of terrace, in heat of summer to feel the pleasant whisking wind above, or delicate coolness of the fountain-spring beneath; to taste of delicious strawberries, cherries, and other fruits, even from their stalks; to smell such fragrancy of sweet odours, breathing from the plants, herbs and flowers; to hear such melodious music and tunes of birds; to have in eye for mirth sometime these underspringing streams; then, the woods, the waters (for both pool and chase were hard at hand in sight), the deer, the people (that out of the east arbour in the base court, also at hand in view), the fruit-trees, the plants, the herbs, the change in colours, the birds flittering, the fountain streaming, the fish swimming, all in such delectable variety, order and dignity. Argument most certain of a right noble mind, that this could have thus all contrived.

& A Princelike Garden

In 1597 Sir Francis Bacon outlined the ideal plan for what he called a 'prince-like' garden. It boasts shady alleys, a mount topped by a banqueting house — and a swimming pool.

The contents ought not well to be under thirty acres of ground; and to be divided into three parts; a green in the entrance; a heath or desert in the going forth; and the main garden in the midst; besides alleys on both sides. And I like well that four acres of ground be assigned to the green; six to the heath; four and four to either side; and twelve to the main garden. The green hath two pleasures: the one, because nothing is more pleasant to the eye than green grass kept finely shorn; the other, because it will give you a fair alley in the midst, by which you may go towards the stately hedge, which is to enclose the garden. But because the alley will be long, and, in great heat of the year or day, you ought not to buy the shade in the garden by going in the sun through the green, therefore you are, of either side the green, to plant a covert alley upon carpenter's work, about twelve foot in height, by which you may go in shade into the garden.

As for the making of knots or figures, with divers coloured earths, that they may lie under the windows of the house on that side which the garden stands, they be but toys; you may see as good sights, many times, in tarts. The garden is best to be square, encompassed on all the four sides with a stately arched hedge. The arches to be upon pillars of carpenter's work, of some ten foot high, and six foot broad; and the spaces between of the same dimension with the breadth of the arch. Over the arches let there be an entire hedge of some four foot high, framed also upon carpenter's work; and upon the upper hedge, over every arch, a little turret, with a belly, enough to receive a cage of birds: and over every space between the arches some other little figure, with broad plates of round coloured glass gilt, for the sun to play upon. But this hedge I intend to be raised upon a bank, not steep, but gently sloping, of some six foot, set all with flowers. Also I understand, that this square of the garden, should not be the whole breadth of the ground, but to leave on either side ground enough for a diversity of side alleys; unto which the two covert alleys of the green may deliver you.

For the ordering of the ground, within the great hedge, I leave it to variety of device; advising nevertheless, that whatsoever form you cast it into, first, it be not too busy, or full of work. Wherein I, for my part, do not like images cut out in juniper or other garden stuff; they be for children. Little low hedges, round, with some pretty pyramids, I like well; and in some places, fair columns upon frames of carpenter's work. I would also have the alleys, spacious and fair. You may have closer alleys, upon the side grounds, but none in the main garden. I wish also, in the very middle, a fair mount, with three ascents, and alleys, enough for four to walk abreast; which I would have to be perfect circles, without any bulwarks or embossments; and the whole mount to be thirty foot high; and some fine banqueting-house, with some chimneys neatly cast, and without too much glass.

For fountains, they are a great beauty and refreshment; but pools mar all, and make the garden unwholesome, and full of flies and frogs. Fountains I intend to be of two natures: the one that sprinkles or spouts water; the other a fair receipt of water, of some thirty or forty foot square, but without fish, or slime, or mud. For the first, the ornaments of images gilt, or of marble, which are in use, do well: but the main matter is so to convey the water, as it never stay, either in the bowls or in the cistern; that the water be never by rest discoloured, green or red or the like; or gather any mossiness or putrefaction. Besides that, it is to be cleansed every day by the hand. Also some steps up to it, and some fine pavement about it, doth well.

As for the other kind of fountain, which we may call a bathing pool, it may admit much curiosity and beauty; wherewith we will not trouble ourselves: as, that the bottom be finely paved, and with images; the sides likewise; and withal embellished with coloured glass, and such things of lustre; encompassed also with fine rails of low statues. But the main point is the same which we mentioned in the former kind of fountain; which is, that the water be in perpetual motion, fed by a water higher than the pool, and delivered into it by fair spouts, and then discharged away under ground, by some equality of bores, that it stay little. And for fine devices, of arching water without spilling, and making it rise in several forms (of feathers, drinking glasses, canopies,

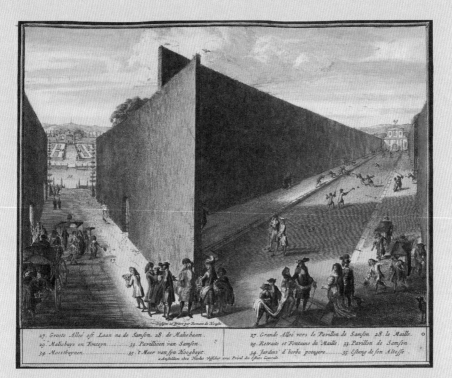

27. Groote Alleé oft Laan na de Samson. 28. de Maliebaan.
29. Malichuys en Fonteyn..............33. Pavillioen van Samson.
34. Moesthuynen.....................35. 't Meer van syn Hooghcyt.
e Amfteldam chez Niclas Vifcher avec Privil. des Eftats Generals.

27. Grande Alleé vers le Pavillon de Samson. 28. le Maille.
29. Retraite et Fontaine du Maille. 33. Pavillon de Samson.
34. Jardins d'herbe potagere..........35. Eftang de son Alteffe.

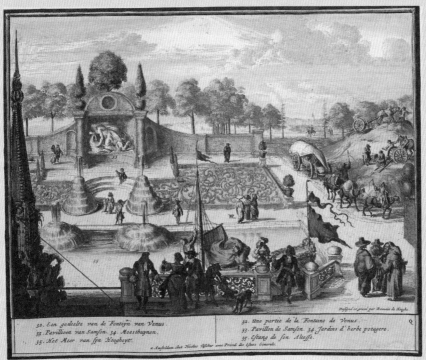

32. Een gedeelte van de Fonteyn van Venus.
33. Pavillioen van Samson. 34. Moesthuynen.
35. Het Meer van syn Hooghcyt.
e Amfteldam chez Niclas Vifcher avec Privil. des Eftats Generals.

32. Une partie de la Fontaine de Venus.
33. Pavillon de Samson. 34. Jardins d'herbe potagere.
35. Eftang de son Alteffe.

and the like), they be pretty things to look on, but nothing to health and sweetness.

For the heath, which was the third part of our plot, I wish it to be framed, as much as may be, to a natural wildness. Trees I would have none in it, but some thickets made only of sweetbriar and honeysuckle, and some wild vine amongst; and the ground set with violets, straw-berries, and primroses. For these are sweet, and prosper in the shade. And these to be in the heath, here and there, not in any order. I like also little heaps, in the nature of mole-hills (such as are in wild heaths), to be set, some with wild thyme; some with pinks; some with germander, that gives a good flower to the eye; some with periwinkle; some with violets; some with strawberries; some, with cowslips; some with daisies; some with red roses; some with lilies of the valley; some with sweet-williams red; some with bear's-foot: and the like low flowers, being withal sweet and sightly. Part of which heaps are to be with standards of little bushes pricked upon their top, and part without. The standards to be roses, juniper, holly, barberries and here and there, because of the smell of their blossoms, red currants, gooseberries, rosemary, bays, sweet-briar and such like. But these standards to be kept with cutting, that they grow not out of course.

&⅌ The Shalimar Bagh

The Mughal emperors excelled in planning gardens that led visitors into ever more enticing retreats. None was so renowned as the Shalimar Bagh, created in 1619 on the banks of the Dal Lake in Kashmir by the Emperor Jahangir to please his queen. In 1910 it was visited by Constance Villiers-Stuart, and described in her pioneering book Gardens of the Great Mughals *(1913), which she illustrated herself.*

A canal about a mile in length and twelve yards broad, runs through the marshy swamps, the willow groves, and the rice-fields that fringe the lower end of the lake connecting the garden with the deep open water. On each side there are broad green paths overshadowed by large chenars; and at the entrance to the canal blocks of masonry indi-cate the site of an old gateway. There are fragments also of the stone embankment which formerly lined the watercourse.

The Shalimar … still shows the charming old plan of a Mughal summer residence. The present enclosure is five hundred and ninety yards long by about two hundred and sixty-seven yards broad, divided, as was usual in royal pleasure-grounds, into three separate parts: the outer gardens, the central, or Emperor's garden, and last and most beautiful of the three, the garden for the special use of the Empress and her ladies.

The outer or public garden, starting with the grand canal leading from the lake, terminates at the first large pavilion, the Diwan-I-'Am. The small black marble throne still stands over the waterfall in the vcentre of the canal which flows through the building into the tank below. From time to time this garden was thrown open to the people so that they might see the Emperor enthroned in his Hall of Public Audience.

The second garden is slightly broader, consisting of two shallow terraces with the Diwan-I-Khas (the Hall of Private Audience) in the centre … On the north-east boundary of this enclosure are the royal bathrooms.

At the next wall, the little guard-rooms that flank the entrance to the ladies garden have been rebuilt in Kashmir style on older stone bases.

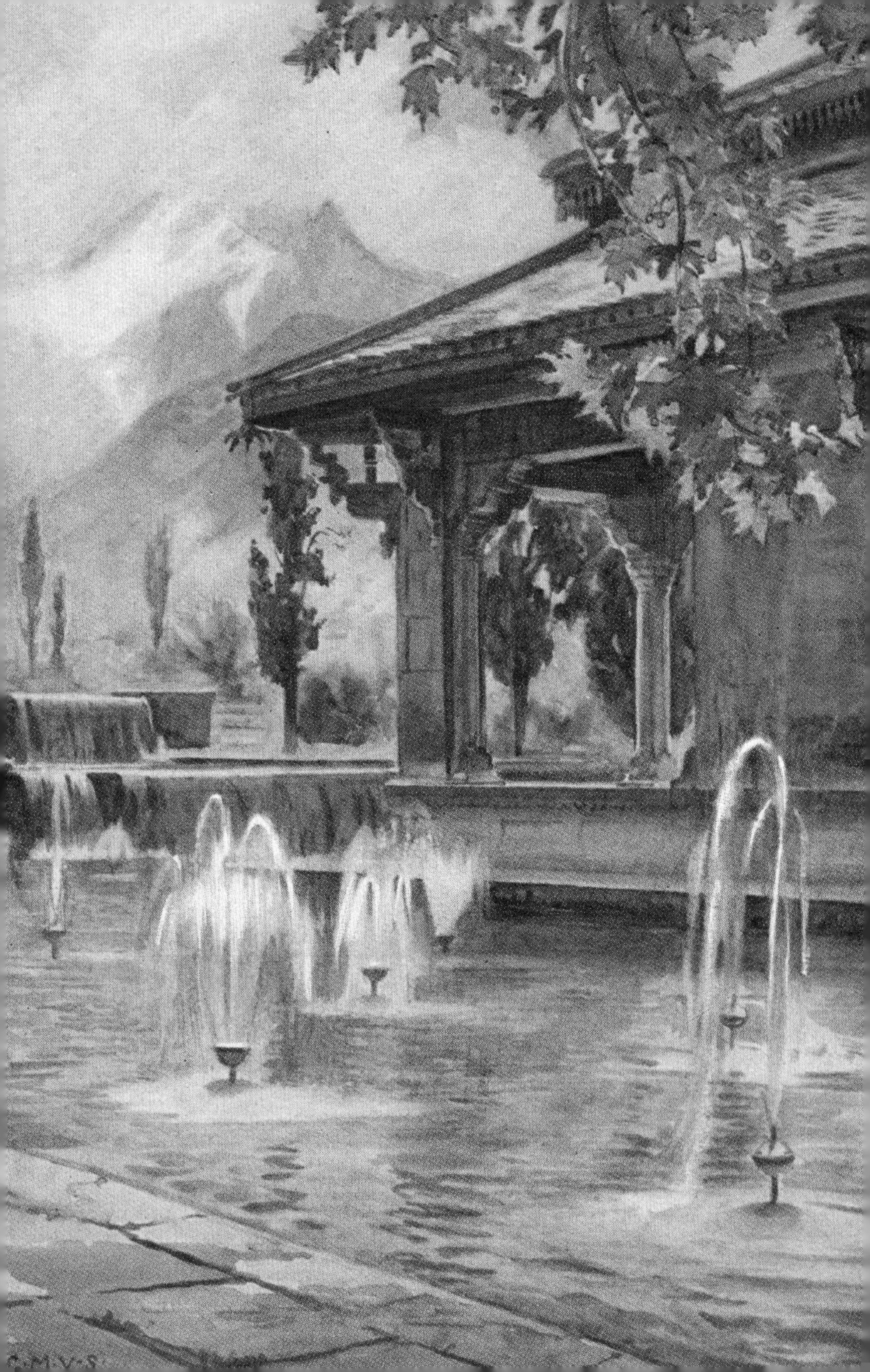

Here the whole effect culminates with the beautiful black marble pavilion built by Shah Jahan, which still stands in the midst of its fountain spray; the green glitter of water shining in the smooth, polished marble, the deep rich tone of which is repeated in the old cypress trees. Round this baradari [pavilion] the whole colour and perfume of the garden is concentrated, with the snows of Mahadev for a background. How well the Mughals understood the principle that the garden, like every other work of art, should have a climax.

This unique pavilion is surrounded on every side by a series of cascades, and at night when the lamps are lighted in the little arched recesses behind the shining waterfalls, it is even more fairy-like than by day... A subtle air of leisure and repose, a romantic but indefinable spell, pervades the royal Shalimar: this leafy garden of dim vistas, shallow terraces, smooth sheets of falling water, and wide canals, with calm reflections broken only by the stepping stones across the streams.

❧ The Genius of the Place

Alexander Pope was fascinated by gardens and parks; he saw them as the settings in which houses lay like jewels. 'Gardening is near-akin to Philosophy,' he once wrote. He repeatedly satirised contemporary garden style, insisting that artificiality was to be abhorred. Nature was the best guide, and the first considera-tion was the existing landscape in which a park or garden was constructed. His ideals were memorably stated in his 'Epistle Of the Use of Riches', written in the 1730s and dedicated to Richard Boyle, Earl of Burlington.

To build, to plant, whatever you intend,
To rear the column, or the arch to bend,
To swell the terrace, or to sink the grot;
In all, let Nature never be forgot.
But treat the goddess like a modest fair,
Nor overdress, nor leave her wholly bare;
Let not each beauty everywhere be spied,
Where half the skill is decently to hide.
He gains all points, who pleasingly confounds,
Surprises, varies, and conceals the bounds.

Consult the genius of the place in all;
That tells the waters or to rise, or fall;
Or helps th'ambitious hill the heavens to scale,
Or scoops in circling theatres the vale;
Calls in the country, catches opening glades,
Joins willing woods, and varies shades from shades,
Now breaks, or now directs, th'intending lines;
Paints as you plant, and, as you work, designs.

Still follow sense, of every art the soul,
Parts answering parts shall slide into a whole,
Spontaneous beauties all around advance,
Start ev'n from difficulty, strike from chance;
Nature shall join you; time shall make it grow
A work to wonder at – perhaps a Stowe!

In an article for The Guardian *in 1713, Pope derided the prevailing fashion for elaborate topiary in a magnificent parody of a commercial gardener's catalogue of greens.*

How contrary to simplicity is the modern practice of gardening! We seem to make it our study to recede from nature, not only in the various tonsure of greens into the most regular and formal shape, but even in monstrous attempts beyond the reach of the art itself: we run into sculpture, and are yet better pleased to have our trees in the most awkward figures of men and animals, than in the most regular of their own...

A citizen is no sooner proprietor of a couple of yews, but he entertains thoughts of erecting them into giants, like those of Guildhall. I know an eminent cook, who beautified his country-seat with a coronation dinner in greens, where you see the champion flourishing on horseback at one end of the table, and the Queen in perpetual youth at the other.

For the benefit of all my loving countrymen of this curious taste, I shall here publish a catalogue of greens to be disposed of by an eminent town gardener, who has lately applied to me upon this head. He represents, that for the advancement of a politer sort of ornament in the villas and gardens adjacent to this great city, and in order to distinguish those places from the mere barbarous countries of gross nature, the world stands much in need of a virtuoso gardener, who has a turn to sculpture, and is thereby capable of improving upon the ancients of his profession, in the imagery of ever-greens. My correspondent is arrived to such perfection that he also cuts family pieces of men, women, or children. Any ladies that please may have their own effigies in myrtle, or their husband's in horn-beam. He is a Puritan wag, and never fails, when he shows his garden, to repeat that passage in the Psalms, 'Thy wife shall be as the fruitful vine, and thy children as olive-branches round thy table.'

I proceed to his catalogue.

Adam and Eve in yew; Adam a little shattered by the fall of the Tree of Knowledge in the great storm; Eve and the serpent very flourishing.

Noah's ark in holly, the ribs a little damaged for want of water.

The Tower of Babel, not yet finished.

St. George in box; his arm scarce long enough, but will be in a condition to stick the dragon by next April.

A green dragon of the same, with a tail of ground-ivy for the present.

N. B. These two not to be sold separately.

Edward the Black Prince in cypress.

A laurustine bear in blossom, with a juniper hunter in berries.

A pair of giants, stunted, to be sold cheap.

A Queen Elizabeth in phyllirea, a little inclining to the green sickness, but of full growth.

Another Queen Elizabeth in myrtle, which was very forward, but miscarried by being too near a savine.

An old maid of honour in wormwood.

A topping Ben Jonson in laurel.

Divers eminent modern poets in bays, somewhat blighted, to be disposed of a pennyworth.

A quick-set hog shot up into a porcupine, by being forgot a week in rainy weather.

A lavender pig, with sage growing in his belly.

A pair of maidenheads in fir, in great forwardness.

When Pope settled in his Thameside house at Twickenham and began to lay out his own garden, however, simplicity was not exactly his watchword. As this letter to his friend Edmund Blount in 1725 reveals, nothing could have been much more artificial than the trompe l'oeil conceits of his villa at Twickenham.

I have put the last hand to my works, finishing the subterraneous way and grotto. I there found a spring of the clearest water, which falls in a perpetual rill, that echoes through the Cavern day and night. From the river Thames, you see through my arch up a walk of the wilderness to

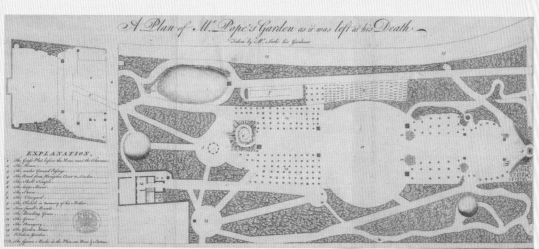

A Plan of Mr Pope's Garden as it was left at his Death.
Taken by Mr Serle his Gardner.

EXPLANATION.

a kind of open temple wholly composed of shells in the rustic manner; and from that distance under the temple, you look down through a sloping arcade of trees, and see the sails on the river passing suddenly and vanishing as through a perspective glass. When you shut the doors of this grotto it becomes on the instant, from a luminous room, a Camera obscura, on the walls of which all the objects of the river, hills, woods and boats are forming a moving picture in their visible radiations; and when you have a mind to light it up, it affords you a very different scene.

It is finished with shells interspersed with pieces of looking-glass in angular forms; and in the ceiling is a star of the same material, at which when a lamp, of an orbicular figure of thin alabaster, is hung in the middle, a thousand pointed rays glitter, and are reflected over the place. There are connected to this grotto by a narrower passage two porches with niches and seats – one towards the river, of smooth stones, full of light and open; the other towards the arch of trees, rough with shells, flints and iron-ore. The bottom is painted with simple pebble, and the adjoining walk up the wilderness to the temple is to be cockle-shells, in the natural taste, agreeing not ill with the little dripping murmur, and the aquatic idea of the whole place. It wants nothing to complete it but a good statue.

❧ A Labyrinth of My Own Raising

*Pope's contemporary Joseph Addison was the first writer to talk, in 1712, of
'making a landscape', and his interest in gardens is celebrated by Addison's Walk
in Magdalen College, Oxford, his alma mater. In* The Spectator *(no. 477), he
describes the careful informality of his own garden at Bilton Hall, near Rugby.*

I have several Acres about my House, which I call my Garden, and
which a skilful Gardener would not know what to call. It is a Confusion
of Kitchin and Parterre, Orchard and Flower-Garden, which lie so
mixt and interwoven with one another, that if a foreigner who had
seen nothing of our country should be convey'd into my garden at his
first landing, he would look upon it as a natural wilderness, and one of
the uncultivated parts of our country.

My flowers grow up in several parts of the garden in the greatest
luxuriancy and profusion. I am so far from being fond of any particular
one, by reason of its rarity, that if I meet with any one in a field which
pleases me, I give it a place in my garden. By this means, when a stranger
walks with me, he is surprised to see several large spots of ground
covered with ten thousand different colours, and has often singled out
flowers that he might have met with under a common hedge, in a field,
or in a meadow, as some of the greatest beauties of the place. The only
method I observe in this particular, is to range in the same quarter
the products of the same season, that they may make their appearance
together, and compose a picture of the greatest variety.

There is the same irregularity in my plantations, which run into as
great a wildness as their natures will permit. I take in none that do not
naturally rejoice in the soil, and am pleased when I am walking in a
labyrinth of my own raising, not to know whether the next tree I shall
meet with is an apple or an oak, an elm or a pear-tree.

My kitchen has likewise its particular quarters assigned it; for
besides the wholesome luxury which that place abounds with, I
have always thought a kitchen-garden a more pleasant sight than the
finest orangery, or artificial greenhouse. I love to see everything in its
perfection, and am more pleased to survey my rows of coleworts and
cabbages, with a thousand nameless pot-herbs, springing up in their

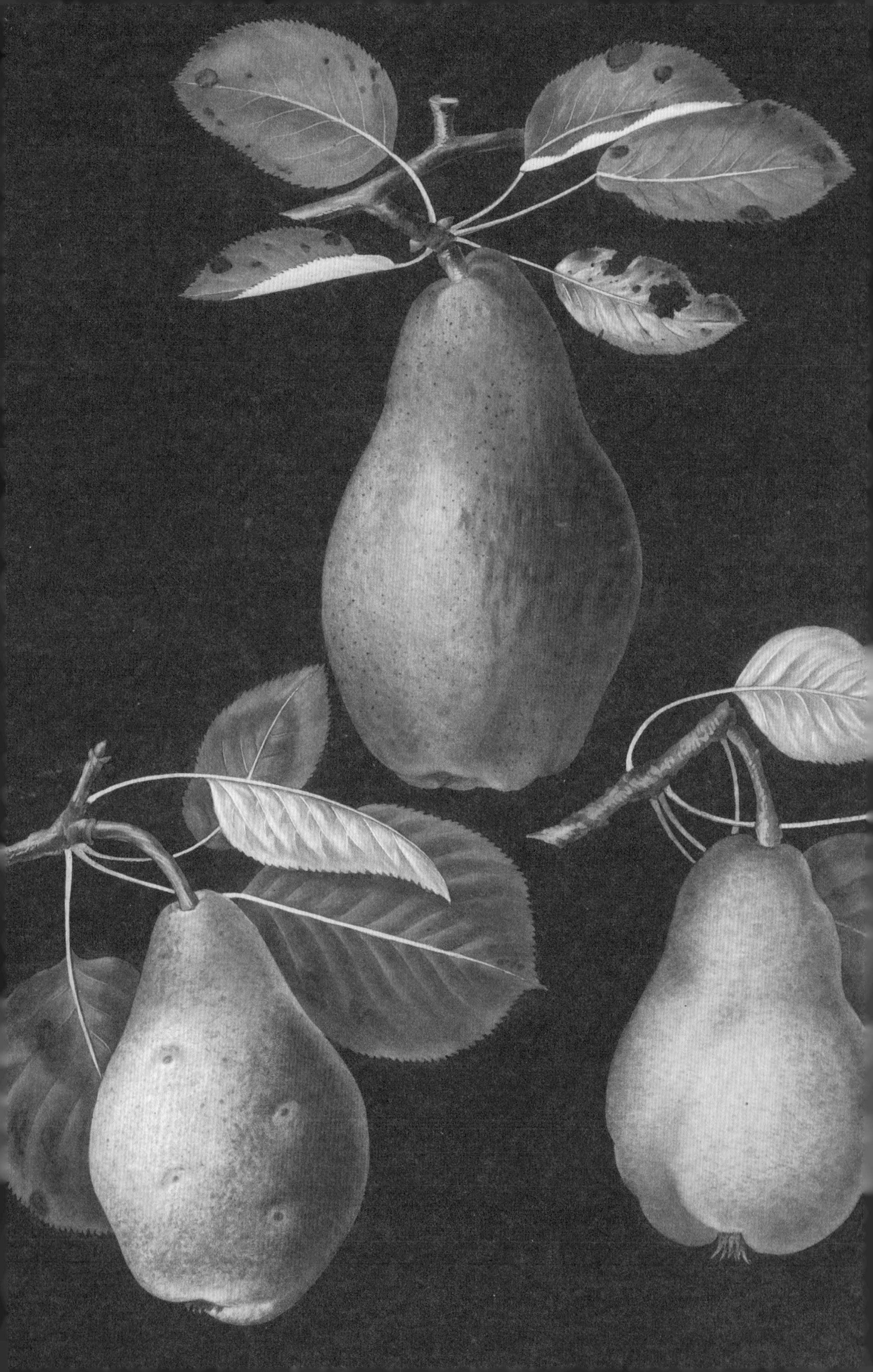

full fragrancy and verdure, than to see the tender plants of foreign countries kept alive by artificial heats, or withering in an air and soil that are not adapted to them.

I must not omit that there is a fountain rising in the upper part of my garden, which forms a little wandering rill, and administers to the pleasure as well as the plenty of the place. I have so conducted it that it visits most of my plantations; and have taken particular care to let it run in the same manner as it would do in an open field, so that it generally passes through banks of violets and primroses, plats of willow, or other plants, that seem to be of its own producing.

There is another circumstance in which I am very particular, or, as my neighbours call me, very whimsical: as my garden invites into it all the birds of the country, by offering them the conveniency of springs and shades, solitude and shelter, I do not suffer any one to destroy their nests in the spring, or drive them from their usual haunts in fruit-time. I value my garden more for being full of blackbirds than cherries, and very frankly give them fruit for their songs. By this means I have always the musick of the season in its perfection, and am highly delighted to see the jay or the thrush hopping about my walks, and shooting before my eye across the several little glades and alleys that I pass thro'.

𝕰𝕾 The Horticultural Xenophobe

Tobias Smollett travelled in France and Italy in the 1760s, sending letters home to be published on his return. His opinionated observations reveal the contrast between continental and English garden design in the eighteenth century.

NICE, MARCH 5, 1765

Dear Sir, In my last I gave you my opinion freely of the modern palaces of Italy. I shall now hazard my thoughts upon the gardens of this country, which the inhabitants extol with all the hyperboles of admiration and applause. I must acknowledge however, I have not seen the famous villas at Frascati and Tivoli, which are celebrated for their gardens and waterworks. I intended to visit these places; but was prevented by an unexpected change of weather, which deterred me from going to the country. On the last day of September the mountains of Palestrina were covered with snow; and the air became so cold at Rome, that I was forced to put on my winter clothes [and] return to Florence. But I have seen the gardens of the Poggio Imperiale, and the Palazzo de Pitti at Florence, and those of the Vatican, of the Pope's palace on Monte Cavallo, of the Villa Ludovisia, Medicea, and Pinciana, at Rome; so that I think I have some right to judge of the Italian taste in gardening. Among those I have mentioned, that of the Villa Pinciana is the most remarkable, and the most extensive, including a space of three miles in circuit, hard by the walls of Rome, containing a variety of situations high and low, which favour all the natural embellishments one would expect to meet with in a garden, and exhibit a diversity of noble views of the city and adjacent country.

In a fine extensive garden or park, an Englishman expects to see a number of groves and glades, intermixed with an agreeable negligence, which seems to be the effect of nature and accident. He looks for shady walks encrusted with gravel; for open lawns covered with verdure as smooth as velvet, but much more lively and agreeable; for ponds, canals, basins, cascades, and running streams of water; for clumps of trees, woods, and wildernesses, cut into delightful alleys, perfumed with honeysuckle and sweet-briar, and resounding with the mingled melody of all the singing birds of heaven: he looks for plats of flowers

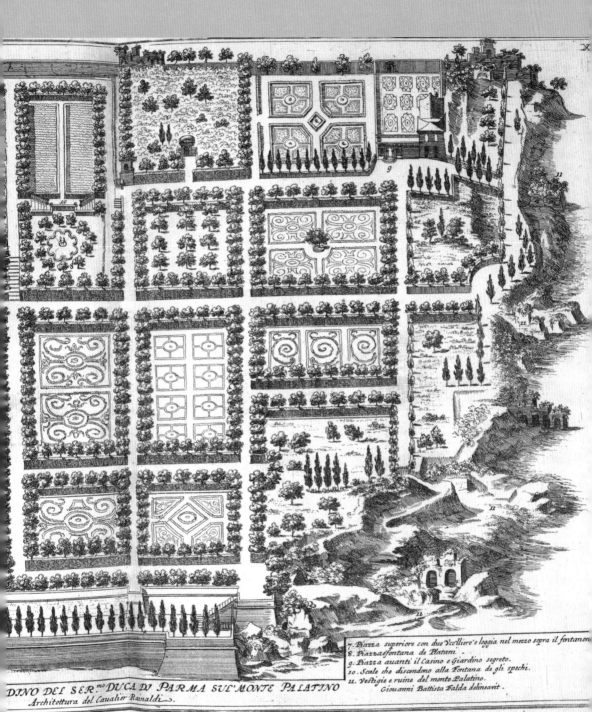

X

9

10

11

11

11

11

7. Piazza superiore con due Vcelliere e loggia nel mezzo sopra il fontanon
8. Piazza e fontana de Platani.
9. Piazza auanti il Casino e Giardino segreto.
10. Scale che discendono alla Fontana de gli spechi.
11. Vestigie e ruine del monte Palatino.
                    Giouanni Battista Falda delineavit.

DINO DEL SER.mo DUCA DI PARMA SUL MONTE PALATINO
     Architettura del Caualier Rainaldi.

in different parts to refresh the sense, and please the fancy; for arbours, grottos, hermitages, temples, and alcoves, to shelter him from the sun, and afford him means of contemplation and repose; and he expects to find the hedges, groves, and walks, and lawns kept with the utmost order and propriety.

He who loves the beauties of simple nature, and the charms of neatness will seek for them in vain amidst the groves of Italy. In the garden of the Villa Pinciana, there is a plantation of four hundred pines, which the Italians view with rapture and admiration: there is likewise a long walk, of trees extending from the garden-gate to the palace; and plenty of shade, with alleys and hedges in different parts of the ground: but the groves are neglected; the walks are laid with nothing but common mould or sand, black and dusty; the hedges are tall, thin and shabby; the trees stunted; the open ground, brown and parched, has scarce any appearance of verdure. The flat, regular alleys of evergreens are cut into fantastic figures; the flower gardens embellished with thin ciphers and flourished figures in box, while the flowers grow in rows of earthen-pots, and the ground appears as dusky as if it was covered with the cinders of a blacksmith's forge.

The water, of which there is great plenty, instead of being collected in large pieces, or conveyed in little rivulets and streams to refresh the thirsty soil, or managed so as to form agreeable cascades, is squirted from fountains in different parts of the garden, through tubes little bigger than common glister-pipes. It must be owned indeed that the fountains have their merit in the way of sculpture and architecture; and that here is a great number of statues which merit attention: but they serve only to encumber the ground, and destroy that effect of rural simplicity, which our gardens are designed to produce.

In a word, here we see a variety of walks and groves and fountains, a wood of four hundred pines, a paddock with a few meagre deer, a flower-garden, an aviary, a grotto, and a fish-pond; and in spite of all these particulars, it is, in my opinion, a very contemptible garden, when compared to that of Stowe in Buckinghamshire, or even to those of Kensington and Richmond. The Italians understand, because they study, the excellencies of art; but they have no idea of the beauties of nature.

❧ In the Hands of the Improvers

In her novels Jane Austen often mentions gardens. She brings air-headed Catherine Morland down to earth in General Tilney's kitchen garden in Northanger Abbey, *and allows Marianne Dashwood to contract a severe chill wandering through the fashionably extensive shrubberies of Cleveland in* Sense and Sensibility. *Here, in* Mansfield Park, *written in 1814, she pokes fun at the improvers – slaves to Repton all.*

'Mr. Rushworth,' said Lady Bertram, 'If I were you, I would have a very pretty shrubbery. One likes to get out into a shrubbery in fine weather.'

Mr. Rushworth was eager to assure her ladyship of his acquiescence, and tried to make out something complimentary; but, between his submission to her taste, and his having always intended the same himself, with the superadded objects of professing attention to the comfort of ladies in general, and of insinuating that there was one only whom he was anxious to please, he grew puzzled, and Edmund was glad to put an end to his speech by a proposal of wine. Mr. Rushworth, however, though not usually a great talker, had still more to say on the subject next his heart.

'Smith has not much above a hundred acres altogether in his grounds, which is little enough, and makes it more surprising that the place can have been so improved. Now, at Sotherton we have a good seven hundred, without reckoning the water meadows; so that I think, if so much could be done at Compton, we need not despair. There have been two or three fine old trees cut down, that grew too near the house, and it opens the prospect amazingly, which makes me think that Repton, or anybody of that sort, would certainly have the avenue at Sotherton down: the avenue that leads from the west front to the top of the hill, you know', turning to Miss Bertram particularly as he spoke. But Miss Bertram thought it most becoming to reply,

'The avenue! Oh! I do not recollect it. I really know very little of Sotherton.'

Fanny, who was sitting on the other side of Edmund, exactly opposite Miss Crawford, and who had been attentively listening, now looked at him, and said in a low voice—

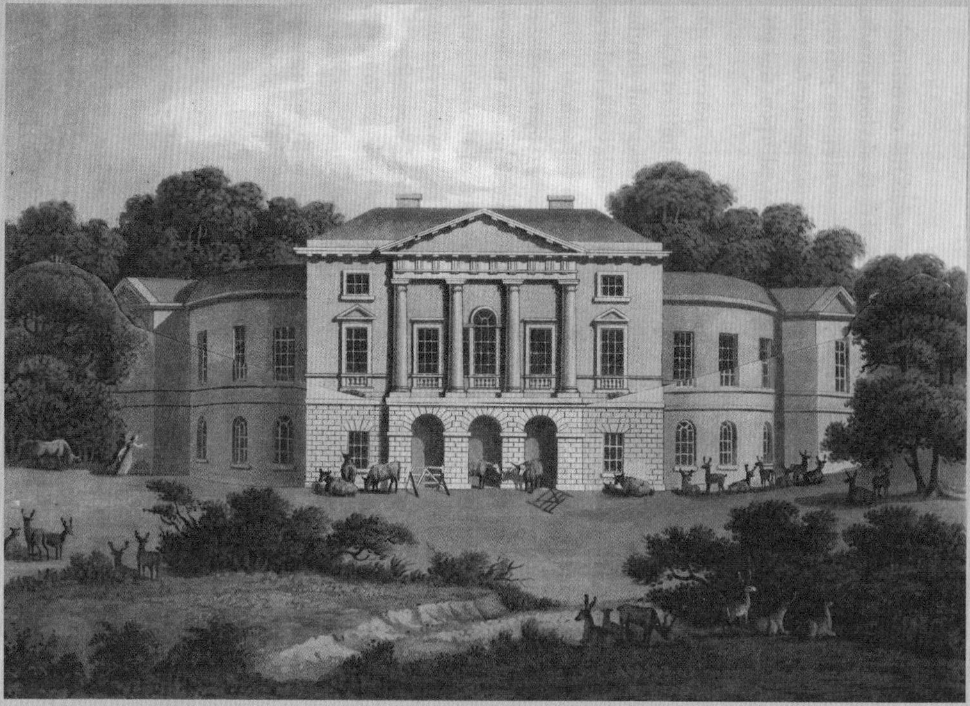

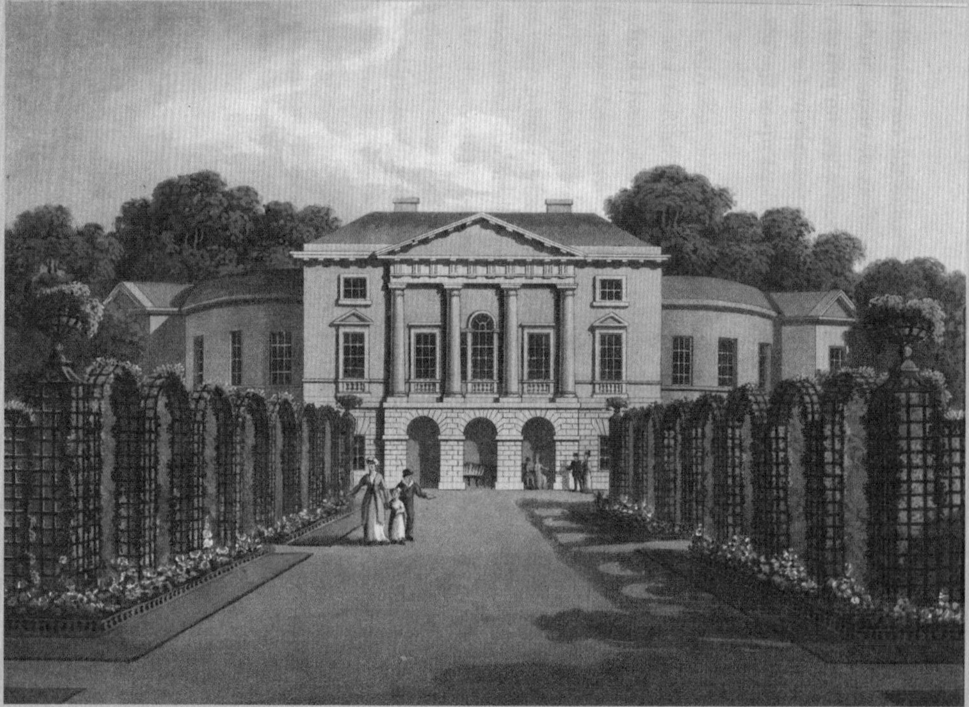

'Cut down an avenue! What a pity! Does it not make you think of Cowper? 'Ye fallen avenues, once more I mourn your fate unmerited.'

He smiled as he answered, 'I am afraid the avenue stands a bad chance, Fanny.'

'I should like to see Sotherton before it is cut down, to see the place as it is now, in its old state; but I do not suppose I shall.'

'Have you never been there? No, you never can; and, unluckily, it is out of distance for a ride. I wish we could contrive it.'

'Oh! it does not signify. Whenever I do see it, you will tell me how it has been altered.'

'I collect,' said Miss Crawford, 'that Sotherton is an old place, and a place of some grandeur. In any particular style of building?'

'The house was built in Elizabeth's time, and is a large, regular, brick building; heavy, but respectable looking, and has many good rooms. It is ill placed. It stands in one of the lowest spots of the park; in that respect, unfavourable for improvement. But the woods are fine, and there is a stream, which, I dare say, might be made a good deal of. Mr. Rushworth is quite right, I think, in meaning to give it a modern dress, and I have no doubt that it will be all done extremely well.'

Miss Crawford listened with submission, and said to herself, 'He is a well-bred man; he makes the best of it.'

'I do not wish to influence Mr. Rushworth,' he continued; 'but, had I a place to new fashion, I should not put myself into the hands of an improver. I would rather have an inferior degree of beauty, of my own choice, and acquired progressively. I would rather abide by my own blunders than by his.'

'You would know what you were about, of course; but that would not suit me. I have no eye or ingenuity for such matters, but as they are before me; and had I a place of my own in the country, I should be most thankful to any Mr. Repton who would undertake it, and give me as much beauty as he could for my money; and I should never look at it till it was complete.'

'It would be delightful to me to see the progress of it all,' said Fanny.

'Ay, you have been brought up to it. It was no part of my education; and the only dose I ever had, being administered by not the first favourite in the world, has made me consider improvements in hand as the greatest of nuisances. Three years ago the Admiral, my honoured

uncle, bought a cottage at Twickenham for us all to spend our summers in; and my aunt and I went down to it quite in raptures; but it being excessively pretty, it was soon found necessary to be improved, and for three months we were all dirt and confusion, without a gravel walk to step on, or a bench fit for use. I would have everything as complete as possible in the country, shrubberies and flower-gardens, and rustic seats innumerable: but it must all be done without my care. Henry is different; he loves to be doing.'

❧ The Simplest Way

Trees, flowers and birds were intrinsic elements of William Morris's creativity. All his houses had gardens, which were as much for living in as the rooms indoors. Those of Kelmscott and the Red House can still be admired. Given in London in 1879, Morris's lecture 'Making the Best of It' explained how the houses and gardens of town dwellers could be arranged according to his principles. He warned against the pretension and artificialities introduced by garden designers and plant-breeders, then known as 'florists'.

Suburban gardeners in London wind about their little bit of gravel walk and grass plot in ridiculous imitation of an ugly big garden of the landscape-gardening style, and then with a strange perversity fill up the spaces with the most formal plants they can get; whereas the merest common-sense should have taught them to lay out their morsel of ground in the simplest way, to fence one part from the other – if it be big enough for that – and the whole from the road, and then to fill up the flower-growing space with things that are free and interesting in their growth, leaving Nature to do the desired complexity, which she will certainly not fail to do, if we do not desert her for the florist, who, I must say, has made it harder work than it should be to get the best of flowers...

When the florists fell upon the rose, they strove for size and got it, a fine specimen of a florist's rose being about as big as a moderate Savoy cabbage. They tried for strong scent and got it – till a florist's rose has not unseldom a suspicion of the scent of the aforesaid cabbage not at its best. They tried for strong colour and got it, strong and bad. They threw away the exquisite subtlety of form, delicacy of texture, and sweetness of colour, which, blended with the richness which the true garden rose shares with many other flowers, yet makes it the queen of them all. These sham roses are driving the real ones out of existence. If we do not look to it our descendants will know nothing of the true cabbage rose, the loveliest in form of all, or the blush rose with its dark green stems and unequalled colour, or the yellow-centred rose of the East, which carries the richness of scent to the very furthest point it can go without losing freshness.

Be very shy of double flowers; choose the old columbine where the clustering doves are unmistakable and distinct, not the double one, where they run into mere tatters. Choose (if you can get it) the old china-aster with the yellow centre, that goes so well with the purple-brown stems and curiously coloured florets, instead of the lumps that look like cut paper, of which we are now so proud. Don't be swindled out of that wonder of beauty, a single snowdrop; there is no gain and plenty of loss in the double one. More loss still in the double sunflower, which is a coarse-coloured and dull plant, whereas the single one, though a late comer to our gardens, is by no means to be despised, since it will grow anywhere, and is both interesting and beautiful, with its sharply chiselled yellow florets relieved by the quaintly patterned sad-coloured centre clogged with honey and beset with bees and butterflies.

Many plants are curiosities only, which Nature meant to be grotesque, not beautiful, and which are generally the growth of hot countries, where things sprout over quick and rank. Take note that the strangest of these come from the jungle and the tropical waste, from places where man is not at home, but is an intruder, an enemy. Go to a botanical garden and look at them, and think of those strange places to your heart's content. But don't set them to starve in your smoke-drenched scrap of ground amongst the bricks, for they will be no ornament to it.

Another thing also much too commonly seen is an aberration of the human mind, which otherwise I should have been ashamed to warn you of. It is technically called carpet-gardening. Need I explain it further? I had rather not, for when I think of it even when I am quite alone I blush with shame at the thought.

And now to sum up as to a garden. Large or small, it should look both orderly and rich. It should be well fenced from the outside world. It should by no means imitate either the wilfulness or wildness of Nature, but should look like a thing never to be seen except near a house. It should, in fact, look like a part of the house. It follows from this that no private pleasure garden should be very big, and a public garden should be divided to look like so many flower-closes in a meadow, or amidst the pavement.

It will be a key to right thinking about gardens if you will consider what kind of places a garden is most desired. In a very beautiful

THIS IS THE PICTURE OF THE OLD
HOUSE BY THE THAMES TO WHICH
THE PEOPLE OF THIS STORY WENT.
HEREAFTER FOLLOWS THE BOOK IT
SELF WHICH IS CALLED NEWS FROM
NOWHERE OR AN EPOCH OF REST &
S WRITTEN BY WILLIAM MORRIS.

country, especially if it be mountainous, we can do without it well enough; whereas in a flat and dull country we crave after it, and there it is often the very making of the homestead. While in great towns, gardens, both private and public, are positive necessities if the citizens are to live reasonable and healthy lives in body and mind.

❧ No Plan of Any Kind

William Robinson was a garden expert of decided opinions who did not suffer fools gladly – and among 'fools' he included most other garden experts. A follower of Ruskin and William Morris, his books waged war against the Victorian garden's ubiquitous carpets of exotic and violently coloured annuals – a trend largely due to the lifting of the tax on glass in 1845, making greenhouses to raise seedlings in much more affordable. Robinson also loathed topiary, likening it to the 'cramming of Chinese feet into impossible shoes'. Instead he called for a return to softly coloured cottage-garden perennials such as lilies, roses and peonies, and walls draped with climbing plants. Towards the end of his most influential book, The English Flower Garden, *published in 1883 and reprinted 16 times between then and 1956, he describes the making of his own garden at Gravetye Manor in Sussex. The manor is now a luxury hotel, and the garden much simplified, but still beautiful.*

When I had a garden of my own to make, I meant it to contain the greatest number of favourite plants in the simplest way. I threw the ground into simple beds, suiting the space for convenience of working and planting, not losing an inch more than was necessary for walks. I did what, so far as we have any evidence to tell us, the Assyrian king and the medieval chatelaine did – that is to say, I cut my limited garden space into simple beds. No plan of any kind was used nor any suggestion sought from any garden, the question being decided in relation to the space. Any talk about styles in relation to such a thing is absurd. Having made my garden, one day a young lady who had been reading one of those mystifying books about formalities and informalities came in, and, instead of warming her eyes at my roses and carnations, said, 'Oh, you, too, have a formal garden!' Just imagine what Nebuchadnezzar or the medieval Lady in their small patches of gardens would think of any silly person who made such a remark instead of looking at the flowers!

Having cut the space up into the simple plan shown, the next question was to make the walks. These are usually of Croydon gravel, but in a real flower garden there is work to do at midsummer as well as in January, and the gravel walk is a serious hindrance if one has

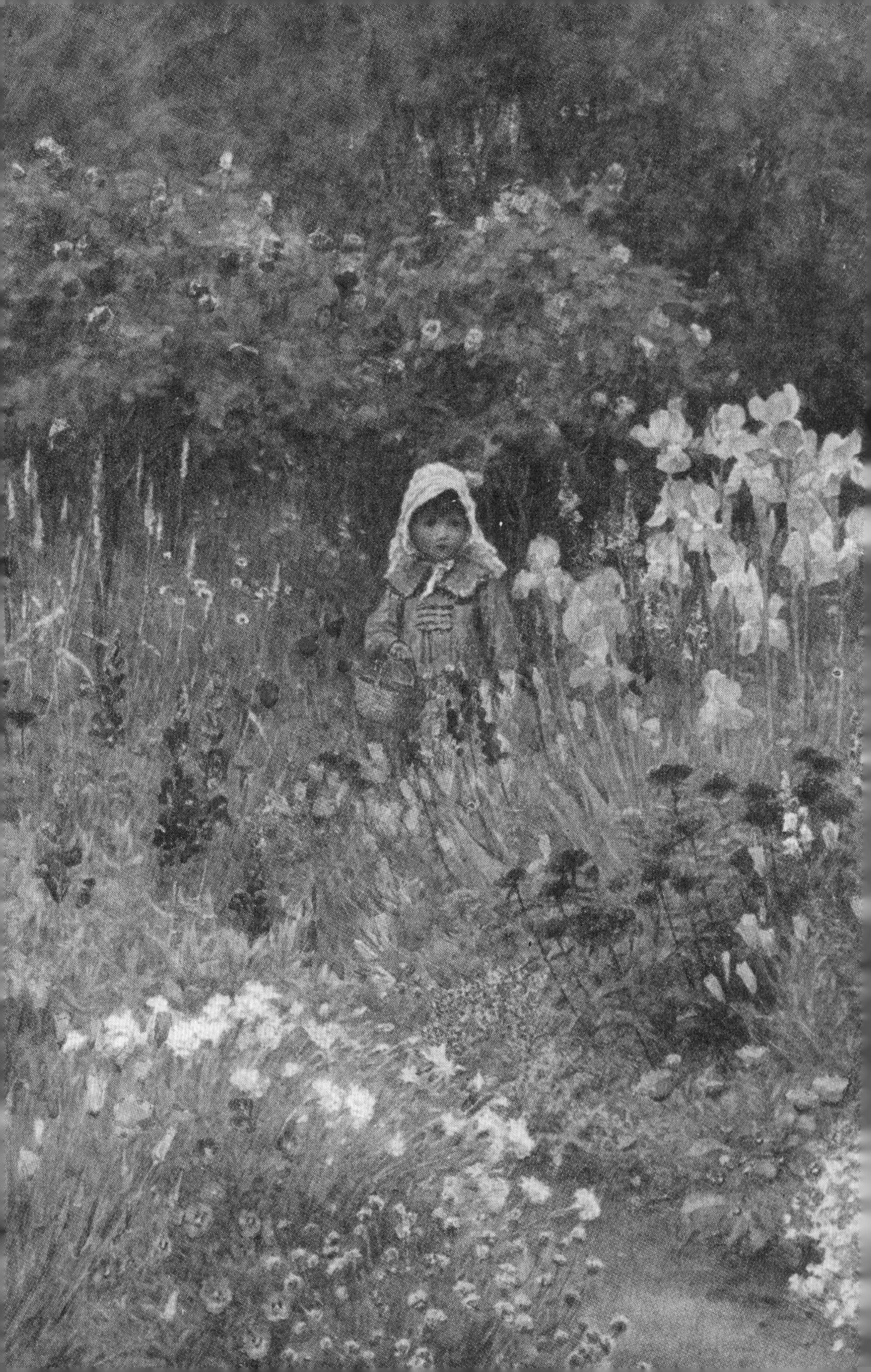

gardening to do all the year round. I made up my mind, therefore, to pave the walks as shown in the plan, using old half-worn London York stone pavings for this purpose, which at that time were often used in making the bottoms of roads, and not of much value. With these, work all the year round is pleasant, as sand, manure, plants or anything else may be spread about on the walks without adding to the labour or causing any unpleasantness. Where the whole flower garden is set out in a week as in bedding-out this would not matter so much; but a real flower garden, which is a thing of varied life, cannot be done in that way. The stones, when in irregular pieces, are sometimes set at random, and they are set in sand only, no cement or mortar being used.

Then came the question of edgings. These in most gardens are a nuisance, and a serious and constant source of labour which can be very often ill spared. Imagine the labour keeping up a large garden with box or other live edgings, harbouring insects and doing other harm. So we had stone edgings made from the same old London flagstones, broken up into handy pieces about 10 inches. These look well at all seasons and make a lasting edging, so the gardeners have time to think of getting beautiful results instead of being bothered with needless labours. In planting we not only seek to get variety, but some difference in the height of things, and thereby obtain a varied surface and not a flat, hard one such as is commonly sought.

Another point gained was that we could devote the beds to permanent planting; we have not to tear up the beds every autumn to plant spring flowers, as is commonly done in the gardens about London and Paris. The spring flowers abound so much in our lawns and woods, and beyond a few pretty edgings of aubrietia, nothing else was done to disturb the beds meant for summer flowers. We can leave our tea roses and carnations alone all the winter, and prepare for the summer garden only. Many fine things in the flower garden will not bear an annual or biennial disturbance, and therefore it is essential to have beds that we can plant with some degree of permanence. When the beds get tired of their contents, we have only to change the plants, but it is a great comfort to have beds which one can leave alone for several years, instead of having the useless labour of disturbing the ground twice a year.

GRAVETYE MANO
EAST GRINSTEA

ALFRED PARSONS

The two flower gardens on slightly different levels are in intimate relation to the house. The old hall door opens into the smaller garden, and the west garden door into the larger. The garden is, in fact, as it should always be – a larger living-room. The varieties of situation are so many that it is not always possible to secure this; but it is by far the best way to have the real garden, where all our precious flowers are, in close relation to the house, so that we can enjoy and see and gather our flowers in the most direct way. The stone paths enable us to do this in all weathers...Always the south and warm sides of the house should be taken advantage of, and the cold side reserved for the entrance.

❧ Tears of Ecstasy

Reginald Farrer was an eccentric and dedicated gardener and plant collector.
Educated at St John's College, Oxford (where he laid out the rock garden), he
travelled into the Alps, the Himalayas and across Japan and China in search
of rare plants. He created a magnificent garden at his home, Ingleborough Hall,
near Clapham in Yorkshire, and seeded the cliffs around it with unusual plants
by peppering the rocks with a shotgun loaded with seeds. The dramatic results
can still be seen. His infectious enthusiasm for alpines made rock gardening, as
defined by his book My Rock Garden *(1920), hugely popular; but he was a*
purist with definite ideas as to what was and wasn't desirable in a rock garden.

The ideal rock-garden must have a plan. But there are three prevailing
plans, none of which are good. The first is what I may call the Almond
Pudding scheme, and obtains generally. You take a round bed; you pile
it up with soil; you then choose out the spikiest pinnacles of limestone
you can find, and you insert them thickly with their points in the air,
until the general effect is that of a tipsy-cake stuck with almonds. In
this vast petrified porcupine nothing will grow except Welsh Poppy,
Ferus, and some of the uglier Sedums. The second style is that of the
Dog's Grave. It marks a higher stage of horticulture, and is affected by
many good growers of alpines. The pudding-shape is more or less the
same in both, but the stones are laid flat in the Dog's Grave ideal. Plants
will grow on this, but its scheme is so stodgy and so abhorrent to
Nature that it should be discarded. The third style is that of the Devil's
Lapful, and prevailed very largely when alpines first began to be used
out of doors. The finest specimens of this style are to be seen in such
gardens as Glasnevin and Edinburgh. The plan is simplicity itself. You
take a hundred or a thousand cartloads of bald square-faced boulders.
Yon next drop them all about absolutely anyhow; and you then plant
things amongst them. The chaotic hideousness of the result is something to be remembered with shudders ever after.

Nurserymen still occasionally pursue this school, which is another
good reason among many why the enthusiast should always insist on
having his rock-garden built under his own eye and on his own plans.
It is as foolish to expect a nurseryman, untrained in design, to build

you a harmonious, genuine, schemed rock-garden, as to ask a journeyman mason to make you a palace. Rule and a knowledge of rule are as necessary to a rock-garden as ever to an architect. In fact, the builder of a rockery must be, on his own different lines, as much of an architect as any planner of houses.

And now, what are these rules that govern the ideal rockery? Briefly, there is but one. Have an idea, and stick to it. Let your rock-garden set out to be something definite, not a mere agglomeration of stones. Let it be a mountain gorge, if you like, or the stony slope of a hill, or a rocky crest, or a peak. But, whatever it be, it must have definiteness of scheme. It is, in effect, an imitation of Nature, and, to be successful, must aim at reproducing with fidelity some particular feature of Nature – whichever you may choose. Kew offers everyone a model which it would be impertinent to praise. The Glen form is apt to be monotonous, perhaps, but climatic conditions make it necessary at Kew, and in many other parts of England; and Kew has triumphed over the problem of how to make a glen perpetually varied and interesting. At Warley Place, Miss Willmott's garden near Brentwood, again, there is the Gorge-design to be studied – to my own personal taste, a trifle too violent to be altogether pleasant, but still a noble example of definite purpose definitely carried out.

Of course the absolute masters of rock-garden, before whose names one must go helpless to one's knees in adoration, are the Japanese. Not to plunge into the bottomless sea of their mysticism and symbolism in design, the sight of a Japanese garden is enough to bring tears of ecstasy to the eyes of any garden-lover. No distortions, no abortion, no discords are there, but some corner of landscape – a rocky gully, a view among the islands – some famous corner of landscape carefully copied to scale, with a sense of harmony and perspective so perfect that in a cottage close four yards square you will seem to have half a mountain-side.

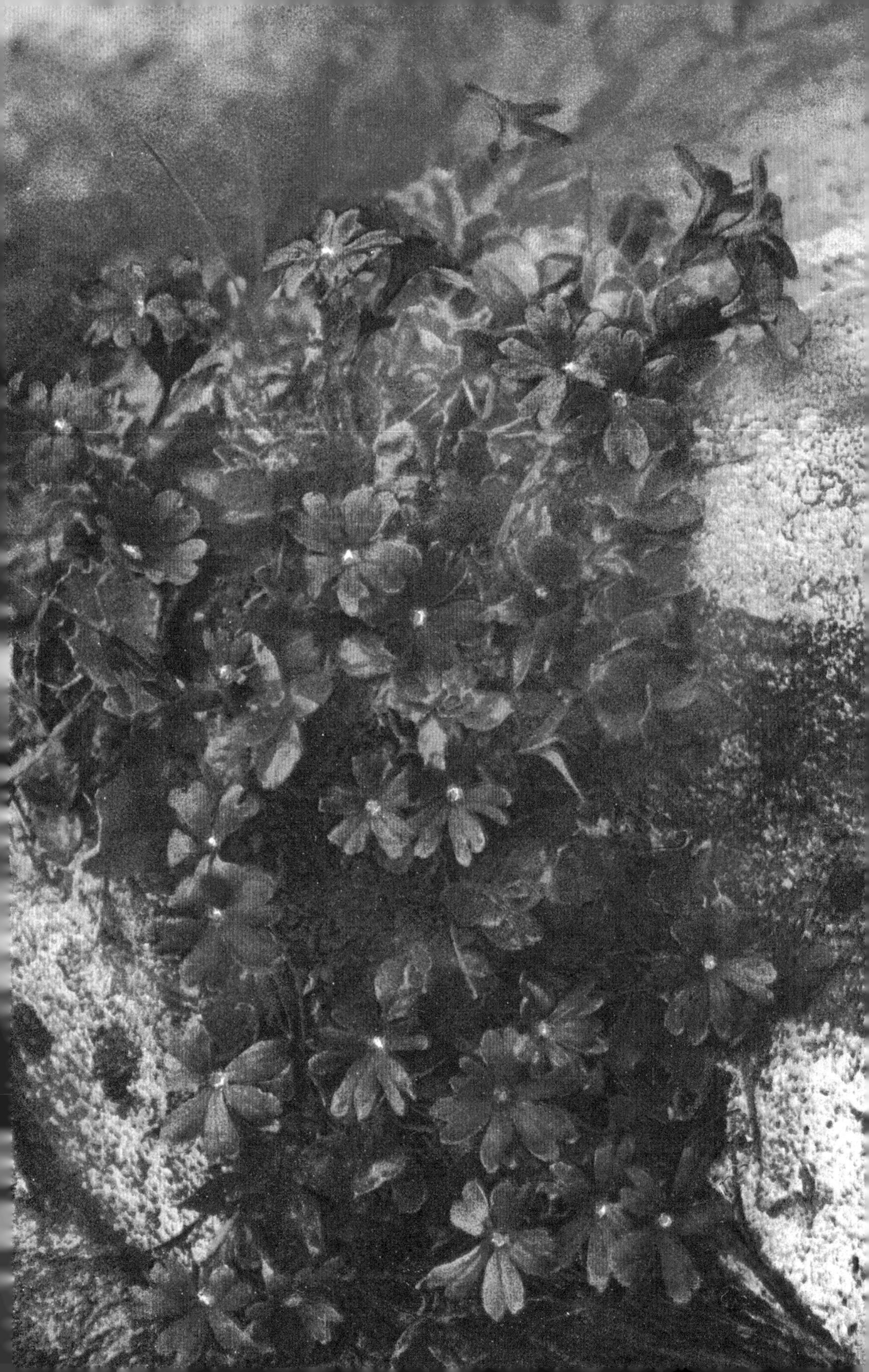

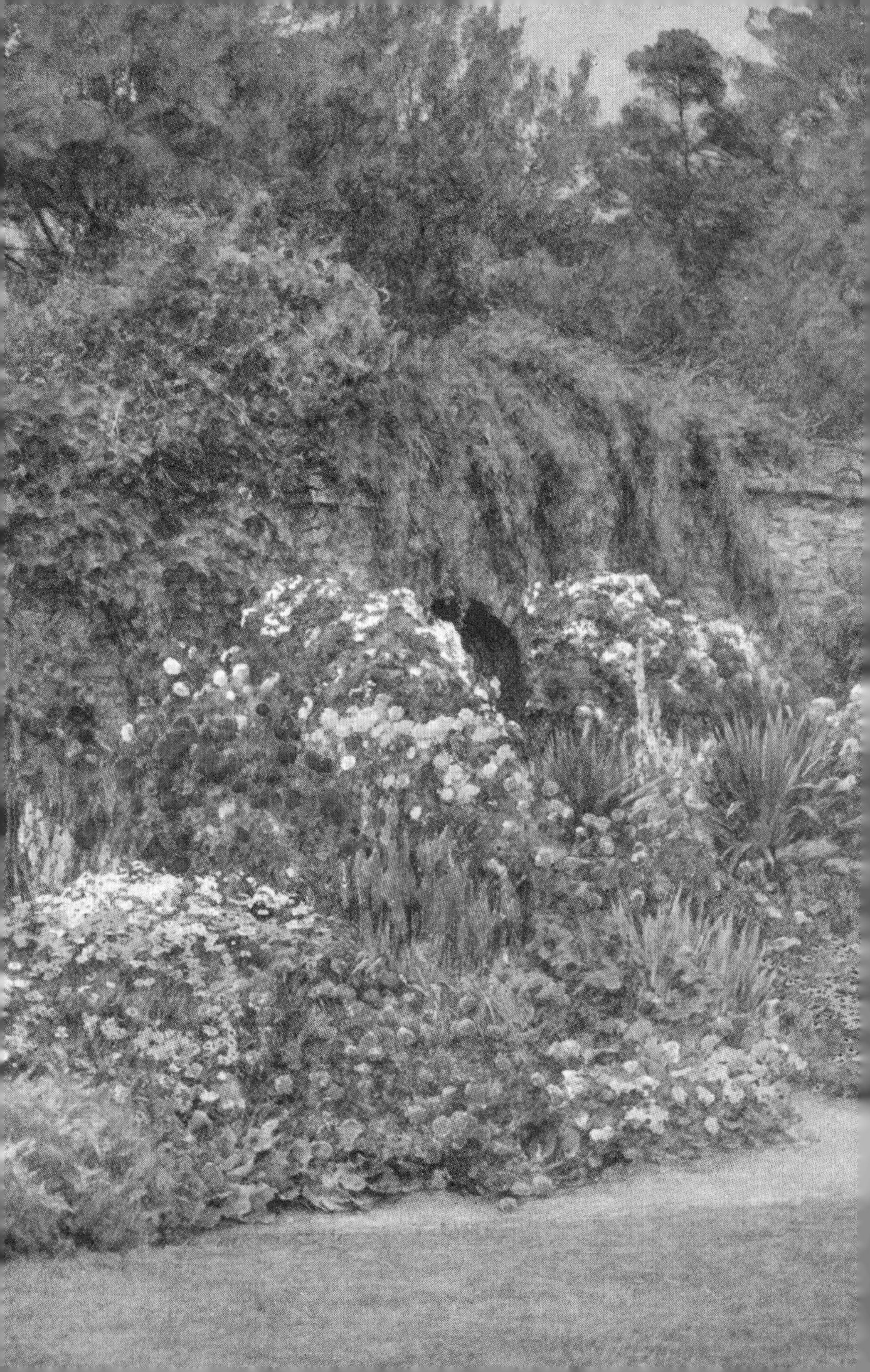

❧ A Garden of Sweet Scents

By the time she died, aged eighty-nine, Gertrude Jekyll had written thirteen books, and today she remains in a class of her own for both her ideas and her inimitable expression of them. She wrote many articles for Country Life, *including this one of 1911 describing the making of a garden that would be scented all year round.*

It is no new idea, that of making a garden where flower and bush of sweet scent only shall be admitted, or where, at least, they shall predominate; but it is worthy of more frequent interpretation. It would be a pleasant thing to know that somewhere in the garden there was a region where nearly everything was not only beautiful, but also fragrant; where, at every step, one would be greeted by some sweet scent – to know that whichever way the wind might blow it would waft some delicious breath of perfume new-distilled. It should be observed that flowers and leaves give off their scent in different ways – one might say, three different ways.

First, there are those that give it off naturally, so that, in passing, it is brought to us by the lightest wind, or even spread abroad in quite still air. This is done by sweet briar, azalea, cistus, azura and French honeysuckle (*Lonicera japonica* var. *repens*) among shrubs, and by wall-flowers, stocks, mignonette and violets among border plants; also three of the grandest of the lilies – the pure and stately white lily, and *Lilum auratum*, the gold-rayed lily of Japan, and the immense *Cardiocrinum giganteum*. Some lowlier plants must be admitted, for of all the sweet scents of the year that of the dying leaves of the little wild straw-berry is one of the most enjoyable; pungent yet delicate, mysterious, elusive, but wholly delightful. Roses in general give off but little scent in the open air, though a bowl of cut roses will scent a room; they are, as Bacon says, 'fast flowers of their smell'. But there is one notable exception in the type *Rosa multiflora* of the Himalayas, the parent of a number of the modern rambling roses. The warm-white flowers, not unlike bramble flowers, and not much larger, are borne in great number at the end of the new shoots. Their scent is carried far and wide. *Clematis montana*, though not usually reckoned among plants of good smell, must admitted, for when the flowers are just passing their best, when the petals, instead of being quite smooth, show a slightly ridged surface, a scent much like vanilla is given off.

Secondly there are the plants with sweet leaves – some of them have sweet flowers also – that do not give off their scent in the air, but yield it to the touch. Such are rosemary and lavender, bay, bog myrtle, candleberry gale and *Rhododendron myrtifolium* among shrubs, sweet geranium, sweet verbena and balm of Gilead among tender plants, and a number of the sweet herbs, their near relatives: balm, marjoram, thyme, savory, sage, hyssop and variegated mint. The last is the variegated form of a native plant, *Mentha suaveolens*; it is a good old garden plant that is too much neglected. Thirdly there are all the other sweet flowers that only ask for slight effort of searching for their sweetness – roses, carnations, peonies, heliotrope, jasmine, sweet peas, lily of the valley and many others. The names are given only as examples, not as complete lists.

It would be well to arrange the garden of sweet scents as a double border, with a path of turf leading to a summerhouse or arbour, which might be covered with honeysuckle and jasmine. The path would be of wild thyme, with, for better wear, a mixture of some of the finer fescue grasses with wiry leaves, that mow and roll into a close short turf. The border would be backed by a planting of sweet briar and two of the cistuses, namely, *C. laurifolius* and *C. ladanifer*. Next the grass, the better to be brushed by foot or skirt, would be bush thyme, winter savory, sage, lavender cotton, catmint and hyssop. Sage should be oftener used as a plant for border or rock garden. It is one of the best of the grey-foliaged plants, and its bright purple bloom is as good as that of any flower of the same colour that blooms at its time of year.

The main planting of the border would be of roses, lilies, peonies, lupins, tulips, rockets and daffodils, the sweetest of which are the poet's daffodil, single and double, the yellow campernelle and the tazettas. Of tender plants there will be heliotrope in plenty and sweet geraniums, and all the sweetest of the annuals, such as sweet peas, mignonette, sweet sultan, night-scented and other stocks, wallflowers and low-growing alyssum. Mignonette should be on the sunny side, as the sun brings out the scent. Night-scented stock (*Matthiola bicornis*) should be freely sown in empty places, not necessarily at the front, though it is a smallish plant, because it has no special beauty. Its delicious fragrance is only given off when the day is dying and through the night. *Nicotiana alata* is another, much larger, plant of the same character, giving off its sweet scent at night, when its flowers expand fully. Lavender and rosemary must also have a place, and *Daphne pontica*, so lavish of its sweetness in the early year.

If there is a wall or a wooden fence, there would be the place for the wintersweet, that gives its sweet, small blooms in the winter months. Such a garden might be still better done if the place were of the more formal type, with the terminal summerhouse of the small temple or pavilion kind. In this case the path would be paved, with here and there an open joint for the planting of the creeping wild thyme, that is so sweet when trodden underfoot. Or the sweet garden may be on quite free lines, that would give a better opportunity for displaying the larger of the scented shrubs. There might be small groves of magnolias and azaleas, of daphne and rosemary, and in some places quite narrow pathways or merely slight openings between the shrubs, so narrow that anyone passing must needs brush up against the plants and bushes. Here would be the place for rosemary and *Rhododendron myrtifolium*, and especially for candleberry gale (*Myrica cerifera*), whose leaves, crushed or bruised, give off an incomparable scent, such as can hardly be matched by that of any other growing thing.

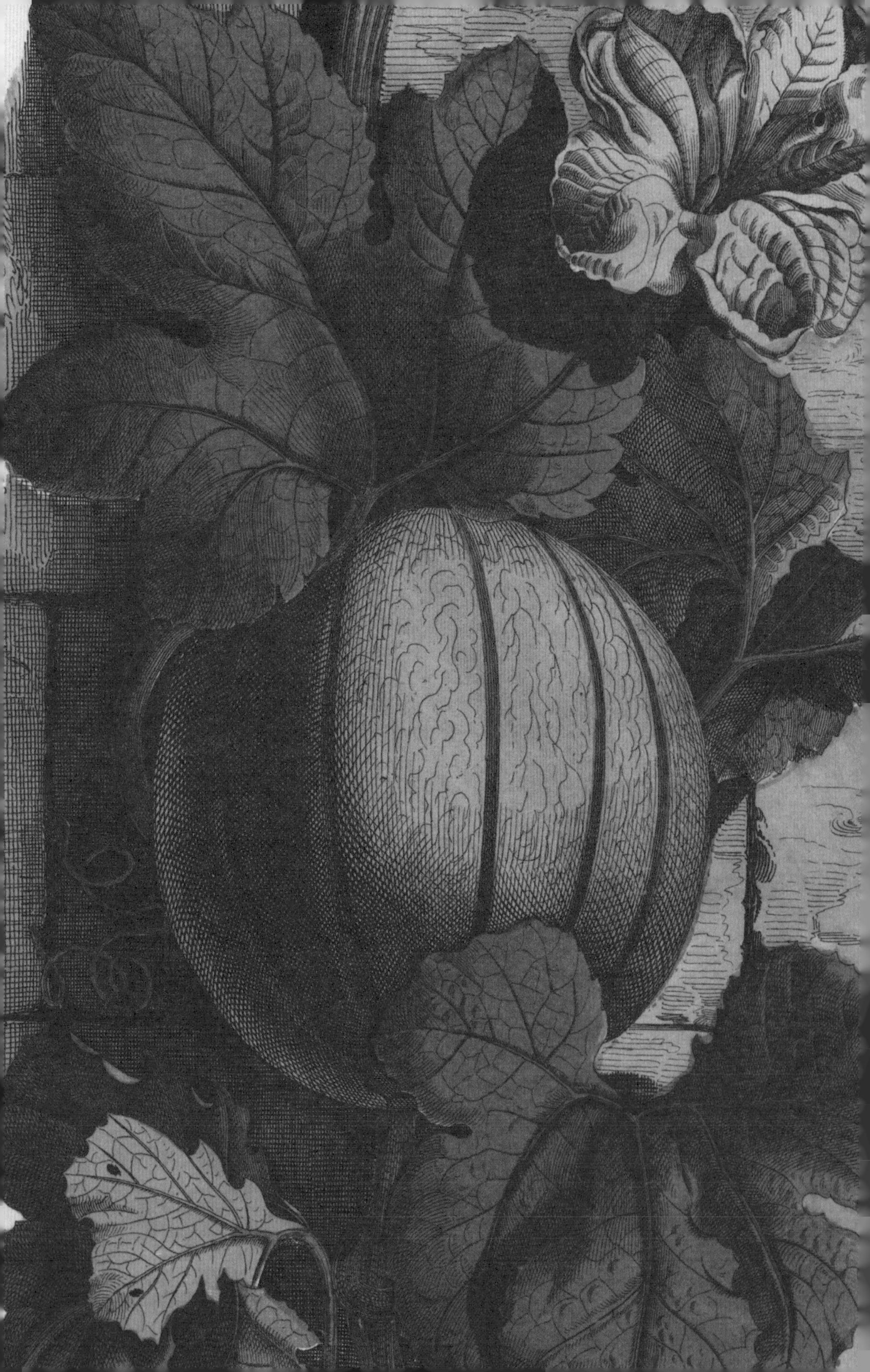

3 Practical Gardening

The third part of this anthology is devoted to the actual grubby business of digging and planting. It celebrates both professional and amateur gardeners, and some notable plantsmen and women. It also reminds us that gardening can be taken light-heartedly as well as seriously.

❧ Whatever Had the Most Blooms

Although it is some twelve centuries old, this Chinese poem will strike a chord with the many modern weekend gardeners who want minimum effort and maximum enjoyment. Bai Juyi was a Tang Dynasty official and a notable poet who lived from AD 772 to 836. His 'Planting Flowers on the Eastern Embankment' was written while he was Governor General of Zhangzhou province.

I took money and bought flowering trees
And planted them out on the bank to the east of the Keep.
I simply bought whatever had most blooms,
Not caring whether peach, apricot, or plum.
A hundred fruits, all mixed up together;
A thousand branches, flowering in due rotation.

Each has its season coming early or late;
But to all alike the fertile soil is kind.
The red flowers hang like a heavy mist;
The white flowers gleam like a fall of snow.
The wandering bees cannot bear to leave them;
The sweet birds also come there to roost.

In front there flows an ever-running stream;
Beneath there is built a little flat terrace.
Sometimes I sweep the flagstones of the terrace;
Sometimes, in the wind, I raise my cup and drink.
The flower-branches screen my head from the sun;
The flower-buds fall down into my lap.

Alone drinking, alone singing my songs,
I do not notice that the moon is level with the steps.
The people of Pa do not care for flowers;
All the spring no one has come to look.
But their Governor-General, alone with his cup of wine,
Sits till evening and will not move from the place!

❧ A Full Dung Barrow

Walafrid Strabo's Hortulus, *or* The Little Garden, *is one of the earliest and most practical horticultural poems. Strabo was a ninth-century Frankish monk and theological writer who became Abbot of Reichenau, near Lake Constance.* Hortulus *is a loving account of preparing raised beds in his own garden, and the uses of the plants that he grows in them; this prose translation is by R. S. Lambert.*

No joy is so great in a life of seclusion as that of gardening. No matter what the soil may be, sandy or heavy clay, on a hill or a slope, it will serve well. The gardener must not be slothful but full of zeal continuously, nor must he despise hardening his hands with toil, or pushing a full dung-barrow out onto the parched earth, and there spreading its contents about.

When the winter has passed and spring has renewed the face of the earth, when the days grow longer and milder, when flowers and herbs are stirred by the west wind, when green leaves clothe the trees, then my little plot is overgrown with nettles. What am I to do? Deep down the roots are matted and linked and riveted like basketwork or the wattled hurdles of a sheepfold. I prepare to attack. Armed with mattock and rake, I tear up the clods and rend them from the clinging network of nettle-roots. Next I leave the whole plot to be baked by the sun. Then I surround the space with a border of stout squared logs, piling the soil within to a convenient height, I spread manure on it, and rake until the surface is powdered and fine. I plant my seeds and the kindly moon moistens each one with dew. Should drought prevail I must water it, running to and fro with full buckets. A casual spurt from the water-pot would disturb my seedlings, so I use the palm of my hand as a sieve. Before long, the whole garden is clothed in a soft robe of green. Part of my garden is bare and dry under the shadow of a roof; in another part a high brick wall robs it of air and sun. But even in these places something will at last succeed.

Amongst my herbs sage holds the place of honour; sweet-scented, it flavours drinks and is full of virtue for many ills. Then there is rue, with its blue-green leaves and short-stemmed flowers, so placed that the sun

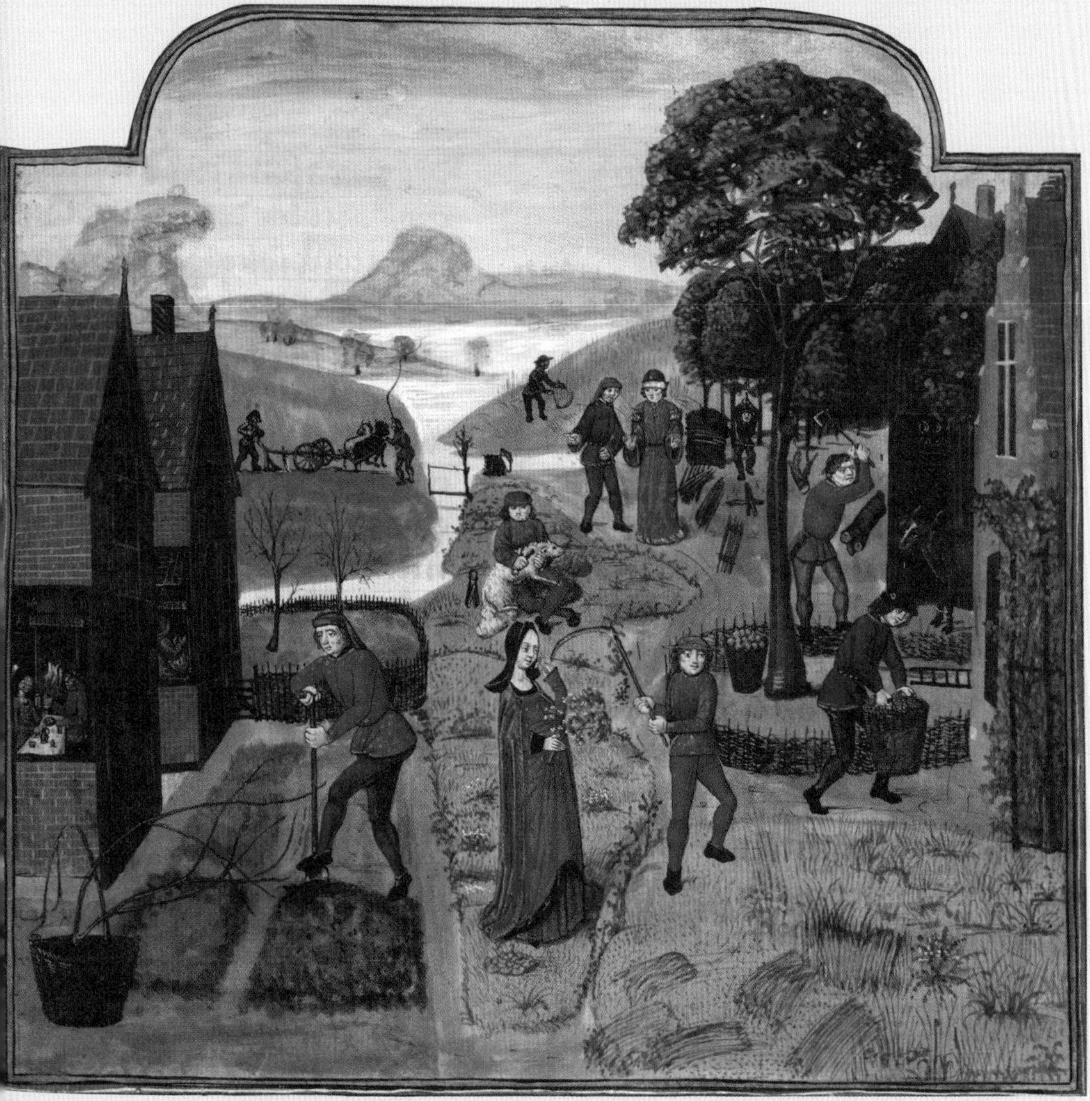

and air can reach all its parts. Great is its power over evil odours and poisons. Southernwood of the hair-like leaves cures fever and wounds; it has well-nigh as many virtues as leaves.

The pumpkin casts its tendrils far and wide. It forms a thick shade with shield-like leaves and throws out tendrils like vines on elms to grapple its supports, and clings as with claws to the alders. There is a tendril for each node and a double thread to each tendril, so it has two hands for climbing, and just as our spinsters transfer their soft work-stuff to their spindles and from wide skeins wind the whole ball of thread, so do these thongs wrap round the stages of their supports. And what beautiful fruit. Slim is the stem from which it hangs, but huge the bulk to which it bulges. Let it harden and you can make utensils of the rind, it will serve to hold a bushel of grain, or caulked inside with resin it will be a jar for wine. The seeds when tender may be used for food, and slices soaked with lard in a hot frying-pan will give a placid relish at dessert.

In the same plot grows the melon. Take not one of the long, thin melons, but the oblong, something between a nut and an egg, work it between your hands like a ball. When there comes a little opening in it, make an incision with your knife and a great quantity of juice will come out with the seed; the whiteness and the flavour please the palate. Nor can you hurt your teeth, it is easy to masticate and swallow.

Next wormwood, what can equal this for fever and gout? For head-ache use an infusion of it and plaster your head with a crown of the wet leaves. Horehound is bitter to the palate yet its scent is sweet. Drink horehound hot from the fire if your stepmother poisons you. Fennel deserves high praise, both for its taste and smell. It is good for weak eyes.

Nor must the gladiolus lily be forgotten; like the hyacinth or the darker violets, it is the glory of purple springtime. It allays all disease of the bladder, and the fullers use it to give whiteness to cloth. The poppy recalls the goddess Demeter, who when unable to find Persephone drank of this herb and sank into slumber oblivious of her anguish.

Amongst the herbs in the shady border I see clary. The leeches avoid the use of it, but it makes excellent beer. Mint I grow in abundance and in all its varieties. How many they are – I might as well try to count the sparks from Vulcan's furnace beneath Etna.

Who can describe the exceeding whiteness of the lily? And the rose – it should be crowned with pearls of Arabia and Lydian gold. Better and sweeter are these flowers than all other plants and rightly called the flower of flowers. Therefore roses and lilies for our church, one for the martyr's blood, the other for the symbol in his hand. Pluck them, O maiden, roses for war and lilies for peace, and think of that Flower of the stem of Jesse, only sower and raiser of man's ancient seed. His words and the hallowed acts of His pleasant life were lilies, but His death dyed the roses red.

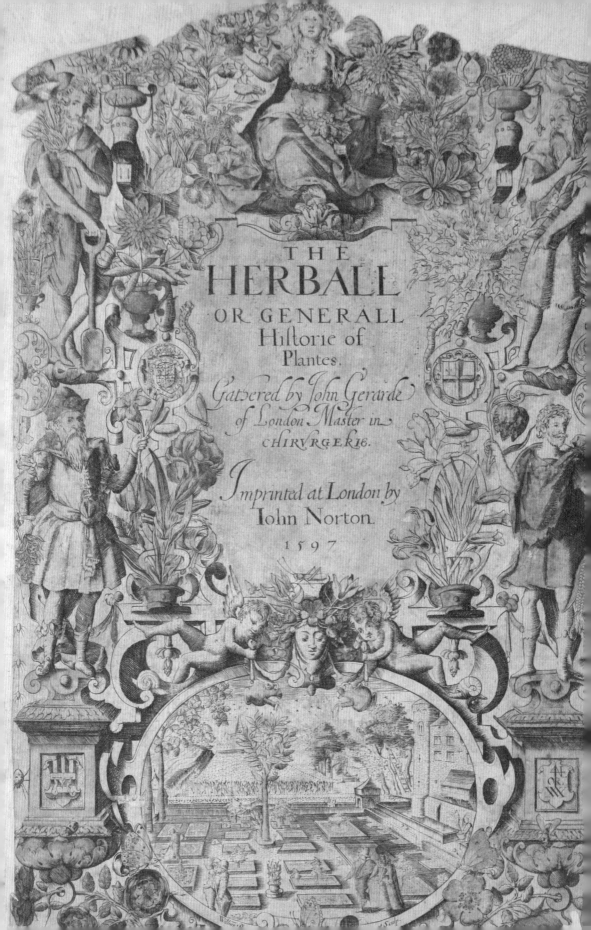

THE
HERBALL
OR GENERALL
Historie of
Plantes.

Gathered by *John Gerarde*
of London Master in
CHIRVRGERIE.

Imprinted at London by
Iohn Norton.
1597

❧ Nosegays and Posies

All the greatest practical gardeners are both observant and curious. The Elizabethan doctor John Gerard filled his famous Herbal *(1597) with fascinating descriptions of plants and their uses, including the Orcadian barnacle tree (from which barnacles were said to fall into the water and hatch into barnacle geese) and the first mention of the Peruvian skirret, or potato. I have chosen his words on two: the garden's humblest inhabitant, the daisy, and the one most beloved for its fragrance, the violet.*

LITTLE DAISIES

The daisy brings forth many leaves from a thread root, smooth, fat, long, and somewhat round withal, very slightly indented about the edges, for the most part lying upon the ground: among which rise up the flower, every one with his own slender stem, almost like those of camomile, but lesser, of a perfect white colour. The double red daisy is like unto the precedent in every respect, saving in the colour of the flowers, for this plant brings forth flowers of a red colour. The double daisies are planted in gardens: the others grow wild everywhere. The daisy is called of some, herba margarita, or Margaret's herb, in French marguerites, in English daisies, and bruisewort. Daisies do mitigate all kinds of pains, but especially in the joints, and gout, if they be stamped with new butter unsalted, and applied upon the pained place, but they work more effectually if mallows be added thereto. The juice of the leaves and roots sniffed up into the nostrils, purges the head mightily, and helps the megrim. The same given to little dogs with milk keeps them from growing great. The leaves stamped take away bruises and swellings proceeding of some stroke, if they be stamped and laid thereon; whereupon it was called in old time bruisewort. The juice put into the eyes clears them, and takes away the watering of them. The decoction of the field daisy (which is the best for physick's use) made in water and drunk, is good against agues.

VIOLETS

Violets of the garden have a great prerogative above others, not only because the mind conceiveth a certain pleasure and recreation by smelling and handling of those most odoriferous flowers, but also for that very many by these violets receive ornament and comely grace: for there be made of them garlands for the head, nosegays and posies, which are delightful to look on, and pleasant to smell to, speaking nothing of their appropriate virtues; yea gardens themselves receive by these the greatest ornament of all, chiefest beauty and most gallant grace; and the recreation of the mind which is taken hereby, cannot be but very good and honest: for they admonish and stir up a man to that which is comely and honest; for flowers through their beauty, variety of colour, and exquisite form, do bring to a liberal and gentlemanly mind, the remembrance of honesty, comeliness and all kinds of virtues. For it would be an unseemly and filthy thing for him that doth look upon and handle fair and beautiful things, and who frequenteth and is conversant in faire and beautiful places, to have his mind not fair, but filthy and deformed.

❧ Bring Your Orange Trees Boldly Out

John Evelyn was the seventeenth century's most authoritative writer on gardening. He was commissioned by the Royal Society to write Sylva, or a Discourse on Forest Trees, *a seminal book on trees and woodlands intended to promote the planting and preservation of timber for the Navy. Although he lived through one of the most turbulent periods of British history – the Civil War, the Dutch war, the plague of 1665 and the Great Fire of London in 1666 – gardening was always his first love. He recorded fascinating descriptions of European gardens as well as English ones, and he used ideas from these to inform the design of the garden of Sayes Court, his great London house close to the royal shipyards on the banks of the Thames near Deptford. He wrote at length on garden design and maintenance, but he never finished* Elysium Britannicum, *which was to be his magnum opus on the subject.*

I have chosen these extracts from Evelyn's most practical book, The Gardener's Almanac. *They detail the work to be done in May and June in the flower garden and in July in the orchard, and conclude with the pay-off: a mouth-watering list of fruits in their prime in August.*

To be done in May in the parterre, and flower-garden
Now bring your orange-trees boldly out of the conservatory; 'tis your only season to transplant and remove them: let the cases be filled with natural earth (such as is taken the first half spit, from just under the turf of the best pasture ground, mixing it with one part of rotten cow-dung, or very mellow soil sifted and prepared some time before; if this be too stiff, sift a little lime discreetly with it, with the rotten sticks of willows: Then cutting the too thick and extravagant roots a little, especially at bottom, set your plant; but not too deep; rather let some of the roots appear. Lastly settle it with temperately enriched water (such as is impregnated with cow and sheep-dung especially set and stirred in the sun some few days before); but be careful not to drench them too much at first; but giving it by degrees day after day, without touching the Stem, having before put some rubbish of lime-stones, pebbles, shells, twigs or the like at the bottom of the cases, to give the

moisture passage, and keep the earth loose for fear of rotting the cases. Then set them in the shade for a fortnight, and afterwards expose them to the sun.

Give now also all your houseplants (such as you do not think requisite to take out) fresh earth at the surface, in place of some of the old earth (a hand-depth or so) and loosen the rest with a fork, without wounding the roots: let this be of excellent rich soil that will be thoroughly consumed, and will wash in the virtue and comfort the plant: brush and cleanse them likewise from the dust contracted during their enclosure. These two last directions have till now been kept as considerable secrets amongst our gardeners.

Shade your carnations, and gillyflowers after mid-day at about this season: plant also your stock-gilly-flowers in beds, at full moon.

Continue watering ranunculuses; transplant forth your amaranthuses, where you would have them stand; sow antirrhinum. Gather what ripe anemone-seed you find that is worth saving, preserving it very dry. Cut likewise the stalks of such bulbous flowers as you find dry.

Towards the end of May take up those tulips which are dried in the stalk; covering them from the sun and showers.

To be done in June

Transplant autumnal cyclamens now if you would change their place, otherwise let them stand. Take up iris chalcedon. Gather the ripe seeds of flowers worth the saving, as of choicest Oriental hyacinth, narcissus (the two lesser, pale spurious daffodils of a whitish green often produce varieties), auricula, ranunculus and so on, and preserve them dry: shade your carnations from the afternoon sun.

You may now begin to lay your gillyflowers. At the end of the month, take up your rarest anemones, and dry the roots well. In mid-June propagate jasmine, roses, and some other fair shrubs.

Sow now also some anemone-seed. Take up the rest of your tulip bulbs, immediately burying such as you find naked upon your beds; or else plant them in some cooler place; and refresh over-parched beds with water. Water your pots of that rare flower narcissus of Japan. Stop some of your scabious from running to seed the first year, by now removing them, and next year they will produce excellent flowers. Also may you now take up all such plants and flower-roots as endure

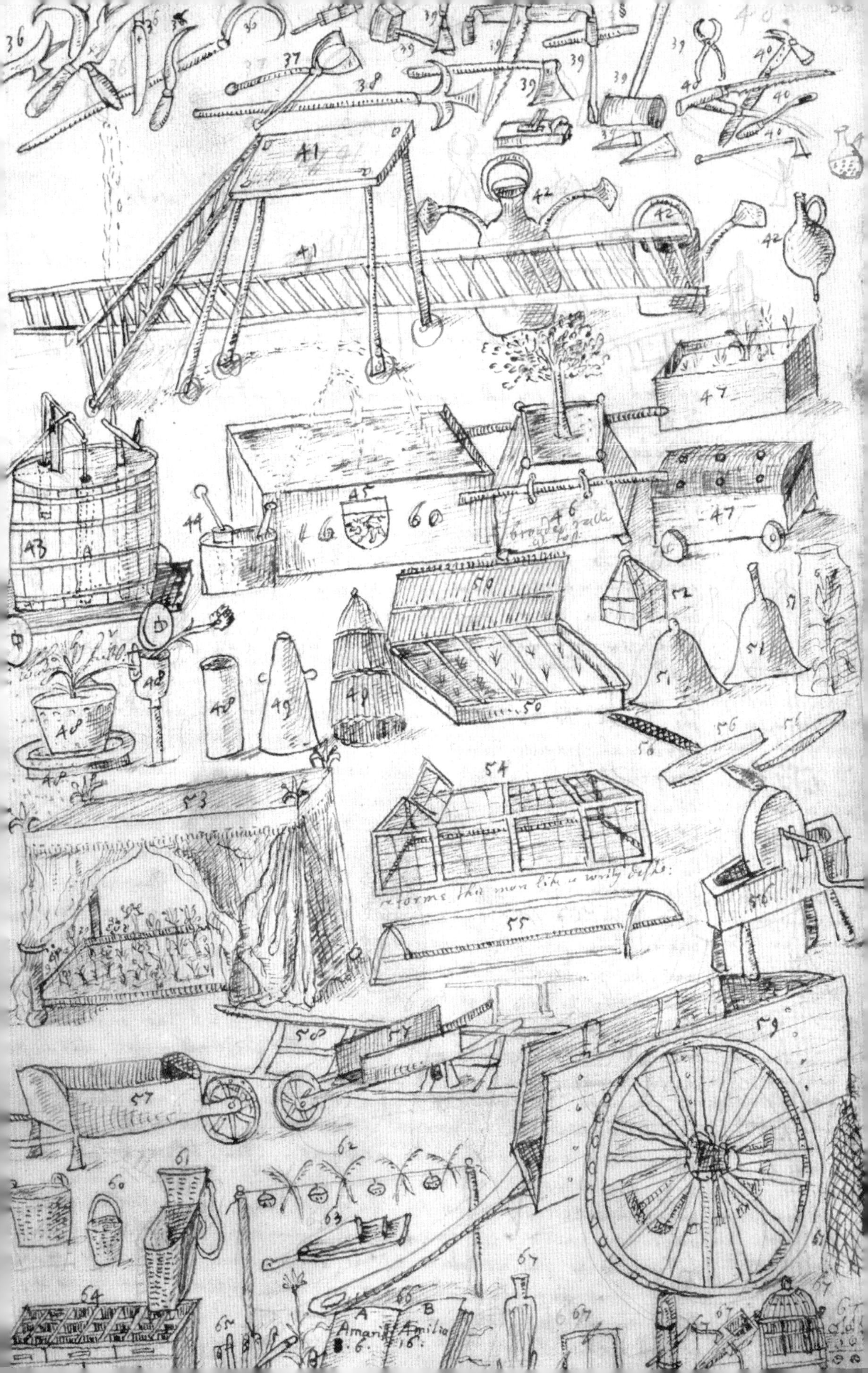
36
37
38
39
40
41
42
43
44
45
46
47
48
49
50
51
52
53
54
55
56
57
58
59
60
61
62
63
64
A
B

not well out of the ground, and replant them again immediately; such as the early cyclamen, Oriental hyacinth, and other bulbous hyacinths, iris, fritillaria, crown-imperial, martagon, muscaris, dens caninus, etc.

JULY: TO BE DONE IN THE ORCHARD
Sow lettuce, radish, etc to have tender salading. Sow later peas to be ripe six weeks after Michaelmas.

Water young planted trees and reprune apricots, and peaches, saving as many of the young likeliest shoots as are well placed; for those now bearing commonly perish, the new ones succeeding. Cut close and even, purging your wall-fruit of superfluous leaves which hinder from the sun, but do it discreetly.

Let such olitory [kitchen garden] herbs run to seed as you would save. Towards the later end, visit your vineyards and stop the exuberant shoots at the second joint above the fruit.

Remove long-sided cabbage planted in May to head in autumn; 'tis the best cabbage in the world.

Set glasses of beer mingled with honey, to entice the wasps, flies, etc which waste your store; also hang bottles of the same mixture near your red Roman-nectarines, and other tempting fruits, for their destruction; else they many times invade your best fruit.

Look now also diligently under the leaves of wall-trees for the snails; they stick commonly somewhat above the fruit; pull not off what is bitten; for then they will certainly begin afresh.

FRUITS IN PRIME IN AUGUST
Apples: Ladies' Longing, Kirkham, John Apple, Seaming Apple, Cushion Apple, Spicing Apple, the Mayflower, the Sheeps Snout.
    Pears: Windsor, Sovereign, Orange, Bergamot, Slipper Pear, Red Catherine, King Catherine, Denny Pear, Prussia Pear, Summer Poppering, Sugar Pear, Lording Pear.
    Peaches: Roman Peach, Man Peach, Quince Peach, Rambouillet, Musk Peach, Grand Carnation, Portugal Peach, Crown Peach, Bordeaux

Peach, Lavar la Belle Chevreuse, the Peach De Peau, Savoy Malacoten (which last till Michaelmas).

Nectarines: The Muroy Nectarine, Tawny, Red-Roman, little Green Nectarine, Cluster Nectarine, Yellow Nectarine.

Plums: Imperial Blue, White Dates, Yellow Pear-Plum, Black Pear-plum, White Nutmeg, late Pear-plum, Great Anthony, Turkey Plum, the Jane Plum

Other Fruit: Cluster-grape, Muscadine, Corinths, Cornelians, Mulberries, Figs, Filberts and Melons.

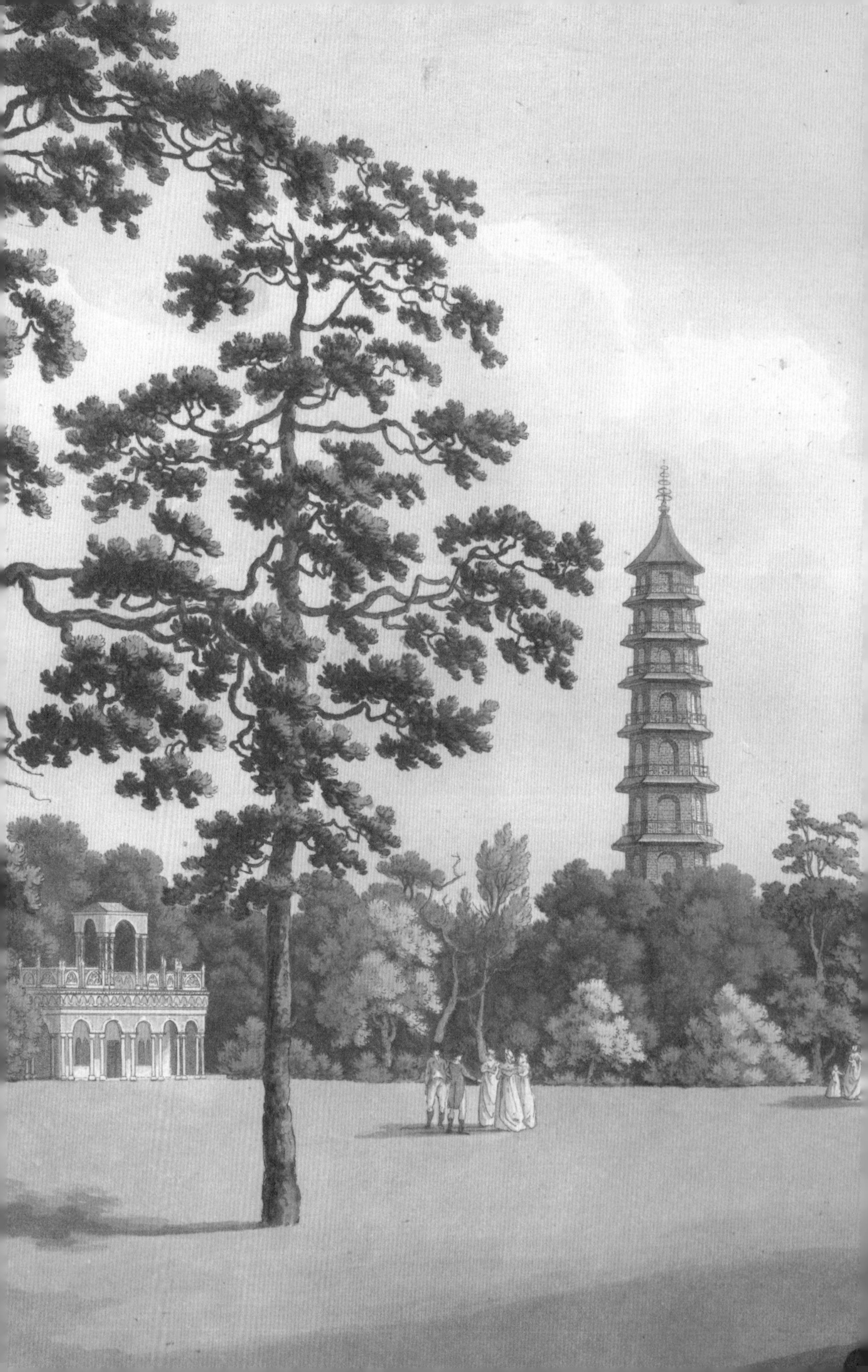

❧ Vegetable Pride

The eighteenth-century botanist Erasmus Darwin had a scientific curiosity as perceptive and far-reaching as that of his more famous descendant, Charles. Written in 1791, his 650-line poem The Botanical Garden *has twice as many words again in its copious notes and touches on innumerable natural phenomena, including electricity, solar volcanoes and the ingredients of gunpowder. The theatre of many of his observations and experiments was the new botanical garden founded by George III at Kew in 1759, which Darwin celebrated towards the end of his poem.*

So sits enthroned in vegetable pride
Imperial KEW by Thames's glittering side;
Obedient sails from realms unfurrowed bring
For her the unnamed progeny of spring;
Attendant Nymphs her dulcet mandates hear,
And nurse in fostering arms the tender year,
Plant the young bulb, inhume the living seed,
Prop the weak stem, the erring tendril lead;
Or fan in glass-built fanes the stranger flowers
With milder gales, and steep with warmer showers.

Delighted Thames through tropic umbrage glides,
And flowers antarctic, bending o'er his tides;
Drinks the new tints, the sweets unknown inhales,
And calls the sons of science to his vales.
In one bright point admiring Nature eyes
The fruits and foliage of discordant skies,
Twines the gay floret with the fragrant bough,
And bends the wreath round GEORGE's royal brow.
—Sometimes retiring, from the public weal
One tranquil hour the ROYAL PARTNERS steal;
Through glades exotic pass with step sublime,
Or mark the growths of Britain's happier clime;
With beauty blossomed, and with virtue blazed,
Mark the fair Scions, that themselves have raised;

Sweet blooms the Rose, the towering Oak expands,
The Grace and Guard of Britain's golden lands.

Apart from this splendid panegyric, Darwin's verse strikes ponderously on the ear today; but his copious notes on its stanzas are enthralling.

Many vegetables during the night do not seem to respire, but to sleep like the dormant animals and insects in winter. This appears from the mimosa and many other plants closing the upper sides of their leaves together in their sleep, and thus precluding that side of them from both light and air. And many flowers close up the polished or interior side of their petals, which we have also endeavoured to show to be a respiratory organ.

The irritability of plants is abundantly evidenced by the absorption and pulmonary circulation of their juices; their sensibility is shown by the approaches of the males to the females, and of the females to the males in numerous instances; and, as the essential circumstance of sleep consists in the temporary abolition of voluntary power alone, the sleep of plants shows that they possess voluntary power; which also indisputably appears in many of them by closing their petals or their leaves during cold, or rain, or darkness, or from mechanic violence.

Linnaeus names buds and bulbs the winter-cradles of the plant, or 'hybernacula', and might have given the same term to seeds. In warm climates few plants produce buds, as the vegetable life can be completed in one summer, and hence the hybernacle is not wanted; in cold climates also some plants do not produce buds, as philadelphus, frangula, viburnum, ivy, heath, wood-nightshade, rue, geranium. The bulbs of plants are another kind of winter-cradle, or hybernacle, adhering to the descending trunk, and are found in the perennial herbaceous plants which are too tender to bear the cold of the winter.

A sun-flower three feet and half high, according to the experiment of Dr Hales, perspired two pints in one day which is many times as much in proportion to its surface, as is perspired from the surface and lungs of animal bodies; it follows that the vital air liberated from the surfaces of plants by the sunshine must much exceed the quantity of it absorbed by their respiration, and that hence they improve the air in which they live during the light part of the day, and thus blanched vegetables will sooner become tanned into green by the sun's light, than etiolated animal bodies will become tanned yellow by the same means.

❧ Gross Fog Boeotian

William Cowper's description of growing cucumbers from Book III of The Task *shows that he was a hands-on gardener as well as an aficionado. It is undoubtedly the most baroque description of preparing a hothouse bed ever written. Boeotia is in Greece, incidentally, and is notorious for the mists and fogs of its soggy, stagnant plain.*

To raise the prickly and green-coated gourd,
So grateful to the palate, and when rare
So coveted, else base and disesteemed –
Food for the vulgar merely – is an art
That toiling ages has but just matured...
The stable yields a stercoraceous [dung-filled] heap
Impregnated with quick fermenting salts,
And potent to resist the freezing blast.
For ere the beech and elm have cast their leaf
Deciduous, and when now November dark
Checks vegetation in the torpid plant
Exposed to his cold breath, the task begins.
Warily therefore, and with prudent heed
He seeks a favoured spot, that where he builds
The agglomerated pile, his frame may front
The sun's meridian disk, and at the back
Enjoy close shelter, wall, or reeds, or hedge
Impervious to the wind. First he bids spread
Dry fern or littered hay that may imbibe
The ascending damps; then leisurely impose,
And lightly, shaking it with agile hand
From the full fork, the saturated straw.
What longest binds the closest, forms secure
The shapely side, that as it rises takes
By just degrees an overhanging breadth,
Sheltering the base with its projected eaves.
The uplifted frame compact at every joint,
And overlaid with clear translucent glass,

He settles next upon the sloping mount,
Whose sharp declivity shoots off secure
From the dashed pane the deluge as it falls.
He shuts it close, and the first labour ends.
Thrice must the voluble and restless earth
Spin round upon her axle, ere the warmth
Slow gathering in the midst, through the square mass
Diffused, attain the surface. When, behold!
A pestilent and most corrosive steam,
Like a gross fog Boeotian, rising fast,
And fast condensed upon the dewy sash,
Asks egress; which obtained, the overcharged
And drenched conservatory breathes abroad,
In volumes wheeling slow, the vapour dank,
And purified, rejoices to have lost
Its foul inhabitant. But to assuage
The impatient fervour which it first conceives
Within its reeking bosom, threatening death
To his young hopes, requires discreet delay.
Experience, slow preceptress, teaching oft
The way to glory by miscarriage foul,
Must prompt him, and admonish how to catch
The auspicious moment, when the tempered heat,
Friendly to vital motion, may afford
Soft fermentation, and invite the seed.
The seed selected wisely, plump and smooth
And glossy, he commits to pots of size
Diminutive, well filled with well-prepared
And fruitful soil, that has been treasured long.

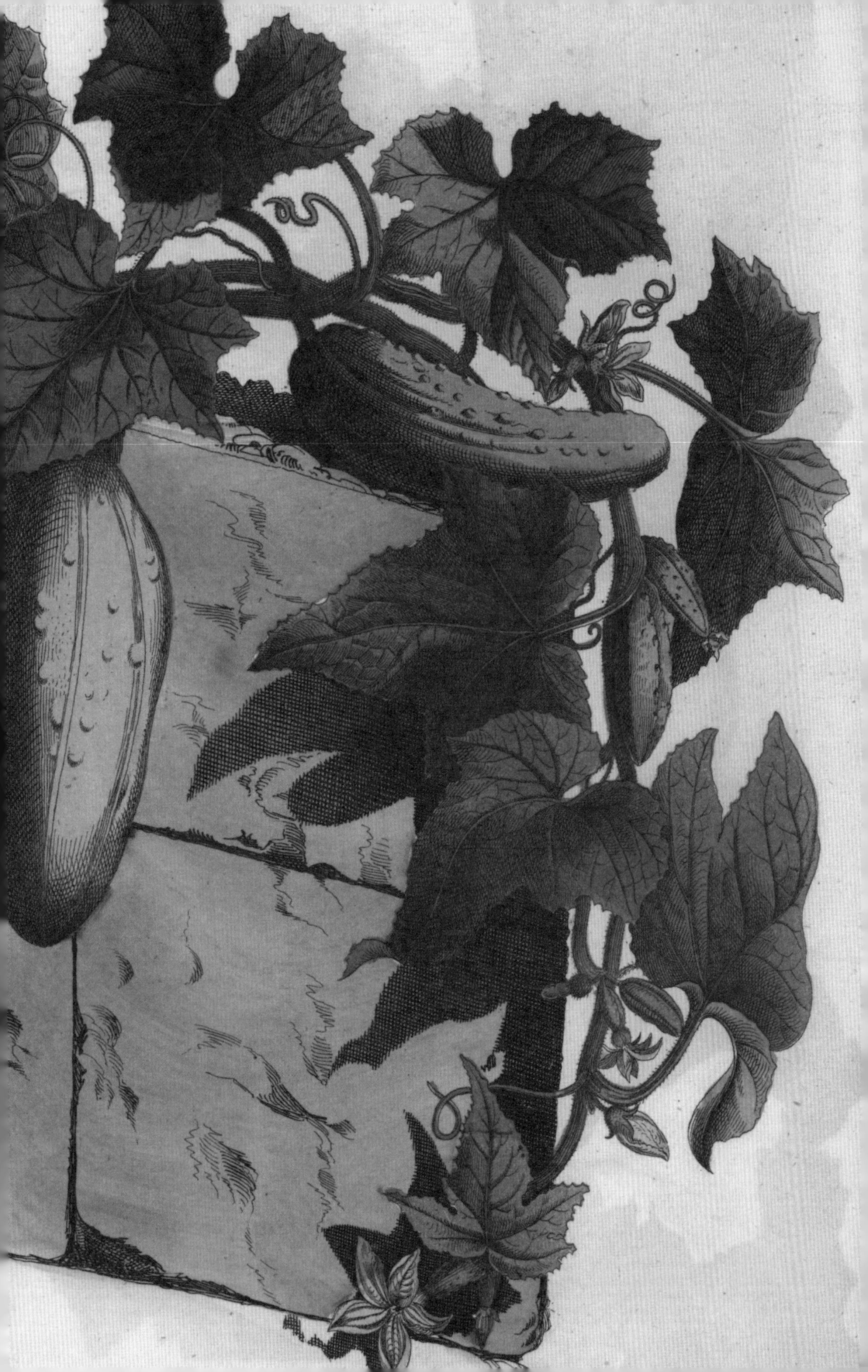

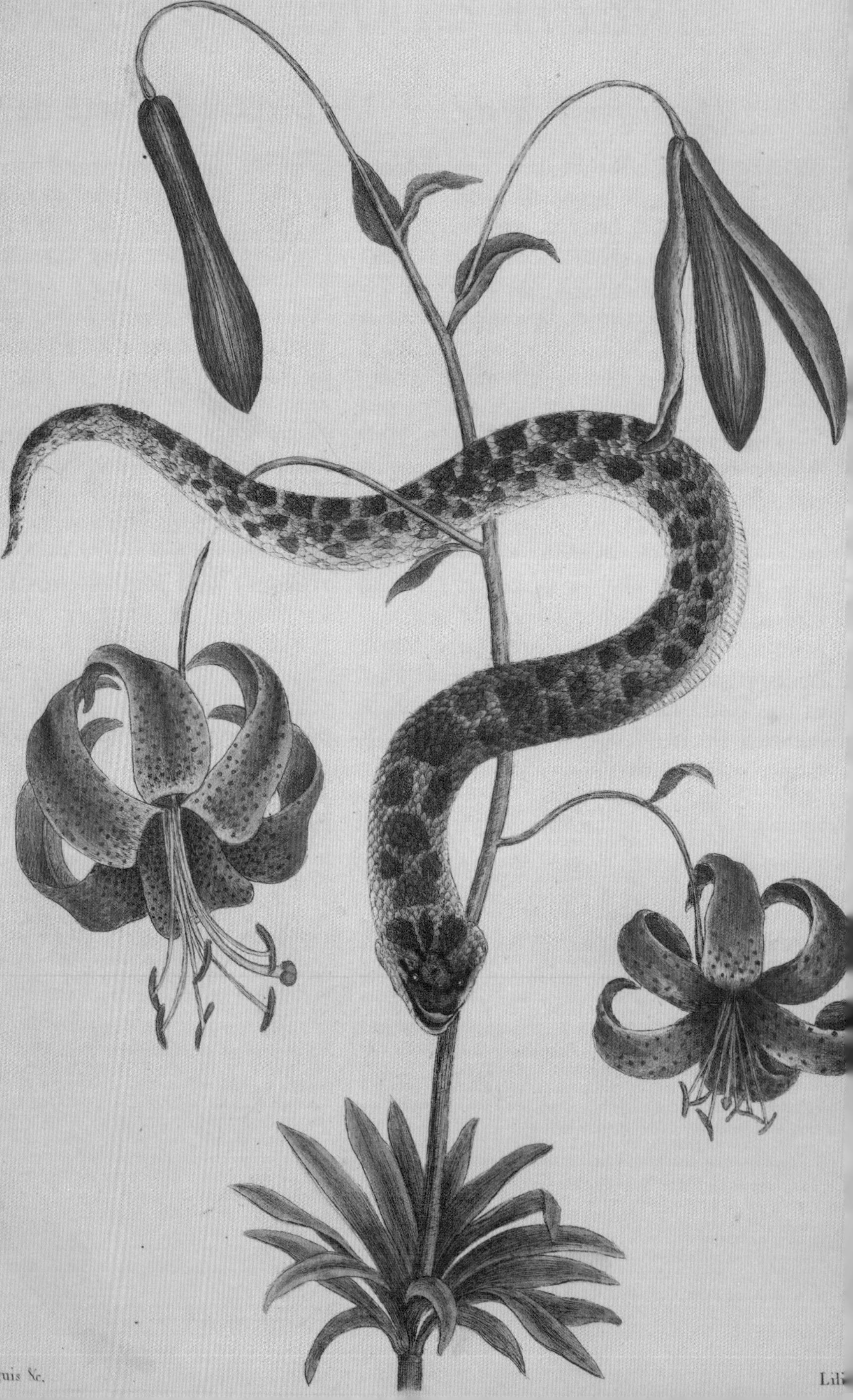

Anguis &c.

Lili

❧ Snapdragons Blooming

Thomas Jefferson, President of the United States from 1801 to 1809, always found gardens an inspiration and a solace. Besides drafting the Declaration of Independence, he introduced the cultivation of olives and rice to South Carolina and invented a new kind of plough. He was immensely knowledge-able about varieties of plants, and was skilled in propagating and raising them. In 1786 he toured England, visiting such great gardens as Alexander Pope's at Twickenham, Charles Bridgeman's at Stowe, William Shenstone's at the Leasowes, Shropshire and William Kent's at Blenheim, making careful notes as he went. These would eventually influence the garden of his dreams, which he constructed at Monticello after his retirement from office.

From an early age Jefferson kept a gardening book, noting what was planted each year and how they fared. Here are his entries for the first three months of 1767, when he was 23.

Feb'ry 20	sowed a bed of forwardest and a bed of middling peas
March 9	both beds of peas up
March 15	planted asparagus seed in 5 beds, 4 rows in each
March 17	sowed a bed of forwardest peas, and a bed of the latest of all.
March 23	purple hyacinth & narcissus bloom; sowed 2 rows of celery and 2 rows of Spanish onions and of lettuce
April 1	peas of March 17 just appearing
April 2	sowed carnations, Indian pink, marigold, globe amaranth, auricula, double balsam, tricolor, Dutch violet, sensitive plant, cockscomb, a flower like the prince's feather, sweet peas, lilac, Spanish broom, umbrella, laurel, almonds, cayenne pepper, cuttings of gooseberries
April 4	planted suckers of roses, seeds of althaea & prince's feather
April 6	planted lilies & wild honeysuckles
April 7	planted strawberry roots
April 9	sowed 3 rows of celery, 2 dozen of lettuce and 2 of radish. Lunaria in full bloom
April 16	sweet williams begin to open
April 24	forwardest peas of February 20 come to table
April 25	asparagus 3 inches high, and branched. Feathered hyacinth

	40 in bloom, also sweet williams. A pink is blooming. Lunaria still in bloom, an indifferent flower
April 27	sowed lettuce, radish, broccoli and cauliflower
April 28	flower-de luce irises just opening! Strawberries come to table. Note this is the first year of their bearing having been planted in the spring of 1766. And on an average the plants bear 20 strawberries each. 100 fill half a pint. Forwardest peas of March 17 come to table. Latest peas of Feb. 20 will come to table within about 4 days. Snapdragons blooming.

Jefferson's letters also show his deep interest in garden design and plants. Many were written to William Hamilton, a renowned botanist and plant collector who had visited the same English gardens a few years before Jefferson and used what he saw to influence his magnificent park and garden at Woodlands, Philadelphia, on the banks of the Schuylkill river. Here, Jefferson outlines his plans for Monticello and begs Hamilton to help him with them.

Washington July 1806

To William Hamilton

Your [note] of the 7th duly came to hand and the plant you are so good as to propose to send me will be thankfully received. The little *Mimosa julibrisin* you were so kind as to send me the last year is flour-ishing.... At a future day, say two years hence I shall ask from you some seeds of the *Mimosa farnesiana* or *nilotica*, of which you were kind enough before to furnish me with some, but the plants have been lost during my absence from home. I remember seeing in your greenhouse a plant a couple of feet in height in a pot the fragrance of which (from its gummy bud if I recollect rightly) was peculiarly agreeable to me and you were so kind as to remark that it required only a greenhouse, and that you would furnish me with one when I should be in a situation to preserve it. But its name has entirely escaped me and I cannot suppose you can recollect or conjecture in your vast collection what particular plant this might be. I must acquiesce therefore in a privation which my own defect of memory has produced...

Having decisively made up my mind for retirement at the end of my present term, my views and attentions are all turned homewards. I have hitherto been engaged in my buildings, which will be finished in the course of the present year. The improvement of my grounds has been reserved for my occupation on my return home. For this reason it is that I have put off to the fall of the year after next the collection of such curious trees as will bear our winters in the open air.

The grounds, which I destine to improve in the style of English gardens, are in a form very difficult to be managed. They compose the northern quadrant of a mountain for about two-thirds of its height and then spread for the upper third over its whole crown. They contain about three hundred acres, washed at the foot for about a mile, by a river of the size of the Schuylkill. The hill is generally too steep for direct ascent, but we make level walks successively along its side, which in its upper part encircle the hill and intersect these again by others of easy ascent in various parts. They are chiefly still in their native woods. These are majestic, and very generally a close undergrowth, which I have not suffered to be touched, knowing how much easier it is to cut away than to fill up. The upper third is chiefly open, but to the South is covered with a dense thicket of Scotch broom which being favourably spread before the sun will admit of advantageous arrangement for winter enjoyment. You are sensible that this disposition of the ground takes from me the first beauty in gardening, the variety of hill and dale, and leaves me as an awkward substitute a few hanging hollows and ridges, this subject is so unique and at the same time refractory, that to make a disposition analogous to its character would require much more of the genius of the landscape painter and gardener than I pretend to... I could never wish your health to be such as to render travelling necessary; but should a journey at any time promise improvement to it, there is no one on which you would be received with more pleasure than at Monticello. Should I be there you will have an opportunity of indulging on a new field some of the taste which has made the Woodlands the only rival which I have known in America to what may be seen in England.

Jefferson had many happy years at Monticello. In 1811, aged sixty-eight, he spelled out just how much gardening meant to him in a letter to Charles Willson Peale, who had painted his portrait twenty years earlier.

I have often thought that if heaven had given me choice of my position and calling, it should have been on a rich spot of earth, well watered and near a good market for the productions of the garden. No occupation is so delightful to me as the culture of the earth, and no culture comparable to that of the garden. Such a variety of subjects, some one always coming to perfection, the failure of one thing repaired by the success of another, and instead of one harvest a continued one through the year. Under a total want of demand except from our family table, I am still devoted to the garden. But though an old man, I am but a young gardener.

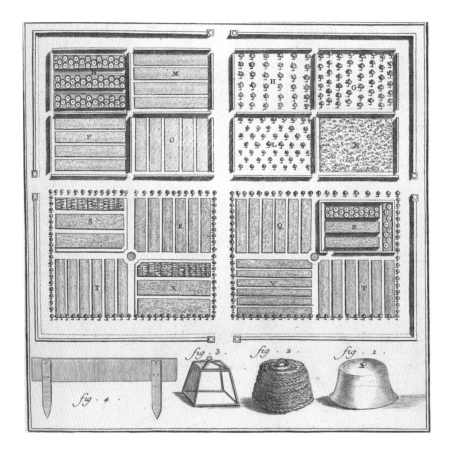

🦋 A Bachelor of Husbandry

The Yorkes, occupants of the remote country house of Erddig, near Wrexham in Clwyd, habitually maintained close and affectionate relations with their estate and household staff. In the 1880s Philip Yorke immortalised many of them in portraits, each bearing a poem singing their praises. Their occupations ranged from cook to spider-brusher – and the gardener, of course, was included.

Our Gardener here, James Phillips, see
A Bachelor of Husbandry
Who did from garden-boy become
The finished grower of the Plum,
Scarce ever absent from our ground
Then only some few miles around.
This Garden formed his chief delight,
And was as Eden in his sight.

Old-fashioned, in his notions, he
With foreign names did not agree
'Quatre-Saisons' 'Quarter-Sessions' meant,
The 'Bijou' as the 'By Joe' went,
'Glory to die John' was the Rose,
Which each as 'Gloire de Dijon' knows.
No Green-house here 'twas his advice
The Antique Frames would well suffice.

Invited by a friend was he
To Leasowe Castle by the Sea
And a day's holiday he took
That he on that Estate might look.
Little regard to it he paid,
This one remark was all he made,
That they, whose Gardens he was shown,
Did 'a fine sheet of water' own...

For three and forty years his name
Was known to all who hither came:
Our gardens under his employ
Did great fertility enjoy:
And visitors did oft declare
They ne'er did taste so good a pear
As 'Winter-nellie', by him grown,
And at our local Contests shown.

This faithful steward, just and true
Died here, in eighteen eighty two,
At the full age of fifty eight,
Like 'shock of corn', mayhap of wheat;
When 'as bare grain' his body sank
Were nigh four thousand pounds in Bank.
A search for next of kin was made,
And to a niece the same was paid.

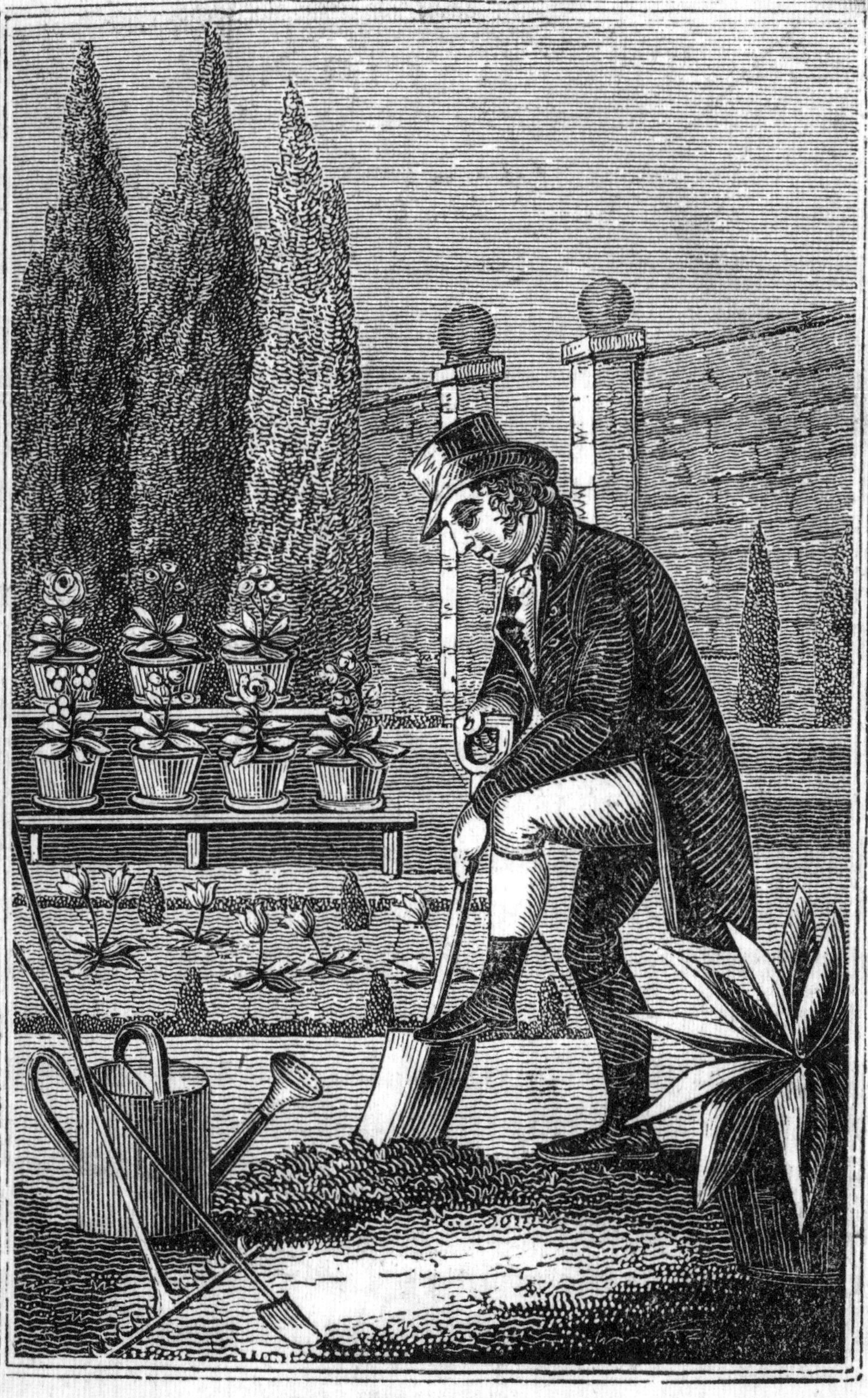

The Gardener.

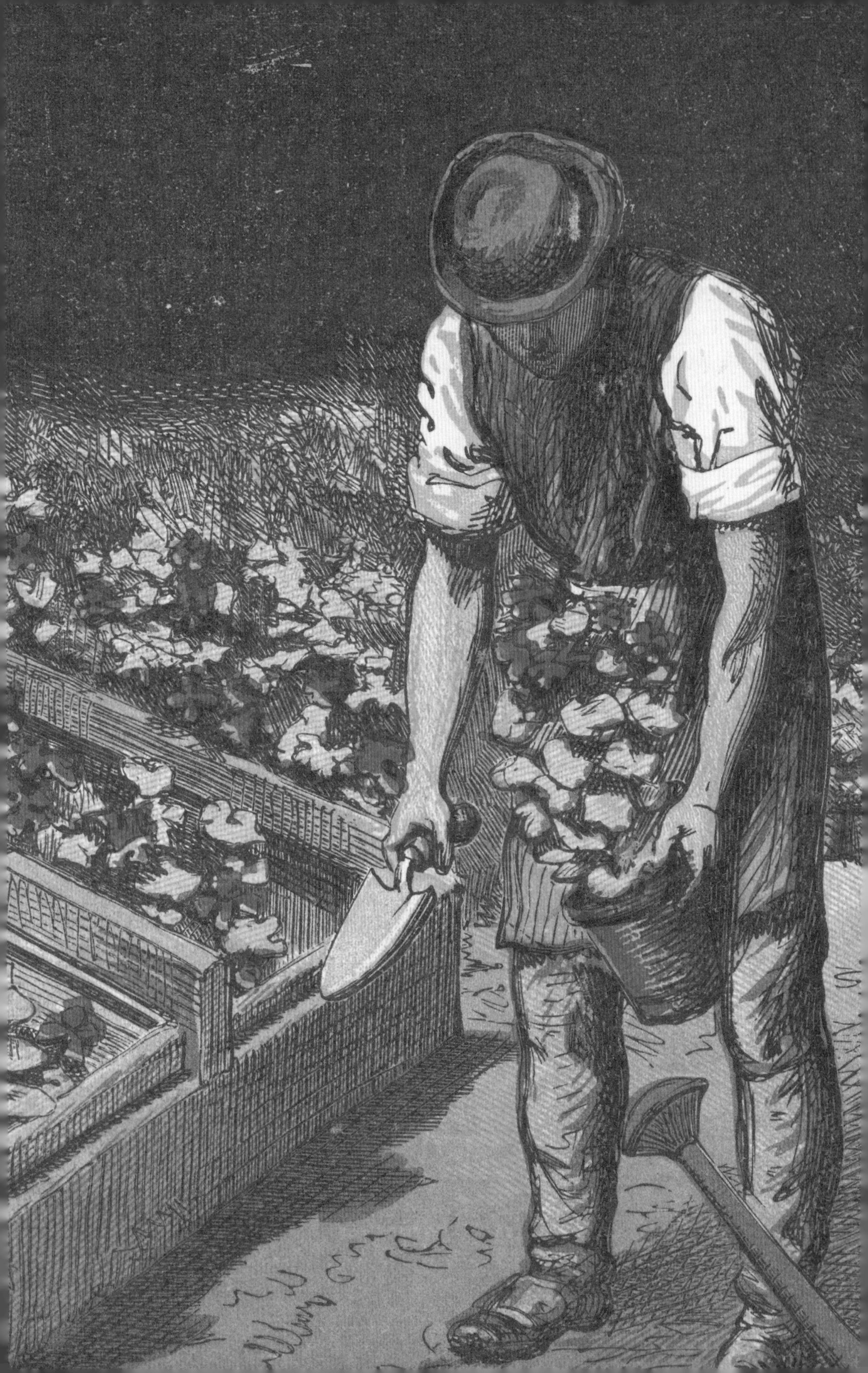

✿ Well Stricken in Years

Robert Louis Stevenson appreciated gardens from childhood, though he only became an active gardener after he settled at Vailima, Samoa, in 1890. There he set about reclaiming a plot of ground from the rampant wilderness around the house. In Memories and Portraits *(1887) he reminisces nostalgically about an aged Scots gardener called Robert.*

He was a man whose very presence could impart a savour of quaint antiquity to the baldest and most modern flower-plots. There was a dignity about his tall stooping form, and earnestness in his wrinkled face that recalled Don Quixote; but a Don Quixote who had come through the training of the Covenant...

To me he stands essentially as a GENIUS LOCI. It is impossible to separate his spare form and old straw hat from the garden in the lap of the hill, with its rocks overgrown with clematis, its shadowy walks, and the splendid breadth of meadow that one saw from the northwest corner. The garden and gardener seem part and parcel of each other. The first time that I saw him, I fancy Robert was pretty old already: he had certainly begun to use his years as a stalking horse. 'I AM OLD AND WELL STRICKEN IN YEARS,' he was wont to say; and I never found any one bold enough to answer the argument.

Apart from this vantage that he kept over all who were not yet octogenarian, he had some other drawbacks as a gardener. He shrank the very place he cultivated. The dignity and reduced gentility of his appearance made the small garden cut a sorry figure. He was full of tales of greater situations in his younger days. He spoke of castles and parks with a humbling familiarity. He told of places where under-gardeners had trembled at his looks, where there were meres and swanneries, labyrinths of walk and wildernesses of sad shrubbery in his control, till you could not help feeling that it was condescension on his part to dress your humbler garden plots. You were thrown at once into an invidious position. You felt that you were profiting by the needs of dignity, and that his poverty and not his will consented to your vulgar rule.

Involuntarily you compared yourself with the swineherd that made Alfred watch his cakes, or some bloated citizen who may have given his sons and his condescension to the fallen Dionysius. Nor were the disagreeables purely fanciful and metaphysical, for the sway that he exercised over your feelings he extended to your garden, and, through the garden, to your diet. He would trim a hedge, throw away a favourite plant, or fill the most favoured and fertile section of the garden with a vegetable that none of us could eat, in supreme contempt for our opinion.

If you asked him to send you in one of your own artichokes, 'THAT I WULL, MEM,' he would say, 'WITH PLEASURE, FOR IT IS MAIR BLESSED TO GIVE THAN TO RECEIVE.' Ay, and even when, by extra twisting of the screw. we prevailed on him to prefer our commands to his own inclination, and he went away, stately and sad, professing that 'OUR WULL WAS HIS PLEASURE,' but yet reminding us that he would do it 'WITH FEELIN'S', –even then, I say, the triumphant master felt humbled in his triumph, felt that he ruled on sufferance only...

In flowers his taste was old-fashioned and catholic; affecting sunflowers and dahlias, wallflowers and roses and holding in supreme aversion whatsoever was fantastic, new-fashioned or wild. There was one exception to this sweeping ban. Foxgloves, though undoubtedly guilty on the last count, he not only spared, but loved; and when the shrubbery was being thinned, he stayed his hand and dexterously manipulated his bill in order to save every stately stem. In boyhood, as he told me once, speaking in that tone that only actors and the old-fashioned common folk can use nowadays, his heart grew 'PROUD' within him when he came on a burn-course among the braes of Manor that shone purple with their graceful trophies; and not all his apprenticeship and practice for so many years of precise gardening had banished these boyish recollections from his heart.

But however his sympathy with his old feelings might affect his liking for the foxgloves, the very truth was that he scorned all flowers together. They were but garnishings, childish toys, trifling ornaments for ladies' chimney-shelves. It was towards his cauliflowers and peas and cabbage that his heart grew warm. His preference for the more useful growths was such that cabbages were found invading the flowerpots, and an outpost of savoys was once discovered in the centre of the lawn. He would hold forth over some thriving plant with wonderful enthusiasm, piling reminiscence on reminiscence of former and perhaps yet finer specimens. Yet even then he did not let the credit leave himself. He had, indeed, raised 'FINER O' THEM'; but it seemed that no one else had been favoured with a like success.

All other gardeners, in fact, were mere foils to his own superior attainments; and he would recount, with perfect soberness of voice and visage, how so and so had wondered, and such another could scarcely give credit to his eyes. Nor was it with his rivals only that he parted praise and blame. If you remarked how well a plant was looking, he would gravely touch his hat and thank you with solemn unction; all credit in the matter falling to him. If, on the other hand, you called his attention to some back-going vegetable, he would quote Scripture: 'PAUL MAY PLANT AND APOLLOS MAY WATER'; all blame being left to Providence, on the score of deficient rain or untimely frosts.

There was one thing in the garden that shared his preference with his favourite cabbages and rhubarb, and that other was the beehive. Their sound, their industry, perhaps their sweet product also, had taken hold of his imagination and heart, whether by way of memory or no I cannot say, although perhaps the bees too were linked to him by some recollection of Manor braes and his country childhood. Nevertheless, he was too chary of his personal safety or (let me rather say) his personal dignity to mingle in any active office towards them. But he could stand by while one of the contemned rivals did the work for him, and protest that it was quite safe in spite of his own considerate distance and the cries of the distressed assistant. In regard to bees, he was rather a man of word than deed, and some of his most striking sentences had the bees for text. 'THEY ARE INDEED WONDERFUL CREATURES, MEM,' he said once. 'THEY JUST MIND ME O' WHAT THE QUEEN OF SHEBA SAID TO SOLOMON — AND I THINK SHE SAID IT WI' A SIGH, — 'THE HALF OF IT HATH NOT BEEN TOLD UNTO ME.'

That essay was not Stevenson's only portrait of Robert. Clearly recognisable, although seen this time from a child's point of view, he is immortalised in A Child's Garden of Verses *(1905).*

The Gardener does not love to talk,
He makes me keep the gravel walk;
And when he puts his tools away,
He locks the door and takes the key.

Away behind the currant row
Where no one else but cook may go,
Far in the plots, I see him dig,
Old and serious, brown and big.

He digs the flowers, green, red, and blue,
Nor wishes to be spoken to.
He digs the flowers and cuts the hay,
And never seems to want to play.

Silly gardener! summer goes,
And winter comes with pinching toes,
When in the garden bare and brown
You must lay your barrow down.

Well now, and while the summer stays,
To profit by these garden days
O how much wiser you would be
To play at Indian wars with me!

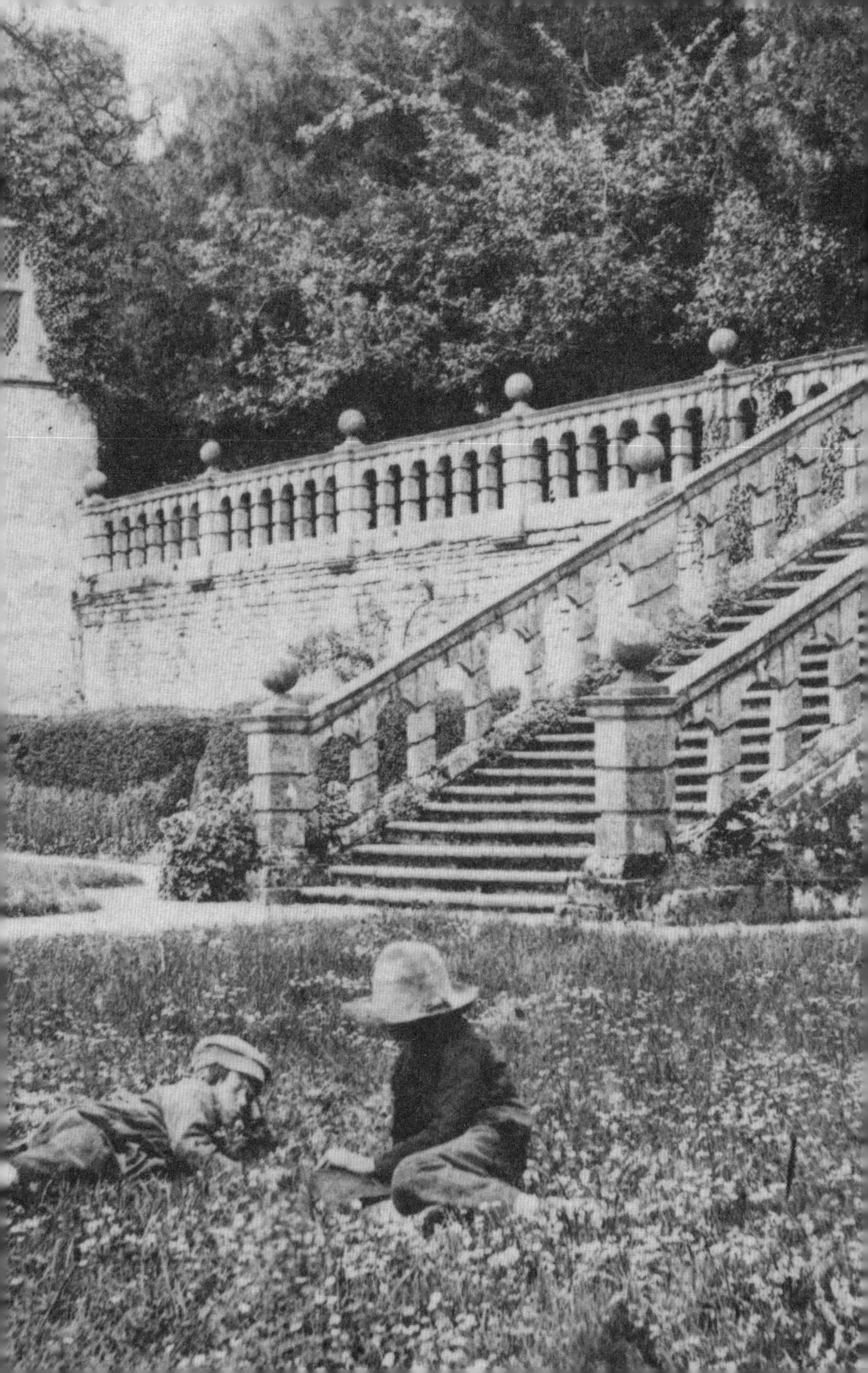

1897
"THE GENTLEWOMAN"
CALENDAR for
March

MARCH

1	Monday
2	Tuesday
3	Wednesday
4	Thursday
5	Friday
6	Saturday
7	SUNDAY
8	Monday
9	Tuesday
10	Wednesday
11	Thursday
12	Friday
13	Saturday
14	SUNDAY
15	Monday
16	Tuesday
17	Wednesday
18	Thursday
19	Friday
20	Saturday
21	SUNDAY
22	Monday
23	Tuesday
24	Wednesday
25	Thursday
26	Friday
27	Saturday
28	SUNDAY
29	Monday
30	Tuesday
31	Wednesday

" "The Gentlewoman" is the Ideal Ladies' Paper "

✸☙ They Gardened in Bloomers

Men were not the only gardeners, of course. Women had long held responsibility for flower gardens, and many found satisfaction in taking on dirty and heavy work themselves – even if they could afford gardeners. Towards the end of the nineteenth century, gardening became a popular career option for women, and in 1896 the first female gardeners were employed at Kew. The satirical magazine Punch *celebrated their arrival – and the new fashion for 'rational dress' in the shape of baggy trousers – in doggerel verse.*

They gardened in bloomers the newspapers said
So to Kew without waiting all Londoners sped.
From the roofs of the bus they had a fine view
Of the ladies in bloomers who gardened at Kew.
The orchids were slighted, the lilies were scorned,
The dahlias were flouted, till botanists mourned,
But the Londoners shouted, 'What ho there, Go to;
Who wants to see blooms now you've bloomers at Kew?'

✌ A Cast-Iron Back with a Hinge in It

Charles Dudley Warner, a writer and humorist who collaborated with Mark Twain on several books, was an equally enthusiastic amateur gardener. His book A Summer in a Garden, *a week-by-week report on his garden at Nook Farm, near Hartford, Connecticut, was originally published in 1870 in the form of columns in the local newspaper.*

The love of dirt is among the earliest of passions, as it is the latest. Mud-pies gratify one of our first and best instincts. So long as we are dirty, we are pure. Fondness for the ground comes back to a man after he has run the round of pleasure and business, eaten dirt, and sown wild-oats, drifted about the world, and taken the wind of all its moods. The love of digging in the ground (or of looking on while he pays another to dig) is as sure to come back to him as he is sure, at last, to go under the ground, and stay there. To own a bit of ground, to scratch it with a hoe, to plant seeds and watch their renewal of life, this is the commonest delight of the race, the most satisfactory thing a man can do...

However small it is on the surface, it is four thousand miles deep; and that is a very handsome property. And there is a great pleasure in working in the soil, apart from the ownership of it. The man who has planted a garden feels that he has done something for the good of the World. He belongs to the producers. It is a pleasure to eat of the fruit of one's toil, if it be nothing more than a head of lettuce or an ear of corn. One cultivates a lawn even with great satisfaction; for there is nothing more beautiful than grass and turf in our latitude. The tropics may have their delights, but they have not turf: and the world without turf is a dreary desert. The original Garden of Eden could not have had such turf as one sees in England.

There is life in the ground; it goes into the seeds; and it also, when it is stirred up, goes into the man who stirs it. The hot sun on his back as he bends to his shovel and hoe, or contemplatively rakes the warm and fragrant loam, is better than much medicine. The buds are coming out on the bushes round about; the blossoms of the fruit trees begin

to show; the blood is running up the grapevines in streams; you can smell the wild flowers on the near bank; and the birds are flying and glancing and singing everywhere. To the open kitchen door comes the busy housewife to shake a white something, and stands a moment to look, quite transfixed by the delightful sights and sounds. Hoeing in the garden on a bright, soft May day, when you are not obliged to, is nearly equal to the delight of going trouting...

The principal value of a private garden is not understood. It is not to give the possessor vegetables or fruit (that can be better and cheaper done by the market-gardeners), but to teach him patience and philosophy and the higher virtues, hope deferred and expectations blighted, leading directly to resignation and sometimes to alienation. The garden thus becomes a moral agent, a test of character, as it was in the beginning.

The first pleasant thing about a garden is, that you never know when to set it going. If you want anything to come to maturity early, you must start it in a hothouse. If you put it out early, the chances are all in favour of getting it nipped with frost. And, if you do not set out plants or sow seeds early, you fret continually; knowing that your vegetables will be late, and that, while Jones has early peas, you will be watching your slow-forming pods. This keeps you in a state of mind. When you have planted anything early, you are doubtful whether to desire to see it above ground, or not. If a hot day comes, you long to see the young plants; but, when a cold north wind brings frost, you tremble lest the seeds have burst their bands. Your spring is passed in anxious doubts and fears, which are usually realized; and so a great moral discipline is worked out for you...

The most humiliating thing to me about a garden is the lesson it teaches of the inferiority of man. Nature is prompt, decided, inexhaustible. She thrusts up her plants with a vigour and freedom that I admire; and the more worthless the plant, the more rapid and splendid its growth. She is at it early and late, and all night; never tiring, nor showing the least sign of exhaustion...There is no liberty in gardening. The man who undertakes a garden is relentlessly pursued. He felicitates himself that, when he gets it once planted, he will have a season of rest and of enjoyment in the sprouting and growing of his seeds. It is a green anticipation. He has planted a seed that will keep him awake nights; drive rest from his bones, and sleep from his pillow. Hardly is the garden planted, when he must begin to hoe it. The weeds have sprung up all over it in a night. They shine and wave in redundant life. The docks have almost gone to seed; and their roots go deeper than conscience. Weeds have hateful moral qualities. To cut down a weed is to do a moral action. I feel as if I were destroying sin. My hoe becomes an instrument of retributive justice. I am an apostle of Nature. This view of the matter lends a dignity to the art of hoeing which nothing else does, and lifts it into the region of ethics. Hoeing becomes, not a pastime, but a duty. And you get to regard it so, as the days and the weeds lengthen. The hoe is an ingenious instrument, calculated to call out a great deal of strength at a great disadvantage. Nevertheless, what a man needs in gardening is a cast-iron back, – with a hinge in it.

❧ Being Entirely Ignorant

The novelist Elizabeth von Arnim was also an enthusiastic amateur gardener. Born Mary Annette Beauchamp in Australia in 1866, she was the neglected youngest child of a large family. She was brought up in England and Switzerland, and married her first husband, the much older Count Henning August von Arnim-Schlagenthin, when she was twenty-four. He is teasingly characterised in several of her novels, including her first and most famous: the autobiographical Elizabeth and Her German Garden. *Published in 1898, it celebrated their life in Nassenheide, Pomerania, where they had moved in 1894. It perfectly captures 'beginner's mind': the indefatigable enthusiasm and occasional genius of the new convert.*

May 10th. I knew nothing whatever last year about gardening and this year know very little more, but I have dawnings of what may be done, and have at least made one great stride – from ipomaea [morning glories] to tea-roses.

The garden was an absolute wilderness. It is all round the house, but the principal part is on the south side and has evidently always been so. The south front is one-storied, a long series of rooms opening one into the other, and the walls are covered with Virginia creeper. There is a little veranda in the middle, leading by a flight of rickety wooden steps down into what seems to have been the only spot in the whole place that was ever cared for. This is a semicircle cut into the lawn and edged with privet, and in this semicircle are eleven beds of different sizes bordered with box and arranged round a sun-dial, and the sun-dial is very venerable and moss-grown, and greatly beloved by me.

These beds were the only sign of any attempt at gardening to be seen (except a solitary crocus that came up all by itself each spring in the grass, not because it wanted to, but because it could not help it), and these I had sown with ipomaea, the whole eleven, having found a German gardening book, according to which ipomaea in vast quantities was the one thing needful to turn the most hideous desert into a paradise. Nothing else in that book was recommended with anything like the same warmth, and being entirely ignorant of the quantity of seed necessary, I bought ten pounds of it and had it sown not only in the eleven beds but round nearly every tree, and then waited in great agitation for the promised paradise to appear. It did not, and I learned my first lesson.

Luckily I had sown two great patches of sweet peas which made me very happy all the summer, and then there were some sunflowers and a few hollyhocks under the south windows, with Madonna lilies in between. But the lilies, after being transplanted, disappeared to my great dismay, for how was I to know it was the way of lilies? And the hollyhocks turned out to be rather ugly colours, so that my first summer was decorated and beautified solely by sweet peas.

At present we are only just beginning to breathe after the bustle of getting new beds and borders and paths made in time for this summer. The eleven beds round the sundial are filled with roses, but I see already that I have made mistakes with some. As I have not a living soul with whom to hold communion on this or indeed on any matter, my only way of learning is by making mistakes. All eleven were to have been carpeted with purple pansies, but finding that I had not enough and that nobody had any to sell me, only six have got their pansies, the others being sown with dwarf mignonette. Two of the eleven are filled with Marie van Houtte roses, two with Viscountess Folkestone, two with Laurette Messimy, one with Souvenir de la Malmaison, one with Adam and Devoniensis, two with Persian Yellow and Bicolor, and one big bed behind the sun-dial with three sorts of red roses (seventy-two in all), Duke of Teck, Cheshunt Scarlet, and Prefet de Limburg. This bed is, I am sure, a mistake, and several of the others are, I think, but of course I must wait and see, being such an ignorant person.

Then I have had two long beds made in the grass on either side of the semicircle, each sown with mignonette, and one filled with Marie van Houtte, and the other with Jules Finger and the Bride; and in a warm corner under the drawing-room windows is a bed of Madame Lambard, Madame de Watteville, and Comtesse Riza du Parc; while farther down the garden, sheltered on the north and west by a group of beeches and lilacs, is another large bed, containing Rubens, Madame Joseph Schwartz, and the Honourable Edith Gifford. All these roses are dwarf; I have only two standards in the whole garden, two Madame George Bruants, and they look like broomsticks. How I long for the day when the tea roses open their buds! Never did I look forward so

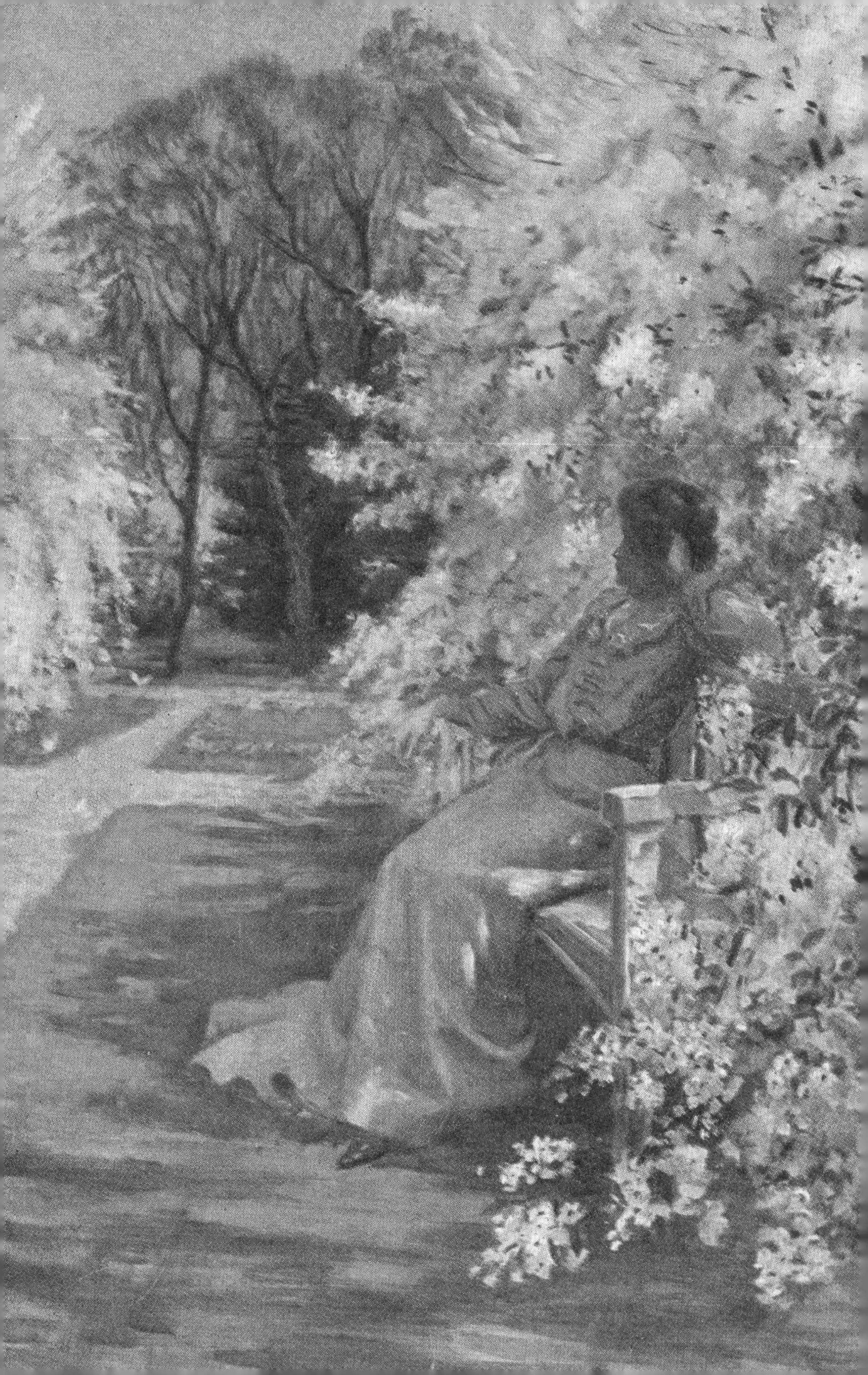

intensely to anything; and every day I go the rounds, admiring what the dear little things have achieved in the twenty-four hours in the way of new leaf or increase of lovely red shoot.

The hollyhocks and lilies (now flourishing) are still under the south windows in a narrow border on the top of a grass slope, at the foot of which I have sown two long borders of sweet peas facing the rose beds, so that my roses may have something almost as sweet as themselves to look at until the autumn, when everything is to make place for more tea-roses. The path leading away from this semicircle down the garden is bordered with China roses, white and pink, with here and there a Persian Yellow. I wish now I had put tea-roses there, and I have mis-givings as to the effect of the Persian Yellows among the Chinas, for the Chinas are such wee little baby things, and the Persian Yellows look as though they intended to be big bushes.

There is not a creature in all this part of the world who could in the least understand with what heart-beatings I am looking forward to the flowering of these roses, and not a German gardening book that does not relegate all tea-roses to hot-houses, imprisoning them for life, and depriving them for ever of the breath of God. It was no doubt because I was so ignorant that I rushed in where Teutonic angels fear to tread and made my tea-roses face a northern winter; but they did face it under fir branches and leaves, and not one has suffered, and they are looking to-day as happy and as determined to enjoy themselves as any roses, I am sure, in Europe.

🍂 The Unkindest Cut

The popular American garden-writer Samuel Reynolds Hole began his book
Our Gardens *(1899) with some disheartening research results.*

I asked a schoolboy 'what he thought a garden was for?' and he said,
'Strawberries.' His younger sister suggested Croquet, and the elder
Garden-parties. The brother from Oxford made a prompt declaration
in favour of Lawn Tennis and Cigarettes, but he was rebuked by a
solemn senior, who wore spectacles, and more back hair than is usual
with males, and was told that 'a garden was designed for botanical
research, and for the classification of plants.' He was about to demon-
strate the differences between the Acoty- and the Monocoty-ledonous
divisions, when the collegian remembered an engagement elsewhere.

I repeated my question to a middle-aged nymph, who wore a feath-
ered hat of noble proportions over a loose green tunic with a silver
belt, and she replied, with a rapturous disdain of the ignorance which
presumed to ask,

'What is a garden for? For the soul, sir, for the soul of the poet!
For visions of the invisible, for grasping the intangible, for hearing
the inaudible, for exaltations' (she raised her hands, and stood tiptoe,
like jocund day upon the misty mountain top, as though she would
soar into space) 'above the miserable dullness of common life into the
splendid regions of imagination and romance.'

I ventured to suggest that she would have to do a large amount of
soaring before she met with anything more beautiful than the flowers,
or sweeter than the nightingale's note; but the flighty one still wished
to fly.

A capacious gentleman informed me that nothing in horticulture
touched him so sensibly as green peas and new potatoes, and he spoke
with so much cheerful candour that I could not be angry; but my indig-
nation was roused by a morose millionaire, when he declared that of
all his expenses he grudged most the outlay on his confounded garden.

The unkindest cut of all comes from those visitors who 'would be
so delighted to see our garden!' and they come and see, and forget to
be delighted. They admire the old city walls which surround it, they

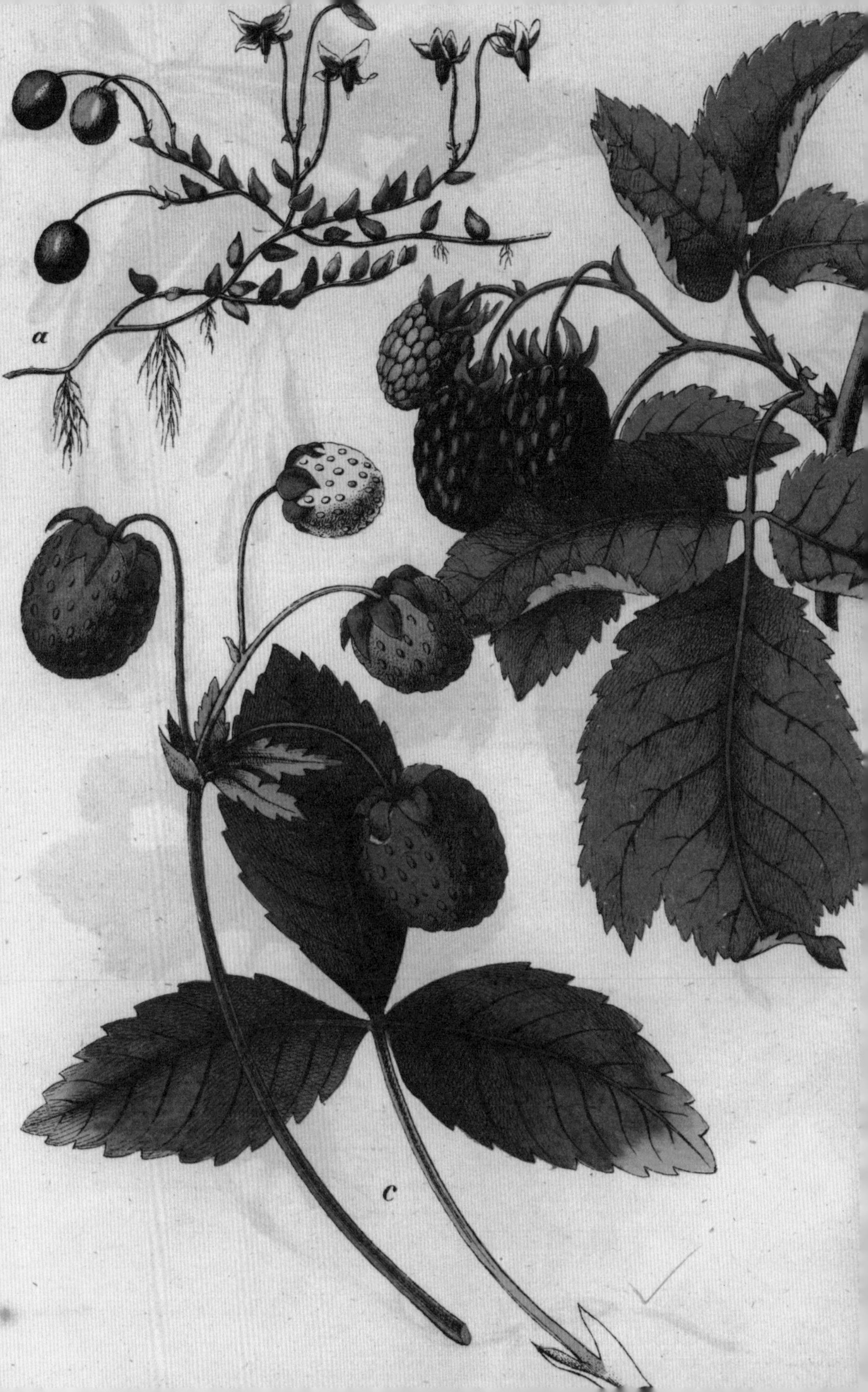
a
c

like to hear the cawing of the rooks, they are pleased with the sundial and the garden-chairs, but as for horticulture they might as well be in Piccadilly! I heard a lady speaking to her companion of 'the most perfect gem she had ever seen', and when, supposing that reference was made to some exquisite novelty in plants, I inquired the name and habitation, I was informed that the subject under discussion was 'Isabel's new baby'!

Iaſminum Indicum,ſeu flos mi,
rabilis peruanus.

❧ Grubbing Weeds from Gravel-paths with Broken Dinner-knives

Rudyard Kipling moved to the Jacobean house called Batemans, near Burwash in East Sussex, in 1902, and lived there until his death thirty-four years later. The countryside around it inspired Puck of Pook's Hill. *Kipling was a keen hands-on gardener, and used some of the 7,000 guineas he was awarded with his Nobel Prize in 1907 to lay out its gardens to his own design (the plan still hangs in his study). Its form reflects his fondness for the Arts and Crafts movement. There is a pear-tree tunnel, a herb garden, a substantial pond on which his two children loved boating, a rose garden full of old roses, a pleached lime walk and encircling yew hedges – all still maintained by the National Trust. Kipling's famous poem 'The Glory of the Garden' is a clarion call to practical action.*

Our England is a garden that is full of stately views,
Of borders, beds and shrubberies and lawns and avenues,
With statues on the terraces and peacocks strutting by;
But the Glory of the Garden lies in more than meets the eye.

For where the old thick laurels grow, along the thin red wall,
You find the tool- and potting-sheds which are the heart of all
The cold-frames and the hot-houses, the dungpits and the tanks
The rollers, carts and drain-pipes, with the barrows and the planks

And there you'll see the gardeners, the men and 'prentice boys
Told off to do as they are bid and do it without noise;
For, except when seeds are planted and we shout to scare the birds
The Glory of the Garden it abideth not in words.

And some can pot begonias and some can bud a rose,
And some are hardly fit to trust with anything that grows;
But they can roll and trim the lawns and sift the sand and loam
For the Glory of the Garden occupieth all who come.

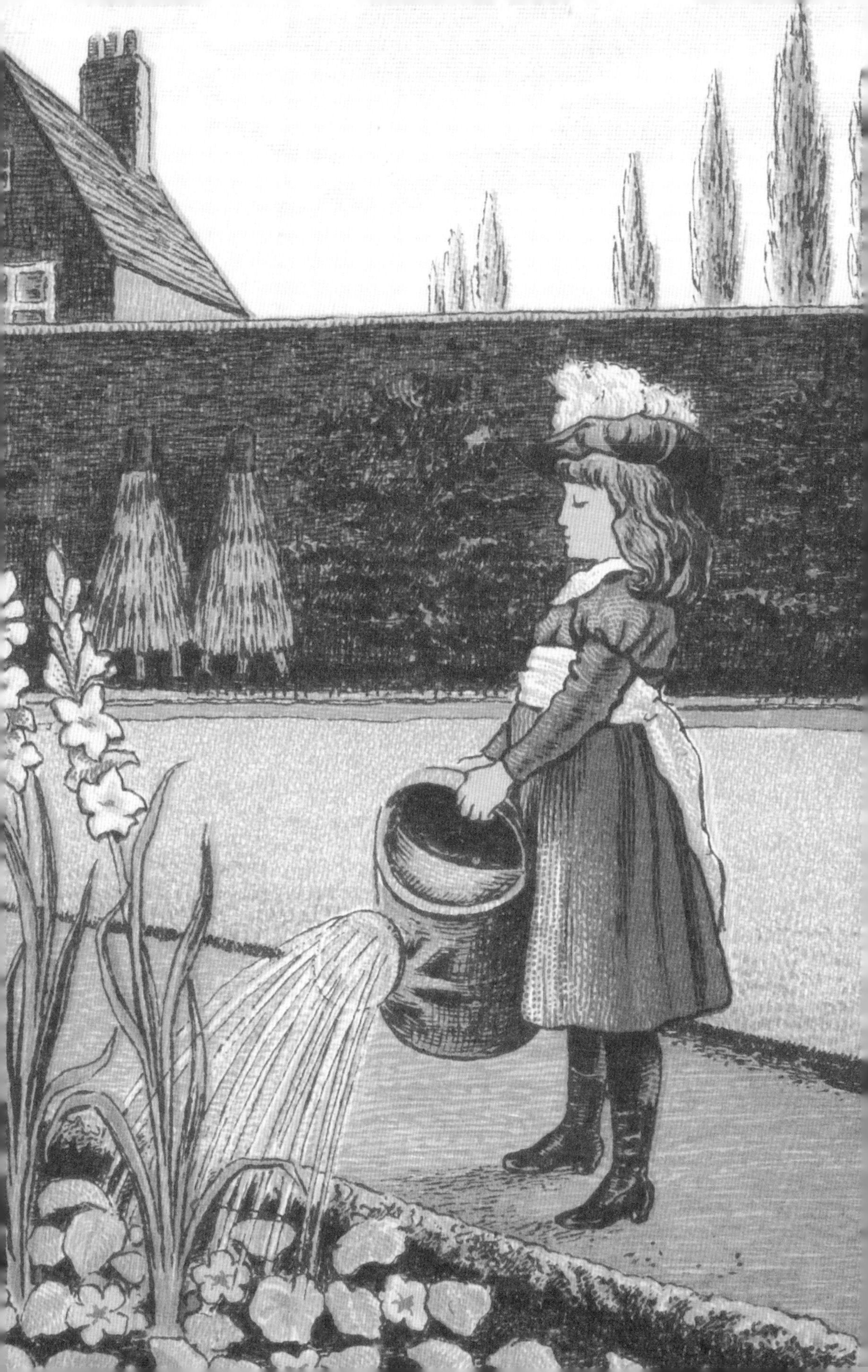

Our England is a garden, and such gardens are not made
By singing: 'Oh, how beautiful!' and sitting in the shade,
While better men than we go out and start their working lives
At grubbing weeds from gravel-paths with broken dinner-knives,

There's not a pair of legs so thin, there's not a head so thick,
There's not a hand so weak and white, nor yet a heart so sick
But it can find some needful job that's crying to be done,
For the Glory of the Garden glorifieth every one.

Then seek your job with thankfulness and work till further orders
If it's only netting strawberries or killing slugs on borders;
And when your back stops aching and your hands begin to harden
You will find yourself a partner in the Glory of the Garden.

Oh, Adam was a gardener, and God who made him sees
That half a proper gardener's work is done upon his knees,
So when your work is finished, you can wash your hands and pray
For the Glory of the Garden, that it may not pass away!
And the Glory of the Garden it shall never pass away!

❧ The Actual Tools

Gertrude Jekyll was always a hands-on gardener. Home and Garden, *published in 1900, describes the making of the garden of Munstead Wood, the house that Edwin Lutyens designed for her in Surrey. It is, more than any of her other books, a personal credo. Munstead Wood is part of the National Gardens Scheme and can still be visited.*

Is it a blessing or a disadvantage to be so made that one take keen interest in many matters; that, seeing something that one's hand may do, one cannot resist doing or attempting it, even though time be already overcrowded, and strength much reduced, and sight steadily failing? Are the people happier who are content to drift comfortably down the stream of life, to take things easily, not to want to take pains or give themselves trouble about what is not exactly necessary? I know not which, as worldly wisdom, is the wiser; I only know that to my own mind and conscience pure idleness seems to me to be akin to folly, or even worse, and that in some form or other I must obey the Divine command: 'Work while ye have the light.'...

There is a lovable quality about the actual tools. One feels so kindly to the thing that enables the hand to obey the brain. Moreover, one feels a good deal of respect for it; without it brain and hand would be helpless. When the knife that has been in one's hand or one's pocket for years has its blade so much worn by constant sharpening that it can no longer be used, with what true regret does one put it aside, and how long it is before one can really make friends with the new one! I do not think any workman really likes a new tool. There is always some feeling about it as of something strange and unfamiliar and uncongenial, somewhat of the feeling that David had about Saul's armour. What an awkward thing a new spade is, how long and heavy and rough of handle! And then how amiable it becomes when it is half worn, when the square corners that made the thrust so hard are ground away, when the whole blade has grown shorter, when the handle has gained that polish, the best polish of all, that comes of long hand-friction. No carpenter likes a new plane; no house painter likes a new brush. It is the same with tools as with clothes; the familiar ease can only come of use and better acquaintance. I suppose no horse likes a new collar; I am sure I do not like new boots!

❧ The Smoke's Smell

Let the last words on the practice of gardening be those of a poem entitled 'Digging'. Haiku-like in its intensity, it is by Edward Thomas, whose word-pictures of the British countryside are his unforgettable legacy.

Today I think
Only with scents, – scents dead leaves yield,
And bracken, and wild carrot's seed,
And the square mustard field;

Odours that rise
When the spade wounds the root of tree,
Rose, currant, raspberry, or goutweed,
Rhubarb or celery;

The smoke's smell, too,
Flowing from where a bonfire burns
The dead, the waste, the dangerous,
And all to sweetness turns.

It is enough
To smell, to crumble the dark earth,
While the robin sings over again
Sad songs of Autumn mirth.

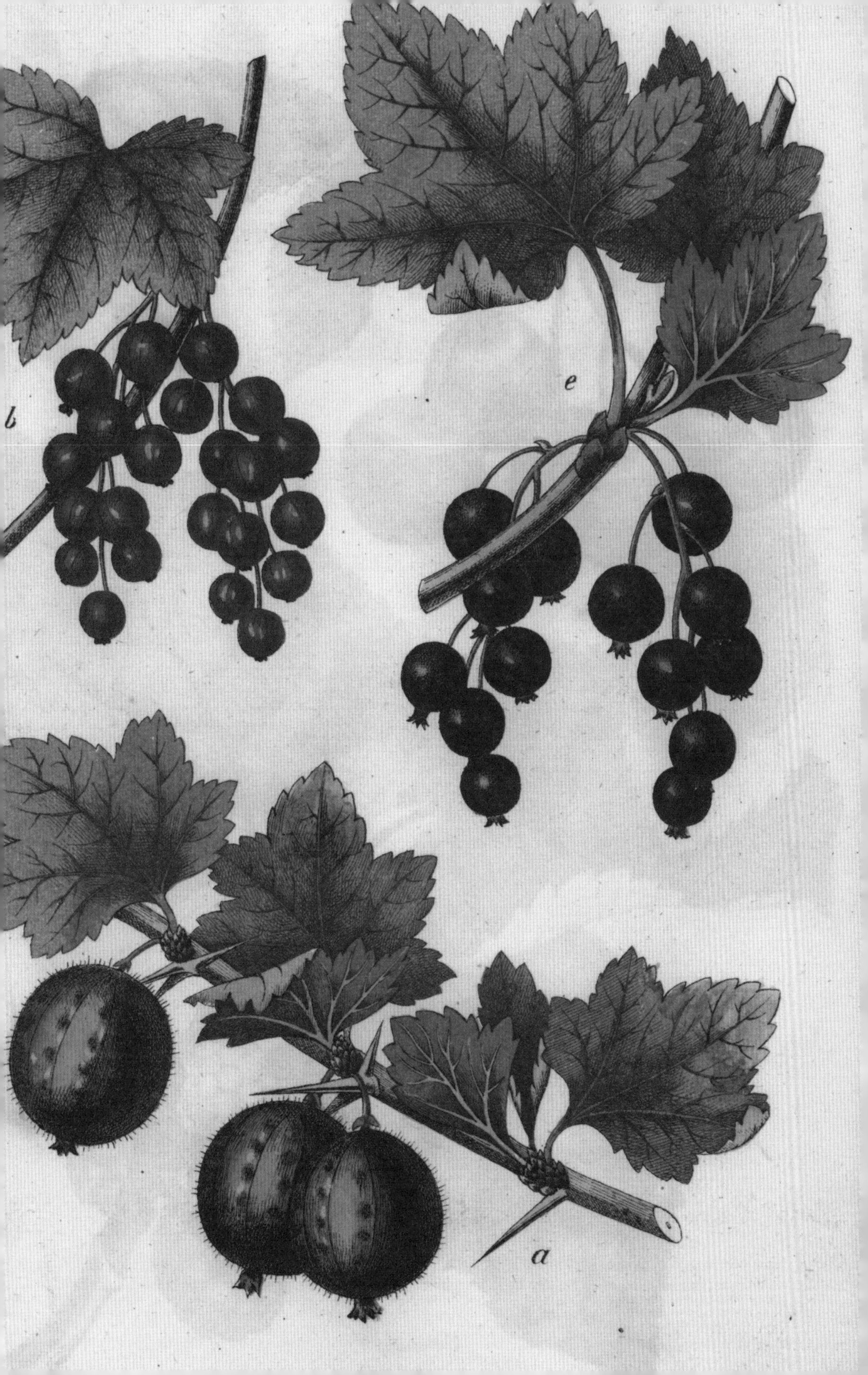
b
e
a

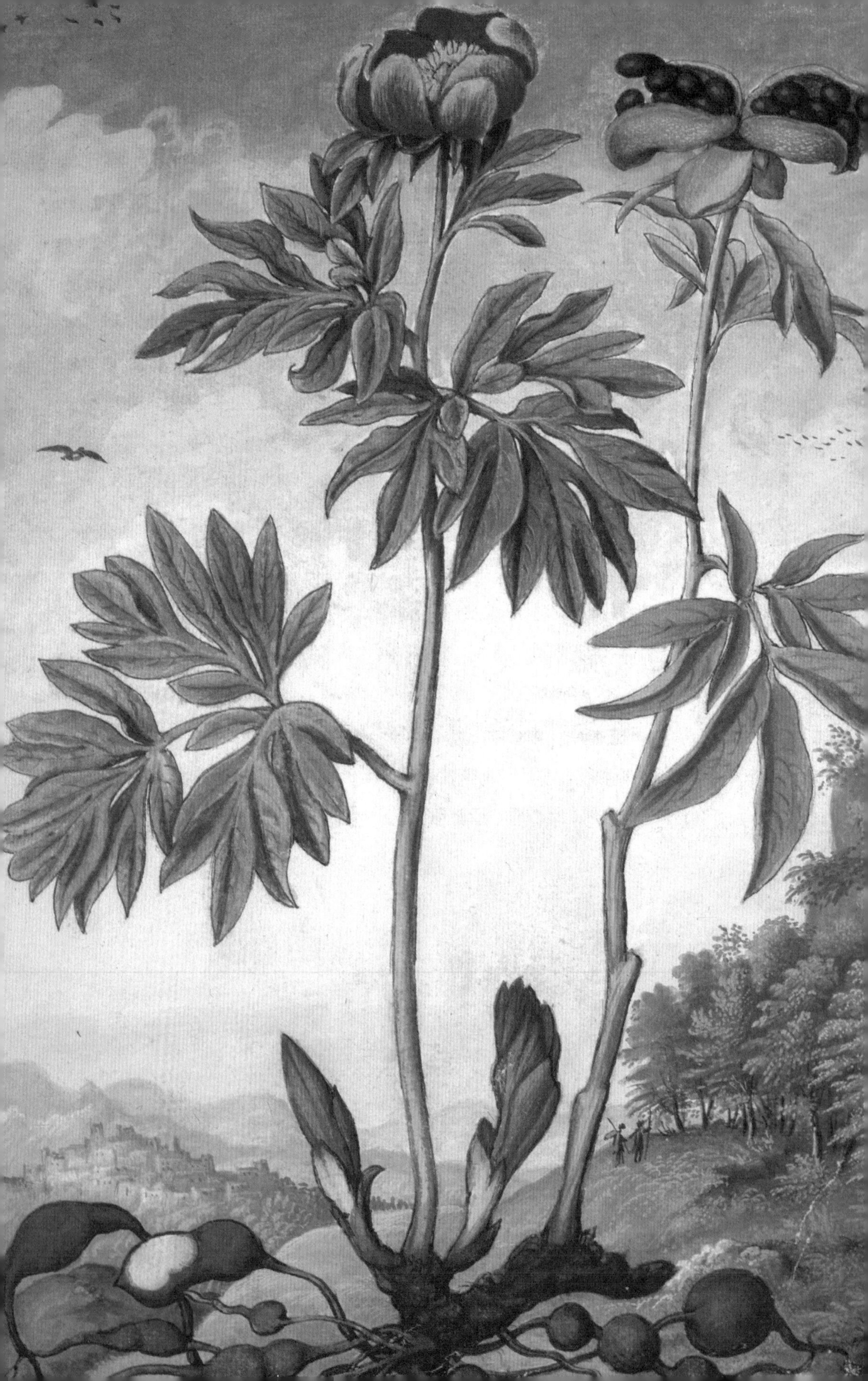

4 Solace for Body and Soul

*Gardens can be all things to all men –
and women. The last part of this anthology
celebrates the deeper meaning and hidden
virtues of gardens, and the uses philosophers
and poets have made of them, both as
metaphors and as rural retreats.*

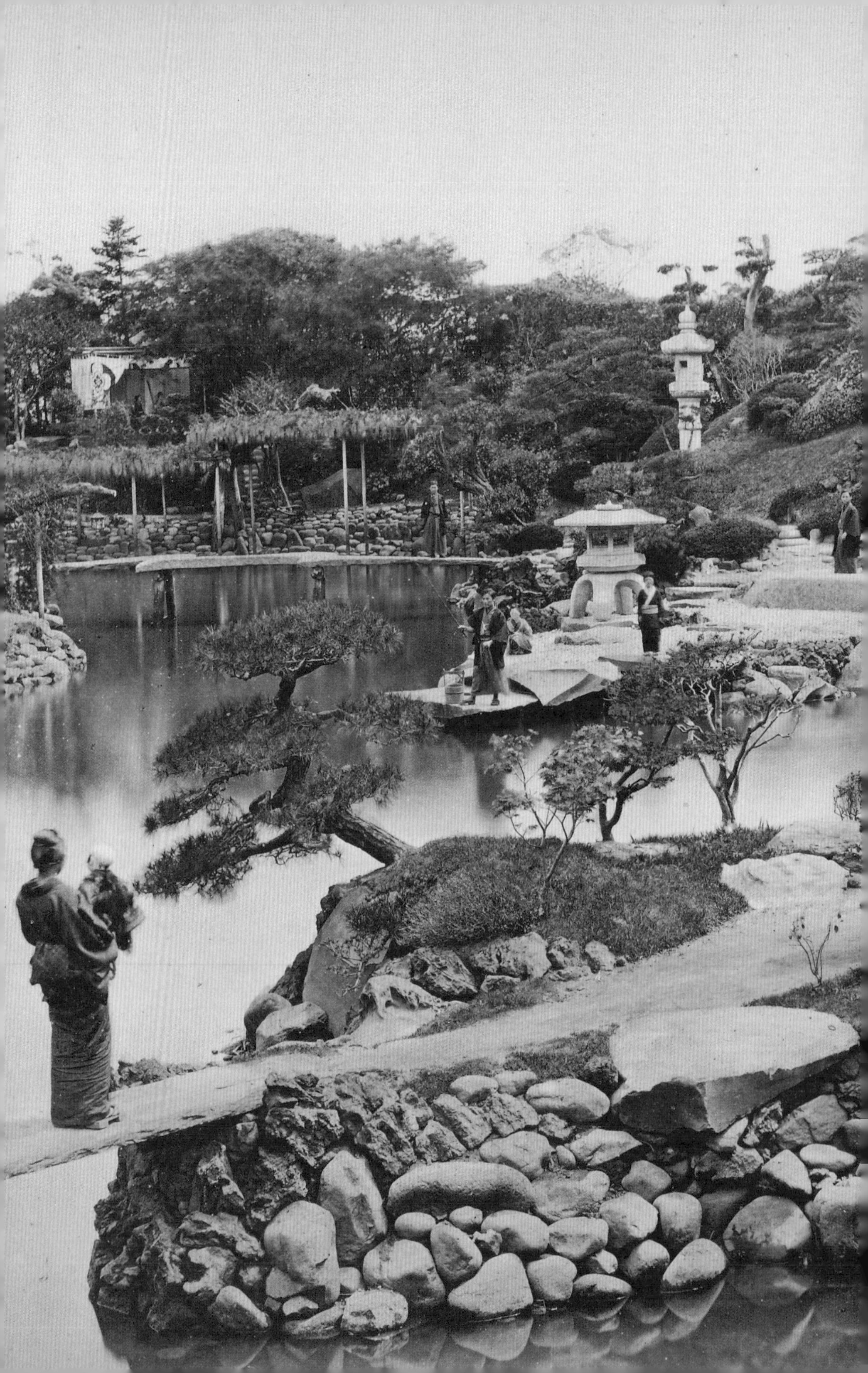

❧ The Belly of the Dragon

Nowhere was symbolic meaning earlier or more pronounced than in ancient China and Japan, where gardens were carefully cosmologically orientated. The Sakutei-ki, the oldest surviving Japanese text on garden architecture, gives a detailed description of the most fortunate garden arrangements. The first two quotes are from Günter Nitschke's book Japanese Gardens, *and the last three are from a modern translation,* Sakutei-ki: Book of the Garden.

To ensure good fortune, water must flow in from the east, pass beneath the floor of the house and flow out to the southwest. For in this way the waters of the Blue Dragon will wash away all the evil spirits from house and garden and carry them to the White Tiger...

The garden stream should flow into the *shinden* area from the east; it should then be directed south and should leave the garden flowing westwards. Even where the water has to come in from the north, it should be allowed to flow eastwards and then exit by the southwest. According to an ancient sutra, the land enclosed in a river bend should be considered the belly of the dragon. To build a house on that belly is to be lucky. But to build a house on the back of the dragon is to invite misfortune...

Even in a flat garden, with neither hills nor meadows, it is appropriate to set stones. However, a stream in a garden with no pond should be made considerably wide and the ground plane kept quite flat, allowing the gently burbling water to be easily seen from the halls nearby…

For a stone that will descend from the shoreline to the depths of the pond, or ascend from the depths out to meet the shore, a majestic stone of grand proportion is best. If this is to be constructed, then gather stones of the same colour, the shapes of which seem like they will fit each other well, and set them together so that they make one huge composite form…

Bear in mind that the stones of steep mountain cliffs rise in the angular manner of folding screens, open shutters or staircases. The stones at the base of a mountain or those of a rolling meadow are like a pack of dogs at rest, wild pigs running chaotically, or calves frolicking with their mothers.

Regarding the placement of stones there are many taboos. If so much as one of these taboos is violated, the master of the household will fall ill and eventually die, his land will fall into desolation and become the abode of devils.

🍀 Your Leaves Are Always at His Lotus Feet

Ancient Indian texts also revel in describing plants and trees in detail. The Bhagavata Purana, *a collection of stories about the incarnation of Vishnu, contains an account of the early life of the god Krishna, in which he is pursued by infatuated* gopis (milkmaids). *During one episode they think Krishna has deserted them and frantically call on the trees and plants by name for help in finding him.*

'Dear banyan tree, have you seen the son of Maharaja Nanda passing this way, laughing and playing on His flute? He has stolen our hearts and has gone away. If you have seen Him, kindly inform us which way He has gone. Dear asoka tree, dear naga flower tree and campaka flower tree, have you seen the younger brother of Balarama pass this way? He has disappeared because of our pride.' The gopis were aware

of the reason for Krishna's sudden disappearance. They could understand that when they were enjoying Krishna, they thought themselves to be the most fortunate women within the universe, and since they were feeling proud, Krishna disappeared immediately just to curb their pride. Krishna does not like His devotees to be proud of their service to Him. He accepts everyone's service, but He does not like one devotee to prouder than others. If sometimes there are such feelings, Krishna ends them by changing His attitude toward the devotee.

The gopis then began to address the tulasi plants: 'Dear tulasi, you are much beloved by Lord Krishna because your leaves are always at His lotus feet. Dear malati flower, dear mallika flower, dear jasmine flower, all of you must have been touched by Krishna while He was passing this way after giving us transcendental enjoyment. Have you seen Madhava passing this way? O mango trees, O trees of jack fruit, O pear trees and asana trees! O blackberries and bael trees and trees of kadamba flower – you are all very pious trees to be living on the bank of Yamuna. Krishna must have passed through this way. Will you kindly let us know which way He has gone?'

❧ Invisible Wisdom

The Elizabethan herbalist John Gerard's own garden was in Fetter Lane, Holborn, but he was also superintendent of the Hatfield gardens of William Cecil, Lord Burghley. He used to grow both native and foreign plants of medicinal value, and the aim of his Herbal, *as its dedication to Cecil made clear, was to record in perpetuity the hidden virtues of plants.*

Among the manifold creatures of God that have in all ages diversely entertained many excellent wits, and drawn them to the contemplation of the divine wisdom, none have provoked men's studies more, or satisfied their desires so much as plants have done, and that upon just and worthy causes: for if delight may provoke men's labour, what greater delight is there than to behold the earth apparelled with plants, as with a robe of embroidered work, set with Orient pearls and garnished with great diversity of rare and costly jewels? If this variety and perfection of colours may affect the eye, it is such in herbs and flowers, that no Apelles, no Zeuxis ever could by any art express the like: if odours or if taste may work satisfaction, they are both so sovereign in plants, and so comfortable that no confection of the Apothecaries can equal their excellent virtue.

But these delights are in the outward senses: the principal delight is in the mind, singularly enriched with the knowledge of these visible things, setting forth to us the invisible wisdom and admirable workmanship of Almighty God. The delight is great, but the use greater, and joined often with necessity. In the first ages of the world they were the ordinary meat of men, and have continued ever since of necessary use both for meats to maintain life, and for medicine to recover health. The hidden virtue of them is such, that, as Pliny notes, the very brute beasts have found it out: and (which is another use that he observes) from thence the dyers took the beginning of their Art.

Furthermore, the use of those fruits of the earth does plainly appear by the great charge and care of almost all men in planting & maintaining of gardens, not as ornaments only, but as a necessary provision also to their houses. And here beside the fruit, to speak again in a word of delight, gardens, furnished with many rare Simples, do singularly delight, when in them a man doth behold a flourishing show of Summer beauties in the midst of Winter's force, and a goodly spring of flowers, when abroad a leaf is not to be seen.

Besides these and other causes, there are many examples of those that have honoured this science. Mithridates the great was famous for his knowledge herein, as Plutarch notes. Euax also King of Arabia, the happy garden of the world for principal simples, wrote of this argument, as Pliny shows. Diocletian likewise, might have had his praise, had he not drowned all his honour in the blood of his persecution. To conclude this point, the example of Solomon is before the rest, and greater, whose wisdom and knowledge was such, that he was able to set out the nature of all plants from the highest Cedar to the lowest Moss.

But that which sometime was the study of great Philosophers and mighty Princes, is now neglected, except it be of some few, whose spirit and wisdom has carried them among other parts of wisdom and counsel, to a care and study of special herbs both for the furnishing of their gardens, and furtherance of their knowledge... I have that way employed my principal study and almost all my time, now by the space of twenty years. To the large and singular furniture of this noble Island I have added from foreign places all the variety of herbs and flowers that I might any way obtain, I have laboured with the soil to make it fit for plants, and with the plants, that they might delight in the soil, so they might live and prosper under our climate, as in their native and proper country. What my success hath been, and what my furniture is, I leave to the report of they that have seen Lord William Cecil's garden and the little plot of mine own especial care and husbandry. But because gardens are private, and many times finding an ignorant or a negligent successor, come soon to ruin, there be that have solicited me, first by my pen, and after by the Press to make my labours common, and to free them from the danger whereunto a garden is subject: wherein when I was overcome, and had brought this History or report of the nature of Plants to a just volume, and had made it (as the Reader may by comparison see) richer than former Herbals... [So] go forth in the name of God; graft, set, plant and nourish up in every corner of your ground.

The grete herball

whiche geueth parfyt knolvlege and vnd
ſtandyng of all maner of herbes & there gracyous vertues Whiche god ha
ozdeyned foz our prosperous Welfare and helth/forthey hele & cure all man
of dyſeaſes and ſekeneſſes that fall oz myſfoztune to all maner of creatou
of god created/pzactyſed by many expert and Wyſe mayſters/as Auicenna
other. &c. Also it geueth full parfyte vnderſtandynge of the booke lately pz
tyd by me(Peter treueris)named the noble experiens of the vertuous ha
warke of ſurgery.

Clad in Tattered Dervish Rags

The sixteenth-century Turkish lyric poet Baqi often used plants as symbols. His poem 'On Autumn' is also, however, a wonderful description of an autumn gale.

Lo, ne'er a trace or sign of springtide's beauty doth remain;
Fall'n 'midst the garden lie the leaves, now all their glory vain.

Bleak stand the orchard trees, all clad in tattered dervish rags;

Dark Autumn's blast hath torn away the hands from off the plane.
From each hill-side they come and cast their gold low at the feet
Of garden trees, as hoped the streams from these some boon to gain.

Stay not within the parterre, let it tremble with its shame:

Bare every shrub, this day doth naught of leaf or fruit retain.
Baqi, within the garden lies full many a fallen leaf;
Low lying there, it seems they 'gainst the winds of Fate complain.

🐝 A Pleasing Savour of Sweet Instructions

John Parkinson was a seventeenth-century apothecary and plantsman who was botanist to Charles I and had a famous botanical garden at Long Acre, near Covent Garden. His books Park-in-Sun's Terrestrial Paradise *(1629) and* The Botanical Theatre *(1640) remained authoritative for centuries, and in 1884 a Parkinson Society was formed to continue his mission to search out and preserve rare garden plants. Like all the pre-Darwinian botanists, he drew moral messages from his observations of plants.*

Truly from all sorts of herbs and flowers we may draw not only matter at all times to magnify the Creator, that hath given them such diversity of forms, scents and colours, and virtues and properties of which many lie hidden and unknown, but many good instructions to ourselves: That, as many herbs and flowers with their fragrant sweet smell do comfort and revive the Spirits and perfume a whole house, even so such men as live virtuously, labouring to do good, and to profit the Church of God and the commonwealth by their pains or pens, do as it were send forth a pleasing savour of sweet instructions, not only to that time wherein they live and are fresh, but being dry, withered and dead, cease not in all after ages to do as much or more.

Many herbs and flowers that have small beauty or savour to commend them, have much good and virtue. So many men of excellent rare parts and good qualities do lie unknown and not respected, until time and use of them do set forth their properties. Again, many flowers have a glorious show, yet are of no other use. So many men do make a glorious ostentation, and flourish in the world – yet surely they have no other virtue than their outside to commend them or leave after them.

The frailty of men's lives is learned by the soon fading of them before their flowering, or in their pride or soon after, being either cropped by the hand of the spectator, or by a sudden blast withered and parched, or by the revolution of time decaying of their own nature: as also that the fairest flowers or fruits first ripe, are soonest and first gathered.

PARADISI IN SOLE
Paradisus Terrestris.
or
A Garden of all sorts of pleasant Flowers which our
English ayre will permitt to be noursed vp:
with
A Kitchen garden of all manner of herbes, rootes, & fruites,
for meate or sause vsed with vs,
and
An Orchard of all sorte of fruitbearing Trees
and shrubbes fit for our Land
together
With the right orderinge planting & preseruing
of them and their vses & vertues
Collected by John Parkinson
Apothecary of London
1629

Qui veut parangonner l'artifice a Nature,
Et nos parcs a l'Eden, indiscret il mesure.

Le pas de l'Elephant par le pas du ciron,
Et de l'Aigle le vol par cil du moucheron.

The mutability also of states or persons [is shown] by this: that as where many goodly flowers and fruits did grow in this year and age, in another they are quite pulled or digged up, and either weeds and grass grow in their place, or some building erected thereon and their place is no more known.

✌ Killing and Quickening

The metaphysical poet George Herbert was educated at Westminster School and at Cambridge, where he was Professor of Rhetoric. He was a friend of Sir Francis Bacon and a protégé of James I. After the death of the king in 1625 and Herbert's mother in 1627, he gave up secular ambitions and was ordained. He spent the last two years of his life as rector of St Andrew's Church, Bemerton, near Salisbury. God's messages to man through natural things are a recurring feature of his writings. In 'The Flower', written in 1633, the last year of his life, Herbert gives thanks for the new hope and happiness he found in his garden at Bemerton.

How Fresh, O Lord, how sweet and clean
Are thy returns! Ev'n as the flowers in spring;
To which, besides their own demean,
The late-past frosts tributes of pleasure bring.
Grief melts away
Like snow in May,
As if there were no such cold thing.

Who would have thought my shrivel'd heart
Could have recover'd greenness? It was gone
Quite under ground; as flowers depart
To see their mother-root, when they have blown;
Where they together
All the hard weather,
Dead to the world, keep house unknown.

These are thy wonders, Lord of power,
Killing and quickening, bringing down to hell
And up to heaven in an hour;
Making a chiming of a passing-bell,
We say amiss,
This or that is:
Thy word is all, if we could spell.

O that I once past changing were;
Fast in thy Paradise, where no flower can wither!
Many a spring I shoot up fair,
Offering at heav'n, growing and groaning thither:
Nor doth my flower
Want a spring-shower,
My sins and I joining together;

But while I grow to a straight line;
Still upwards bent, as if heav'n were mine own,
Thy anger comes, and I decline:
What frost to that? what pole is not the zone,
Where all things burn,
When thou dost turn,
And the least frown of thine is shown?

And now in age I bud again,
After so many deaths I live and write;
I once more smell the dew and rain,
And relish versing: O my only light,
It cannot be
That I am he
On whom thy tempests fell all night.

These are thy wonders, Lord of love,
To make us see we are but flowers that glide:
Which when we once can find and prove,
Thou hast a garden for us, where to bide.
Who would be more,
Swelling through store,
Forfeit their Paradise by their pride.

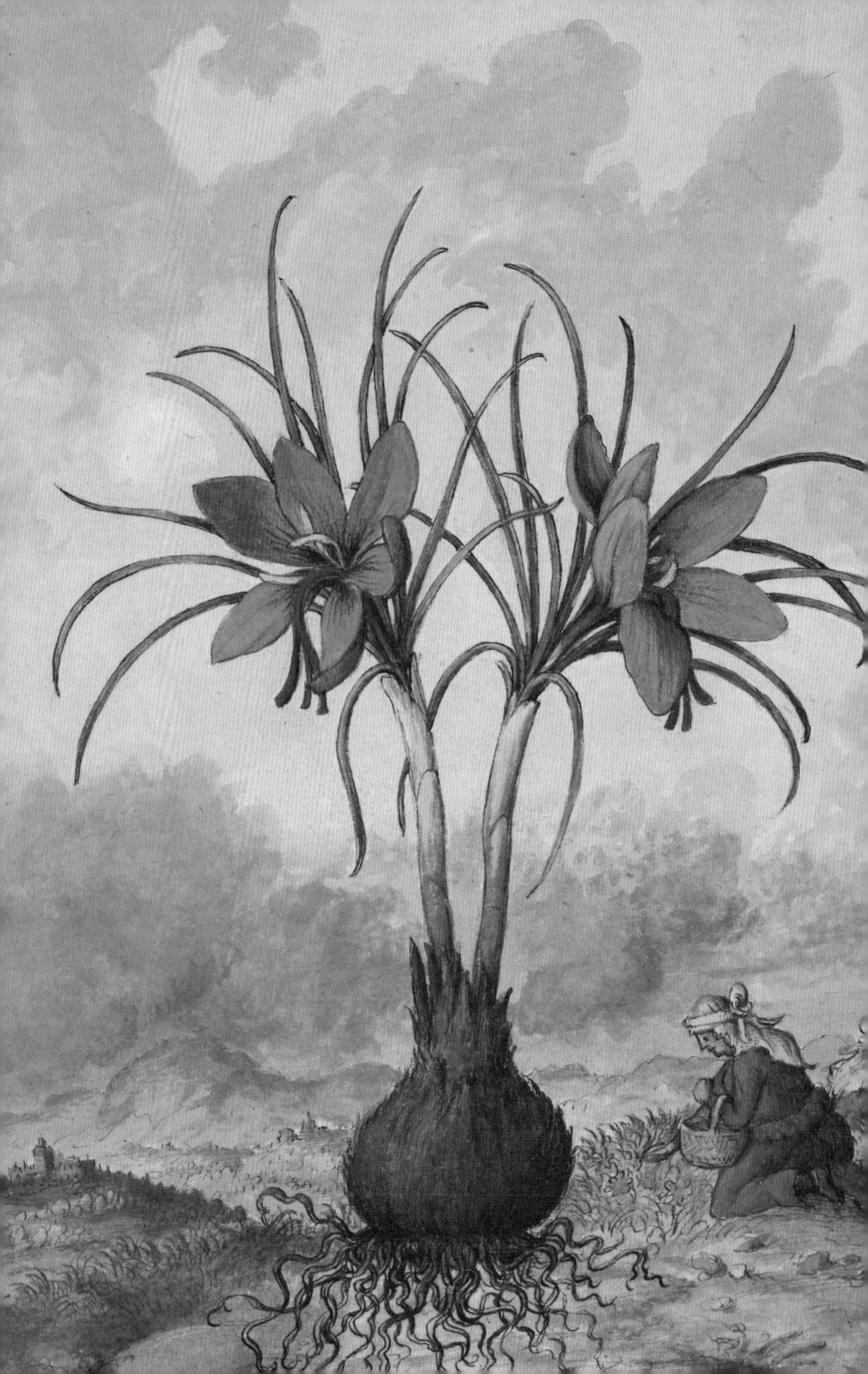

❧ Fresh and Spruce

In his elegantly brief 'Contemplation upon Flowers', Henry King, Bishop of Chichester during the troubled years of the English Civil War, found comfort in the humble gallantry of flowers.

Brave flowers – that I could gallant it like you,
And be as little vain.
You come abroad, and make a harmless show,
And to your beds of earth again.
You are not proud: you know your birth:
For your embroidered garments are from earth.

You do obey your months and times, but I
Would have it ever Spring:
My fate would know no Winter, never die,
Nor think of such a thing.
O that I could my bed of earth but view
And smile, and look as cheerfully as you.

O teach me to see Death and not to fear,
But rather to take truce.
How often have I seen you at a bier,
And there look fresh and spruce.
You fragrant flowers – then teach me, that my breath
Like yours may sweeten and perfume my death.

❧ A Green Thought in a Green Shade

The seventeenth-century poet Andrew Marvell was a Parliamentarian who was apprehensive of the worldliness and corruption of the Restoration monarchy. In his poem 'The Garden' he welcomes the peace and solitude to be found among trees and flowers.

How vainly men themselves amaze
To win the palm, the oak, or bays;
And their uncessant labours see
Crowned from some single herb or tree,
Whose short and narrow-vergèd shade
Does prudently their toils upbraid;
While all the flowers and trees do close
To weave the garlands of repose.

Fair Quiet, have I found thee here,
And Innocence, thy sister dear!
Mistaken long, I sought you then
In busy companies of men:
Your sacred plants, if here below,
Only among the plants will grow;
Society is all but rude,
To this delicious solitude.

No white nor red was ever seen
So amorous as this lovely green;
Fond lovers, cruel as their flame,
Cut in these trees their mistress' name.
Little, alas, they know or heed,
How far these beauties hers exceed!
Fair trees! wheresoe'er your barks I wound
No name shall but your own be found.

When we have run our passion's heat,
Love hither makes his best retreat:
The gods who mortal beauty chase,
Still in a tree did end their race.
Apollo hunted Daphne so,
Only that she might laurel grow,
And Pan did after Syrinx speed,
Not as a nymph, but for a reed.

What wondrous life is this I lead!
Ripe apples drop about my head;
The luscious clusters of the vine
Upon my mouth do crush their wine;
The nectarine and curious peach
Into my hands themselves do reach;
Stumbling on melons as I pass,
Insnared with flowers, I fall on grass.

Meanwhile the mind, from pleasure less,
Withdraws into its happiness:
The mind, that ocean where each kind
Does straight its own resemblance find;
Yet it creates, transcending these,
Far other worlds, and other seas;
Annihilating all that's made
To a green thought in a green shade.

Here at the fountain's sliding foot,
Or at some fruit-tree's mossy root,
Casting the body's vest aside,
My soul into the boughs does glide:
There like a bird it sits and sings,
Then whets and combs its silver wings;
And, till prepared for longer flight,
Waves in its plumes the various light.

Such was that happy garden-state,
While man there walked without a mate;
After a place so pure and sweet,
What other help could yet be meet!
But 'twas beyond a mortal's share
To wander solitary there:
Two paradises 'twere in one
To live in Paradise alone.

How well the skilful gard'ner drew
Of flowers and herbs this dial new;
Where from above the milder sun
Does through a fragrant zodiac run;
And, as it works, th' industrious bee
Computes its time as well as we.
How could such sweet and wholesome hours
Be reckoned but with herbs and flowers!

❧ Slow but Sure

Slugs and snails and caterpillars are anathema to most gardeners. But bear in mind as you curse such things that they have their own point of view – never more beautifully observed than by John Bunyan in his poem 'Upon a Snail'.

She goes but softly, but she goeth sure;
She stumbles not, as stronger creatures do;
Her journey's shorter, so she may endure
Better than they which do much farther go.
She makes no noise, but stilly seizeth on
The flower or herb appointed for her food,
The which she quietly doth feed upon,
While others range and glare, but find no good.
And though she doth but very softly go,
However 'tis not fast, nor slow, but sure;
And certainly they that do travel so,
The prize they do aim at they do procure.

❧ Human Grandeur is Very Dangerous

The Enlightenment writer Voltaire wrote his novella Candide *in 1759 as a fantastical satire on optimism – made incarnate in the complacent Pangloss. Its conclusion, which offers its protagonists their best hope of contentment in the practical cultivation of Candide's farm and garden, reflected Voltaire's deep admiration for the English enthusiasm for gardens, as well as their political arrangements.*

Pangloss, Candide, and Martin, as they were returning to the little farm, met with a good-looking old man, who was taking the air at his door, under an alcove formed of the boughs of orange trees. Pangloss, who was as inquisitive as he was disputative, asked him what was the name of the mufti who was lately strangled.

'I cannot tell,' answered the good old man; 'I never knew the name of any mufti, or vizier breathing. I am entirely ignorant of the event you speak of; I presume that in general such as are concerned in public affairs sometimes come to a miserable end; and that they deserve it: but I never inquire what is doing at Constantinople; I am contented with sending thither the produce of my garden, which I cultivate with my own hands.'

After saying these words, he invited the strangers to come into his house. His two daughters and two sons presented them with divers sorts of sherbet of their own making; besides mimosa, heightened with the peels of candied citrons, oranges, lemons, pineapples, pistachio nuts, and Mocha coffee unadulterated with the bad coffee of Batavia or the American islands. After which the two daughters of this good Mussulman perfumed the beards of Candide, Pangloss, and Martin.

'You must certainly have a vast estate,' said Candide to the Turk.

'I have no more than twenty acres of ground,' he replied, 'the whole of which I cultivate myself with the help of my children; and our labour keeps off from us three great evils – idleness, vice, and want.'

Candide, as he was returning home, thought deeply about the Turk's discourse.

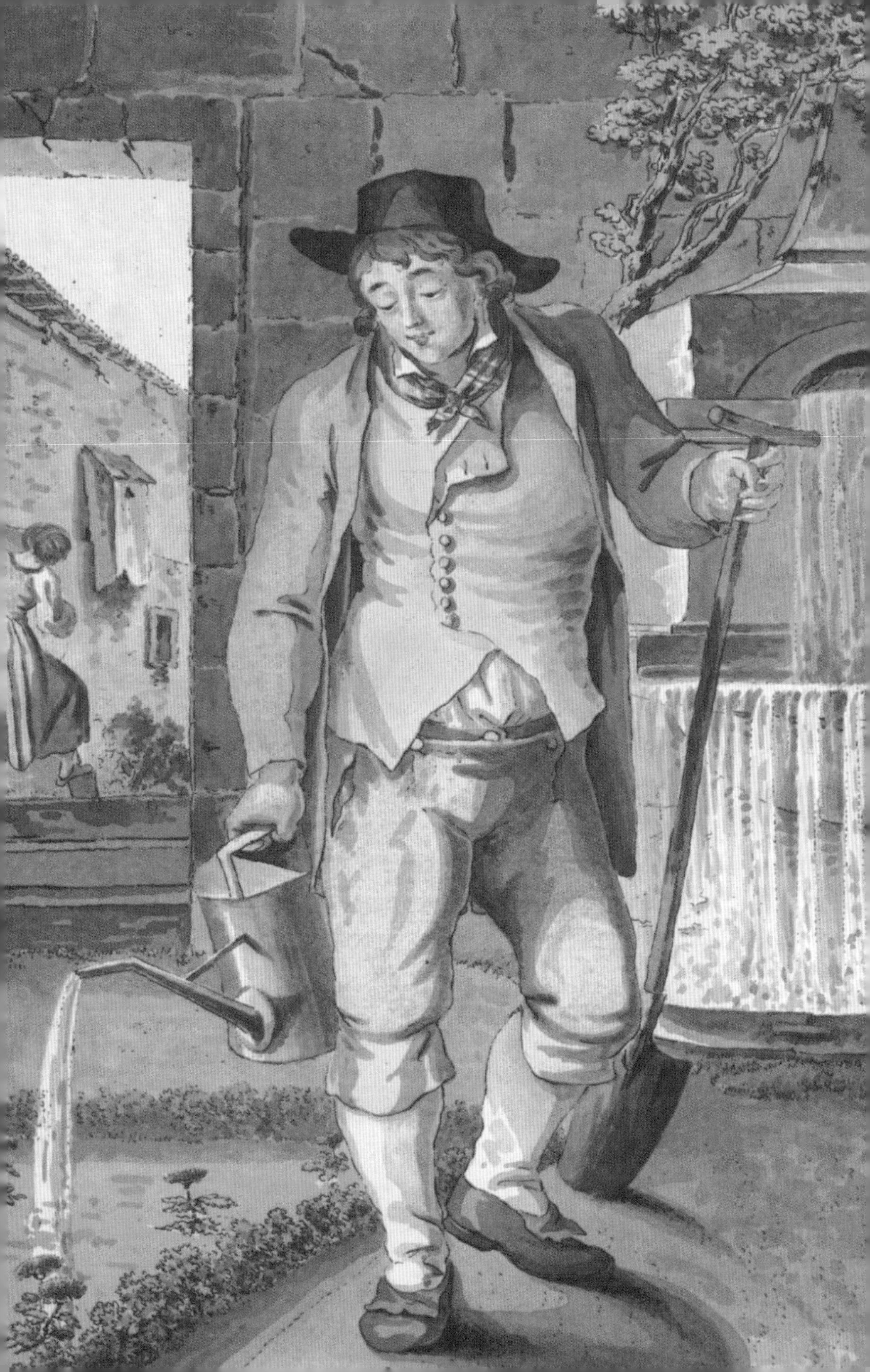

'This good old man,' said he to Pangloss and Martin, 'appears to me to have chosen for himself a lot much preferable to that of the six Kings with whom we had the honour to sup.'

'Human grandeur,' said Pangloss, 'is very dangerous, if we believe the testimonies of almost all philosophers; for we find Eglon, King of Moab, was assassinated by Aod; Absalom was hanged by the hair of his head, and run through with three darts... the Kings Jehooiakim, Jeconiah, and Zedekiah, were led into captivity: I need not tell you what was the fate of Croesus, Darius, Dionysius of Syracuse, Pyrrhus, Perseus, Hannibal, Caesar, Pompey, Nero, Otho, Vitellius, Domitian, Richard II of England, Edward II, Henry VI, Richard III, Mary Stuart, Charles I, the three Henrys of France, and the Emperor Henry IV.'

'Neither need you tell me,' said Candide, 'that we must take care of our garden.'

'You are in the right,' said Pangloss; 'for when man was put into the garden of Eden, it was with an intent to dress it; and this proves that man was not born to be idle.'

'Work then without disputing,' said Martin; 'it is the only way to render life supportable.'

The little society, one and all, entered into this laudable design and set themselves to exert their different talents. The little piece of ground yielded them a plentiful crop. Cunegund indeed was very ugly, but she became an excellent hand at pastrywork: Pacquette embroidered; the old woman had the care of the linen. There was none, down to Brother Giroflee, but did some service; he was a very good carpenter, and became an honest man. Pangloss used now and then to say to Candide:

'There is a concatenation of all events in the best of possible worlds; for, in short, had you not been kicked out of a fine castle for the love of Miss Cunegund; had you not been put into the Inquisition; had you not travelled over America on foot; had you not run the Baron through the body; and had you not lost all your sheep, which you brought from the good country of El Dorado, you would not have been here to eat preserved citrons and pistachio nuts.'

'Excellently observed,' answered Candide; 'but let us cultivate our garden.'

The End.

&❧ Prostrate Peas

Henry Jones was an Irish bricklayer from Louth with a poetic talent. He offered complimentary poems to Lord Chesterfield when he was appointed Viceroy of Ireland in 1745. Chesterfield became his patron, later inviting him to London. His Bricklayer's Poems on Several Occasions *was published in 1749. Every gardener is familiar with the hubris and subsequent nemesis Jones describes in his poem 'On a Fine Crop of Peas Being Spoiled By A Storm', but not all would find the experience a memento mori.*

When Morrice views his prostrate peas,
By raging whirlwinds spread,
He wrings his hands, and in amaze
He sadly shakes his head.

'Is this the fruit of my fond toil,
My joy, my pride, my cheer!
Shall one tempestuous hour thus spoil
The labours of a year!

Oh what avails, that day to day
I nursed the thriving crop,
And settled with my foot the clay,
And reared the social prop!

Ambition's pride had spurred me on
All gard'ners to excel.
I often called them one by one,
And boastingly would tell,

How I prepared the furrowed ground
And how the grain did sow,
Then challenged all the country round
For such an early blow [ripening],

How did their bloom my wishes raise!
What hopes did they afford,
To earn my honoured master's praise,
And crown his cheerful board!'

Poor Morrice, wrapt in sad surprise,
Demands in sober mood,
'Should storms molest a man so
A man so just and good?'

Ah! Morrice, cease thy fruitless moan,
Nor at misfortunes spurn,
Misfortune's not thy lot alone;
Each neighbour hath his turn,

Thy prostrate peas, which low recline
Beneath the frowns of fate,
May teach much wiser heads than thine
Their own uncertain state,

The sprightly youth in beauty's prime,
The lovely nymph so gay,
Oft victims fall to early time,
And in their bloom decay,

In vain th'indulgent father's care
In vain wise precepts form;
They droop, like peas, in tainted air,
Or perish in a storm.

🐝 Good Taste and Not a Gaudy Pride

John Clare, who was born in 1793 and died in 1864, was the son of a day labourer in the village of Helpston, near Peterborough. For a time he was a gardener at Burghley House, and later he worked in a nursery garden at Newark-on-Trent and for other noblemen. After 1820 he became famous for his poems about nature and the countryside. In his wistful poem 'The Wish', written in about 1809, before he had been discovered as a poet and had occasionally to survive on parish relief, Clare fantasised about having a home of his own in his old village. This is how he pictured the garden.

And now a garden planned with nicest care
Should be my next attention to prepare;
For this I'd search the soil of different grounds
Nor small nor great should mark its homely bound
Between these two extremes the plan should be
Complete throughout and large enough for me;
A strong brick wall should bound the outward fen
Where by the sun's all-cheering influence
Wall-trees should flourish in a spreading row
And Peach and Pear in ruddy lustre glow.
A five-foot bed should follow from the wall
To look complete or save the trees withal
On which small seeds for sallading I'd sow
While curl-leaf Parsley should for edges grow.
My Garden in four quarters I'd divide
To show good taste and not a gaudy pride.
In this the middle walk should be the best
Being more to sight exposèd than the rest,
At whose south end an arbour should be made
So well belov'd in summer for its shade:
For this the rose would do or jessamine
With virginbower or the sweet woodbine,
Each one of these would form exactly well
A complete arbour both for shade or smell.

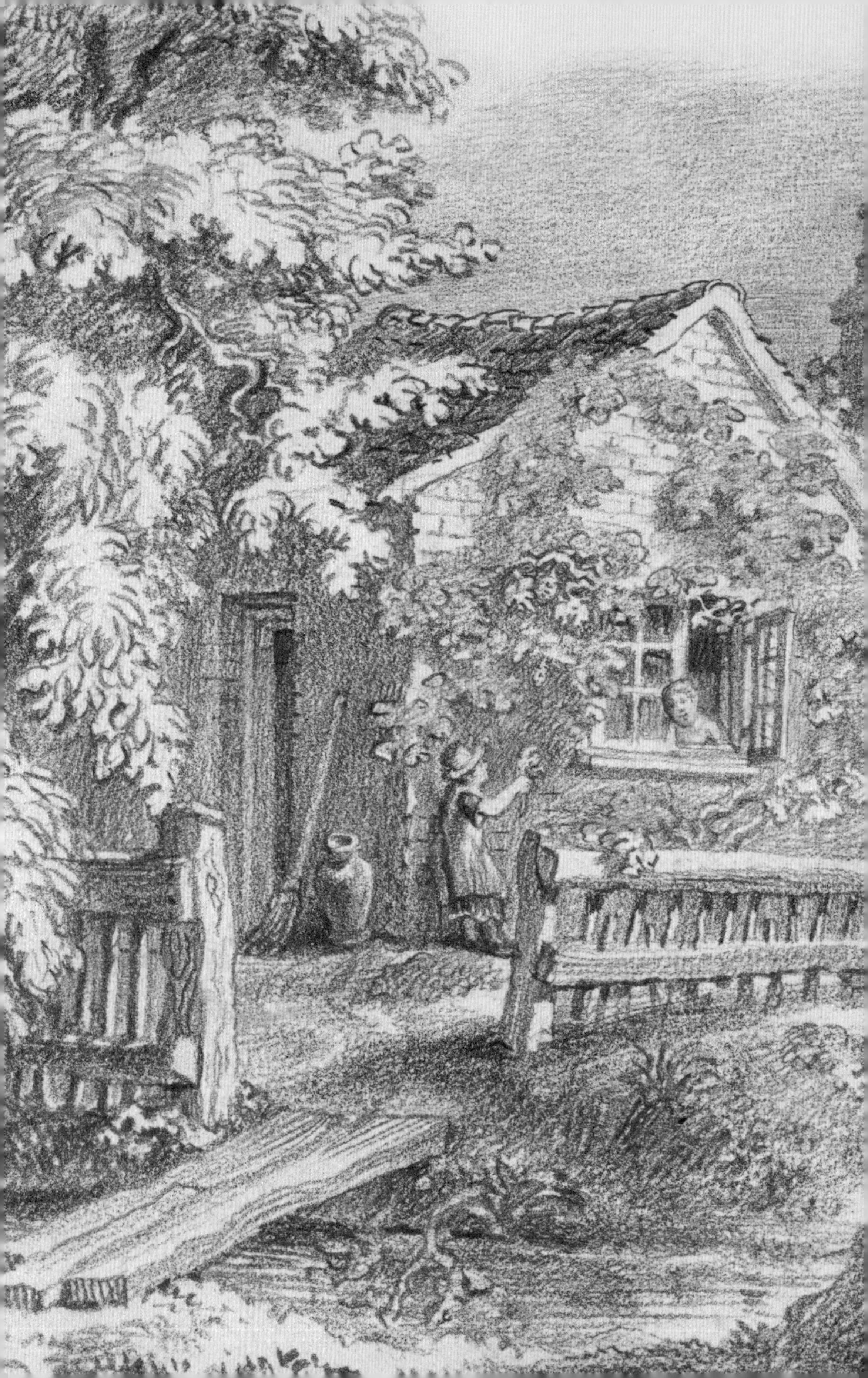

Here would I sit when leisure did agree
To view the pride of summer scenery,
See the productions promis'd from my spade
While blest with liberty and cooling shade.
But now a spot should be reserv'd for flowers
That would amuse me in those vacant hours
When books and study cease their charms to bring
And Fancy sits to prune her shatter'd wing,
Then is the time I'd view the flowrets' eye
And all loose stragglers with scotch-mattin tie;
The borders too I'd clean with nicest care
And not one smothering weed should harbour there.
In trifling thus I should such pleasure know
As nothing but such trifles could bestow.
This charming spot should boast a charming place
Southwardly plan'd my cottage front to grace.
There a nice grass plat should attract the eye,
Mow'd every week more level than the dye.
Ah! think how this would decorate the scene
So fine a level and a finer green.
My borders they should lie a little flue [wide]
And rear the finest flowers that sip the dew.
The roses blush, the lilies vying snow
Should uniform their nameless beauties show,
With fine ranunculus and jonquil fair
That sweet perfumer of the evening air.
The scabious too so jocularly dusk
Should there be seen with tufts of smelling musk.
The woodbine tree should all her sweets unfurl
Close to my door in many a wanton curl.
Aside my wall the vine should find a place
While damask roses did my window grace:
And now a walk as was the plan before
Exactly corresponding with the door
Should lead my footsteps to another bower
Whenever leisure gave the pleasant hour.
But once again the greens delightful spot

Should wear an ornament I quite forgot;
A little pond within a circle laid
It would look nice and might be useful made:
The side with freestone should be walled round
And steps the same to bevel with the ground.
There sweet Nymphea lover of the tide
Should deck my mimic pool with spangling pride
Oft would I seek the steps in midday hour
When Sol mounts high in full meridian power
To see its leaves that on the surface lie
Prove Boats of Pleasure to the dragon fly.
Ah scenes so happy void of all control
Your seeming prospects heightens up my soul;
E'en now so bright the fairy vision flies,
I mark its flight as with possessing eyes
But that's in vain – to hope the wish was gave
It clogs the mind and binds the heart a slave.
Tis nothing but a wish one vents at will
Still vainly wishing and be wanting still
For when a wishing mind enjoys the view
He don't expect it ever will come true,
Yet when he cherishes the pleasing thought
He still is wishing till he wants for nought,
And so will I.

John Clare did eventually achieve his dream, albeit for a short while. His cottage at Helpston was acquired by the John Clare Trust in 2005. The garden has been restored and can be visited.

❧ Paying Back the Garden

Always master of the overblown cliché, and now notorious for beginning his 1830 novel Paul Clifford *'It was a dark and stormy night', Edward Bulwer-Lytton was in his day an immensely popular novelist. In* Eugene Aram *he puts homespun horticultural wisdom into the mouth of an inn landlord.*

The next morning Walter rose early, and descending into the court-yard of the inn, he there met with the landlord, who, a hoe in his hand, was just about to enter a little gate that led into the garden. He held the gate open for Walter.

'It is a fine morning, Sir; would you like to look into the garden?' Walter accepted the offer, and found himself in a large and well-stocked garden, laid out with much neatness and some taste; the Landlord halted by a parterre which required his attention, and Walter walked on in solitary reflection. The morning was serene and clear, but the frost mingled the freshness with an 'eager and nipping air', and Walter unconsciously quickened his step as he paced to and fro the straight walk that bisected the garden, with his eyes on the ground, and his hat over his brows... The young adventurer paused at last opposite his host, who was still bending over his pleasant task, and every now and then, excited by the exercise and the fresh morning air, breaking into snatches of some old rustic song. The contrast in mood between himself and this 'Unvexed loiterer by the world's green ways' struck forcibly upon him.

Mine host might have told some three-and-sixty years, but it was a comely and green old age; his cheek was firm and ruddy, not with nightly cups, but the fresh witness of the morning breezes it was wont to court; his frame was robust, not corpulent; and his long grey hair, which fell almost to his shoulder, his clear blue eyes, and a pleasant curve in a mouth characterized by habitual good humour, completed a portrait that even many a dull observer would have paused to gaze upon. He had seen enough of life to be intelligent, and had judged it rightly enough to be kind...

As Walter stood, and contemplated the old man bending over the sweet fresh earth (and then, glancing round, saw the quiet garden stretching away on either side with its boundaries lost among the thick evergreen), something of that grateful and moralizing stillness with which some country scene generally inspires us, when we awake to its consciousness from the troubled dream of dark and unquiet thought, stole over his mind...

The old man stopped from his work, as the musing figure of his guest darkened the prospect before him, and said:

'A pleasant time, Sir, for the gardener!'

'Ay, is it so... you must miss the fruits and flowers of summer.'

'Well, Sir, but we are now paying back the garden, for the good things it has given us. It is like taking care of a friend in old age, who has been kind to us when he was young.'

Walter smiled at the quaint amiability of the idea.

''Tis a winning thing, Sir, a garden! It brings us an object every day; and that's what I think a man ought to have if he wishes to lead a happy life.'

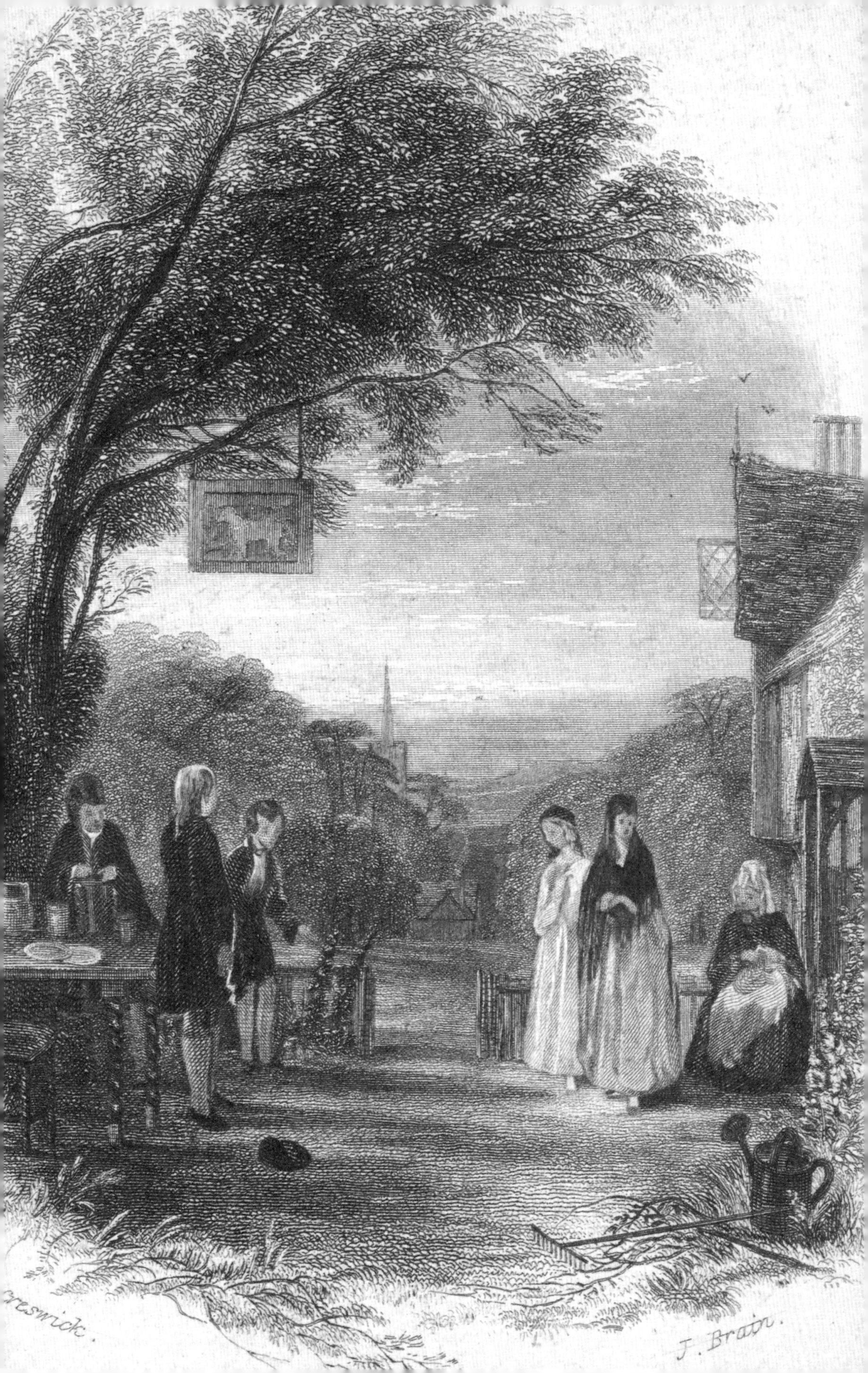
Creswick.
J. Brain.

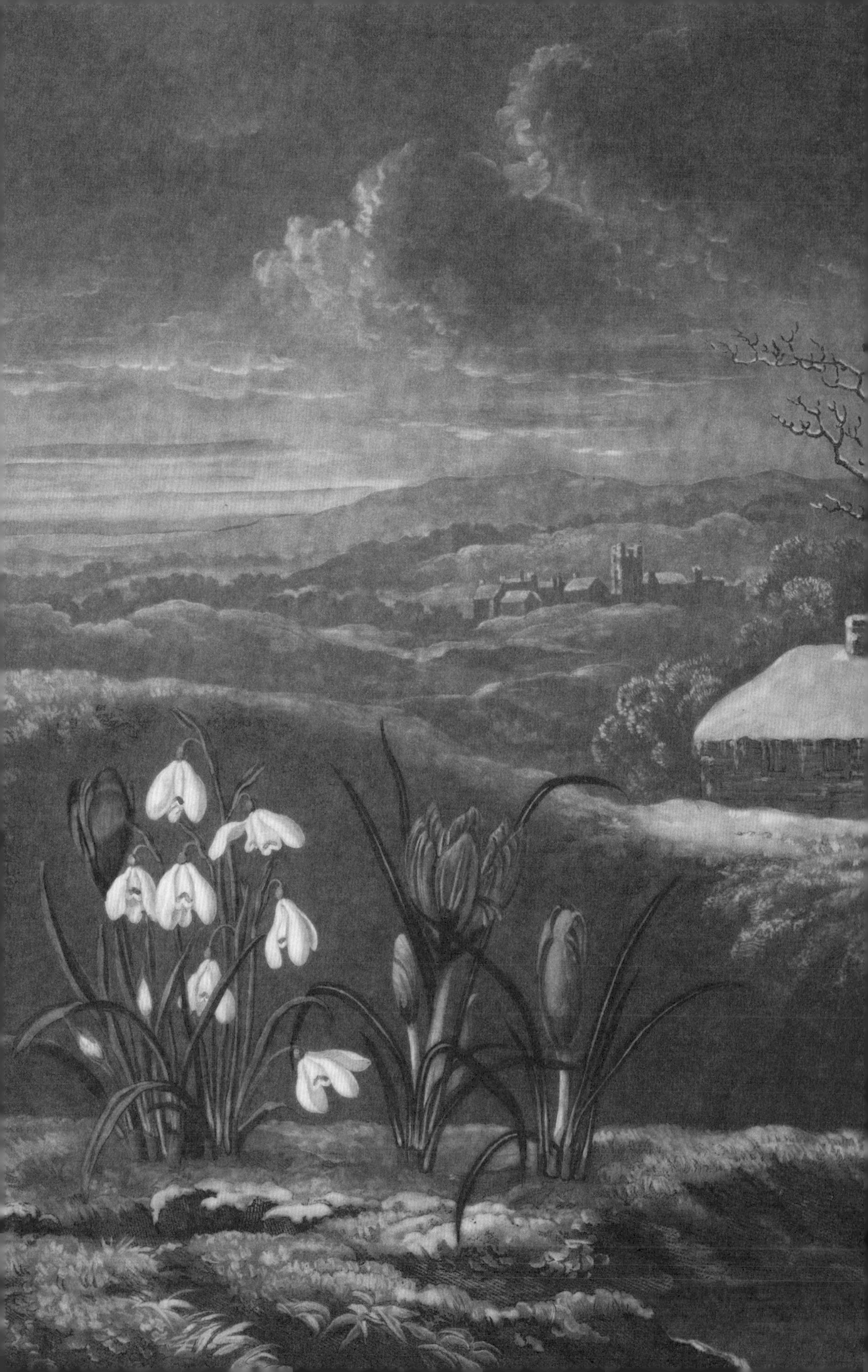

❧ Roses and Lovers

Like an old and empty house, an ancient and neglected garden conjures up both past glories and future potential. Algernon Charles Swinburne's wildly romantic poem 'A Forsaken Garden' was written in 1878. It may well have been inspired by the holidays he spent in Northumberland, at the family seat of Capheaton Hall.

In a coign of the cliff between lowland and highland,
At the sea-down's edge between windward and lee,
Walled round with rocks as an inland island,
The ghost of a garden fronts the sea.
A girdle of brushwood and thorn encloses
The steep square slope of the blossomless bed
Where the weeds that grew green from the graves of its roses
Now lie dead.

The fields fall southward, abrupt and broken,
To the low last edge of the long lone land.
If a step should sound or a word be spoken,
Would a ghost not rise at the strange guest's hand?
So long have the grey bare walks lain guestless,
Through branches and briars if a man make way,
He shall find no life but the sea-wind's, restless
Night and day.

The dense hard passage is blind and stifled
That crawls by a track none turn to climb
To the strait waste place that the years have rifled
Of all but the thorns that are touched not of time.
The thorns he spares when the rose is taken;
The rocks are left when he wastes the plain.
The wind that wanders, the weeds wind-shaken,
These remain.

Not a flower to be pressed of the foot that falls not;
As the heart of a dead man the seed-plots are dry;

From the thicket of thorns whence the nightingale calls not,
Could she call, there were never a rose to reply.
Over the meadows that blossom and wither
Rings but the note of a sea-bird's song;
Only the sun and the rain come hither
All year long.

The sun burns sere and the rain dishevels
One gaunt bleak blossom of scentless breath.
Only the wind here hovers and revels
In a round where life seems barren as death.
Here there was laughing of old, there was weeping,
Haply, of lovers none ever will know,
Whose eyes went seaward a hundred sleeping
Years ago.

Heart handfast in heart as they stood, 'Look thither,'
Did he whisper? 'Look forth from the flowers to the sea;
For the foam-flowers endure when the rose-blossoms wither,
And men that love lightly may die – but we?'
And the same wind sang and the same waves whitened,
And or ever the garden's last petals were shed,
In the lips that had whispered, the eyes that had lightened,
Love was dead.

Or they loved their life through, and then went whither?
And were one to the end – but what end who knows?
Love deep as the sea as a rose must wither,
As the rose-red seaweed that mocks the rose.
Shall the dead take thought for the dead to love them?
What love was ever as deep as a grave?
They are loveless now as the grass above them
Or the wave.

All are at one now, roses and lovers,
Not known of the cliffs and the fields and the sea.
Not a breath of the time that has been hovers

In the air now soft with a summer to be.
Not a breath shall there sweeten the seasons hereafter
Of the flowers or the lovers that laugh now or weep,
When as they that are free now of weeping and laughter
We shall sleep.

Here death may deal not again for ever;
Here change may come not till all change end.
From the graves they have made they shall rise up never,
Who have left nought living to ravage and rend.
Earth, stones, and thorns of the wild ground growing,
While the sun and the rain live, these shall be;
Till a last wind's breath upon all these blowing
Roll the sea.

Till the slow sea rise and the sheer cliff crumble,
Till terrace and meadow the deep gulfs drink,
Till the strength of the waves of the high tides humble
The fields that lessen, the rocks that shrink,
Here now in his triumph where all things falter,
Stretched out on the spoils that his own hand spread,
As a god self-slain on his own strange altar,
Death lies dead.

🪶 Manifest Autobiography

Deeply fond of nature, Alfred Austin was a middlebrow versifier who only succeeded Tennyson as Poet Laureate in 1896 because William Morris turned down the post and Swinburne had too outrageous a reputation. His prose hymn to his own garden in Kent, The Garden that I Love, *ran through many editions.*

A garden that one makes oneself becomes associated with one's personal history and that of one's friends, interwoven with one's tastes, preferences, and character, and constitutes a sort of unwritten, but withal manifest, autobiography. Show me your garden, provided it be your own, and I will tell you what you are like. It is in middle life that the finishing touches should be put to it; and then, after that, it should remain more or less in the same condition, like oneself, growing more deep of shade, and more protected from the winds.

I am well aware that, according to orthodox notions, against which I have not a word to say, the approach to a house in the country should not be through the garden, but on the other and northern side of the dwelling, so that seclusion should be secured against carriage-wheels, and you may be able to say 'Not at home' without incurring suspicion of inhospitality or unfriendliness. But we are humble folk, with a home which, if beautiful, is unpretentious, and when you drive through the orchard-walk to see us, you come on the front door, standing wide open, on the dining room and drawing-room windows, and on a cascade of foam-white roses, so that you see the whole charm of the greater portion of the garden at once; north border, south border, the front of the house, the lawn, the tennis-garden, the oak, the orchard; only the South Enclosure, Poet's Walk, and, of course, the little walled garden behind the older part of the manor, being withheld from your view.

There are seventeen beds on the lawn, and there is a wide border of flowers under the dining room and drawing room windows. But the beds on the lawn are not congregated close together, as in a terraced or strictly formal garden. They lie upon the lawn, some of them being at considerable distance from each other, but none of them losing touch, so to speak, of the rest; and, if one of them even were removed, the entire harmony or balance would be destroyed. In the centre of the lawn are two crescent-shaped beds of rhododendrons, enclosing in their curve, but with a circle of grass between them, a round bed whose chief glory are two well-established and profusely flowering *Clematis jackmannii*, clambering up rough pine-stems.

Of the seventeen beds, twelve are what I may call permanent beds, containing either herbaceous plants eked out in spring with bulbs and in summer and autumn with annuals, or tea roses and their carpet of violas. These last are four in number, and run round the edge of the gravel curve immediately in front of the house two and two, with a non-permanent star-shaped bed between them. There are only five beds not thus disposed of; but I dwell on them because they provide for me the solution of a controversy about which so much has been said and written. In spring, as I have said, they contain tulips and forget-me-not. But in summer they are reserved for and dedicated – yes – to geraniums, iresine, white-leaved centaurea, ageratum, and even sometimes to calceolarias, geraniums, and lobelia.

No one can admire less than I do a so-called garden – for a garden it is not – surrendered wholly to symmetrical lines or groups of colour; and I once nearly banished them from the Garden that I Love. But careful experience showed me that they serve as an invaluable foil to the other and more numerous beds I have called permanent, and whose flowers soar irregularly into the air, and which are orderly without being prim or trim. I have a great liking for the strong-growing cannae; and this year I have a couple of beds which Veronica declares are already most successful, and which will look much more luxurious a month hence, and will continue in that condition till supervenes the first sharp frost. The beds are parallelograms twelve feet by eight. In their centre are the cannae, liberally manured and copiously watered. Outside them are rows of scarlet zinnias, and outside these grows variegated maize, green-and-white. The bed is edged with the dwarf profusely flowering yellow zinnia.

There is nothing formal about these beds any more than there is in the neighbouring ones, where larkspur, evening primroses, ribbon grass or gardeners' garters, phloxes, fuchsias, everlastings, blue cornflowers, annual gaillardias, clarkias, lupins, dahlias, sweet-williams, pinks, and mignonette, fight it out among themselves as to which shall have the lion's share of the space. But these carelessly-ordered and high-growing flowers would not be a hundredth part so effective as they are, were it not for the contrast afforded by the beds of regular and low-lying plants in their vicinity.

Have I said, before, that exclusiveness in a garden is a mistake as great as it is in society? If I have, may I say it again, for it is an important truth that needs to be reiterated. Moreover, it will sometimes happen that, towards the beginning of October, if not before, the more rampant flowers, having nearly outbloomed themselves, begin to wane; and then the lingering bloom of the less beautiful bedded-out things acts as a sort of compensation, and prolongs the life of the garden, indeed even of the Summer. And then their extremely brilliant hues suit the natural mood of autumn.

'It is all very well,' said Lamia, 'to prate of your beds and your borders, your perpetuals and your annuals, your tea-roses and your peonies; but I shall never believe in you till you turn your little walled kitchen-garden into a real pleasance, intersect it with box edgings and paths of broken brick, grow rosemary, rue, lavender, old-fashioned hearts-ease, little China-roses, and dwarf fuchsias, in rectangular beds, have a sun-dial in the centre with a sage apophthegm in a dead language inscribed on it, educate a peacock to strut slowly along the coping of the wall, and induce Veronica to let her maids lean out of those fascinating windows in mob-caps and purfled aprons. To Jericho with your Jerusalem artichokes, your early strawberries, and your sybaritic asparagus. Grub up your Walburton Admirable, your Kirk's Blue, and your Louise Bonne, and let hollyhock and sunflower use the old red brick for background.'

'Dear Lamia,' I replied, 'why do you probe an ever open wound? I shall not die in peace unless I fulfil that dream. The place is made for it, and I plan it over and over again, day and night, night and day. But what would Veronica say? Already she protests against the narrow space dedicated to potato and onion, to cos lettuce and to curly kale, and declares she is ashamed sometimes of the paucity of our winter vegetables. Moreover, she bewails, not without some justification, my lavishness on the Garden that I Love, and she knows perfectly well, as I do myself, that the sun-dial and the peacock project would mean another gardener, to say nothing of the incidental making of kitchen-garden ground elsewhere.'

'What cowards men are!' murmured my companion. 'Veronica might be your wife instead of your sister.'

'Are you calculating,' I asked, 'on intimidating your husband? Do not make too sure of that. And then, you see, Veronica is very good about it, for I have flowers along all the kitchen-garden paths, in the copse garden as well as in the walled garden; and if you will go and look, you will see sunflowers and hollyhocks coming up there in various places to bloom in September. Those white sweet peas you are wearing, and that become you so admirably, were plucked where the sundial haply might stand; and scarlet-runners, later on, will diversify the sober utility of cauliflower and parsnip. Life, Lamia, is a lesson in compromise; and we are never further from being satisfied than when we have got all we want. That unattainable peacock is perhaps the surest guarantee of my content.'

'I shall never stir you into insurrection,' she said.

❧ Persevere!

The American garden-writer Helena Rutherford Ely wrote A Woman's Hardy Garden *in 1903 to urge the well-off American woman to take the 'personal interest in her gardens and conservatories' habitually taken by the Englishwoman.*

Love of flowers and all things green and growing is with many men and women a passion so strong that it often seems to be a sort of primal instinct, coming down through generation after generation, from the first man who was put into a garden 'to dress it and to keep it'. People whose lives, and those of their parents before them, have been spent in dingy tenements, and whose only garden is a rickety soap-box high up on a fire-escape, share this love, which must have a plant to tend, with those whose gardens cover acres and whose plants have been gathered from all the countries of the world. How often in summer, when called to town, and when driving through the squalid streets to the ferries or riding on the elevated road, one sees these gardens of the poor. Sometimes they are only a geranium or two, or the gay petunia. Often a tall sunflower, or a tomato plant red with fruit. These efforts tell of the love for the growing things, and of the care that makes them live and blossom against all odds.

It is the overcoming of the difficulties in the gardener's way, the determination to succeed, that gives zest to the occupation. Did everything planted grow and flourish, gardening would be too tame. Rust and blight, cutworms, rose beetles and weeds, afford the element of sport so attractive to us all. A lesson must be learned from every failure; with renewed patience persevere until success is reached.

I would make the strongest plea in favour of a garden to all those who are so fortunate as to possess any land at all. The relaxation from care and toil and the benefit to health are great, beyond belief, to those who may have to work with head or hands. If you can snatch a few minutes in early morning or late afternoon, to spend among plants, life takes on a new aspect, health is improved, care is dissipated, and you get nearer to Nature, as God intended.

If the rich and fashionable women of this country took more interest and spent more time in their gardens, and less in frivolity, fewer would

1. *Pæonia edulis.* — 2. *Pæonia albiflora.* — 3. *Pæonia tenuifolia.*
4. *Pæonia Hybrida.* — 5. *Pæonia Russi.*

Day & Haghe Lith.rs to the Queen.

suffer from nervous prostration, and the necessity for the multitude of sanatoriums would be avoided.

As a rule, young people do not care for gardening. They lack the necessary patience and perseverance. But in the years of middle life, when one's sun is slowly setting and interest in the world and society relaxes, the garden, with its changing bloom, grows ever dearer.

Prunus Myrobalanus rotundus.

❧ It Isn't a Quite Dead Garden

It was another keen American woman gardener who wrote the most famous of all books about children in a garden. In 1898 Frances Hodgson Burnett walked through a door hidden by ivy to discover the neglected garden of Great Maytham Hall, near Rolvenden in Kent. She rented the house for the next nine years, and gradually restored it. The experience was immortalised in her most famous book, The Secret Garden, *which she wrote in 1911, soon after she returned to America. Its theme is the power of positive thinking, with gardening as therapy – for the book's second inspiration was the tragic death of Burnett's oldest son Lionel, who, unlike Colin, did not recover from consumption. Here, the novel's cross and contrary little heroine discovers the secret garden.*

It was the sweetest, most mysterious-looking place any one could imagine. The high walls which shut it in were covered with the leafless stems of climbing roses, which were so thick that they were matted together. Mary Lennox knew they were roses because she had seen a great many roses in India. All the ground was covered with grass of a wintry brown and out of it grew clumps of bushes which were surely rosebushes if they were alive. There were numbers of standard roses which had so spread their branches that they were like little trees. There were other trees in the garden, and one of the things which made the place look strangest and loveliest was that climbing roses had run all over them and swung down long tendrils which made light swaying curtains, and here and there they had caught at each other or at a far-reaching branch and had crept from one tree to another and made lovely bridges of themselves. There were neither leaves nor roses on them now and Mary did not know whether they were dead or alive, but their thin grey or brown branches and sprays looked like a sort of hazy mantle spreading over everything, walls, and trees, and even brown grass, where they had fallen from their fastenings and run along the ground. It was this hazy tangle from tree to tree which made it all look so mysterious. Mary had thought it must be different from other gardens which had not been left all by themselves so long; and indeed it was different from any other place she had ever seen in her life.

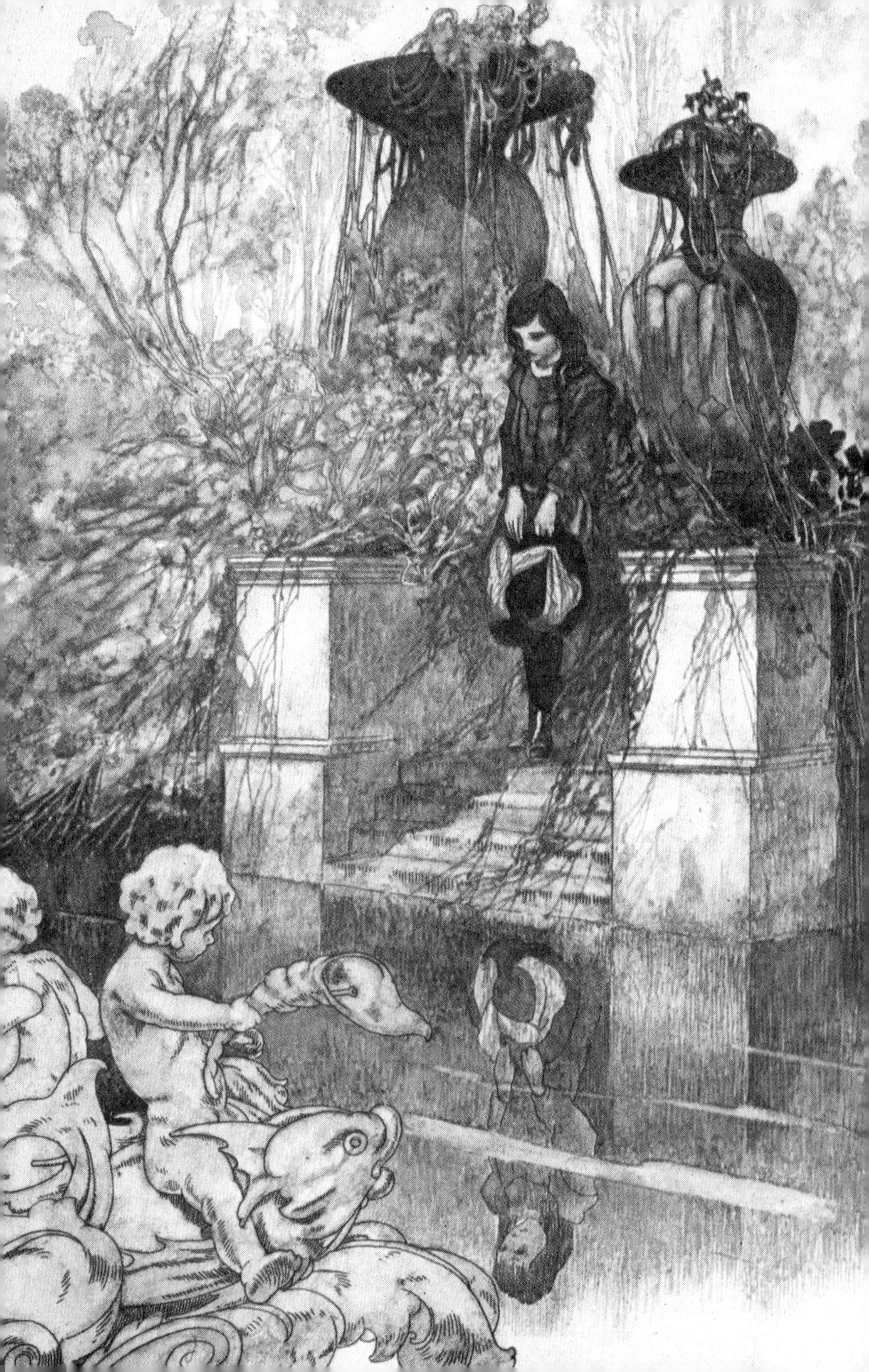

'How still it is!' she whispered. 'How still!'

Then she waited a moment and listened at the stillness. The robin, who had flown to his treetop, was still as all the rest. He did not even flutter his wings; he sat without stirring, and looked at Mary.

'No wonder it is still,' she whispered again. 'I am the first person who has spoken in here for ten years.'

She moved away from the door, stepping as softly as if she were afraid of awakening some one. She was glad that there was grass under her feet and that her steps made no sounds. She walked under one of the fairy-like grey arches between the trees and looked up at the sprays and tendrils which formed them.

'I wonder if they are all quite dead,' she said. 'Is it all a quite dead garden? I wish it wasn't.'

If she had been Ben Weatherstaff she could have told whether the wood was alive by looking at it, but she could only see that there were only grey or brown sprays and branches and none showed any signs of even a tiny leaf-bud anywhere. But she was inside the wonderful garden and she could come through the door under the ivy any time and she felt as if she had found a world all her own.

The sun was shining inside the four walls and the high arch of blue sky over this particular piece of Misselthwaite seemed even more brilliant and soft than it was over the moor. The robin flew down from his treetop and hopped about or flew after her from one bush to another. He chirped a good deal and had a very busy air, as if he were showing her things. Everything was strange and silent and she seemed to be hundreds of miles away from any one, but somehow she did not feel lonely at all. All that troubled her was her wish that she knew whether all the roses were dead, or if perhaps some of them had lived and might put out leaves and buds as the weather got warmer. She did not want it to be a quite dead garden. If it were a quite alive garden, how wonderful it would be, and what thousands of roses would grow on every side!

Her skipping-rope had hung over her arm when she came in and after she had walked about for a while she thought she would skip round the whole garden, stopping when she wanted to look at things. There seemed to have been grass paths here and there, and in one or two corners there were alcoves of evergreen with stone seats or tall moss-covered flower urns in them.

As she came near the second of these alcoves she stopped skipping. There had once been a flowerbed in it, and she thought she saw something sticking out of the black earth--some sharp little pale green points. She remembered what Ben Weatherstaff had said and she knelt down to look at them.

'Yes, they are tiny growing things and they might be crocuses or snowdrops or daffodils,' she whispered. She bent very close to them and sniffed the fresh scent of the damp earth. She liked it very much.

'Perhaps there are some other ones coming up in other places,' she said. 'I will go all over the garden and look.'

She did not skip, but walked. She went slowly and kept her eyes on the ground. She looked in the old border beds and among the grass, and after she had gone round, trying to miss nothing, she had found ever so many more sharp, pale green points, and she had become quite excited again.

'It isn't a quite dead garden,' she cried out softly to herself. 'Even if the roses are dead, there are other things alive.'

She did not know anything about gardening, but the grass seemed so thick in some of the places where the green points were pushing their way through that she thought they did not seem to have room enough to grow. She searched about until she found a rather sharp piece of wood and knelt down and dug and weeded out the weeds and grass until she made nice little clear places around them.

'Now they look as if they could breathe,' she said, after she had finished with the first ones. 'I am going to do ever so many more. I'll do all I can see. If I haven't time today I can come tomorrow.'

She went from place to place, and dug and weeded, and enjoyed herself so immensely that she was led on from bed to bed and into the grass under the trees. The exercise made her so warm that she first threw her coat off, and then her hat, and without knowing it she was smiling down on to the grass and the pale green points all the time.

The robin was tremendously busy. He was very much pleased to see gardening begun on his own estate. He had often wondered at Ben Weatherstaff. Where gardening is done all sorts of delightful things to eat are turned up with the soil. Now here was this new kind of creature who was not half Ben's size and yet had had the sense to come into his garden and begin at once.

Mistress Mary worked in her garden until it was time to go to her midday dinner. In fact, she was rather late in remembering, and when she put on her coat and hat, and picked up her skipping-rope, she could not believe that she had been working two or three hours. She had been actually happy all the time; and dozens and dozens of the tiny, pale green points were to be seen in cleared places, looking twice as cheerful as they had looked before when the grass and weeds had been smothering them.

'I shall come back this afternoon,' she said, looking all round at her new kingdom, and speaking to the trees and the rosebushes as if they heard her. Then she ran lightly across the grass, pushed open the slow old door and slipped through it under the ivy.

❧ A Nation of Gardeners

Deeply learned in garden history, Avray Tipping was one of the most influential garden writers of the 1920s thanks to his regular articles in The Morning Post. *Among the gardens he designed were Chequers in Buckinghamshire, Dartington Hall in Devon and Greynog in Powys. During his term as Architectural Editor of* Country Life, *it changed from a sporting journal to an unrivalled gazetteer of Britain's greatest historic houses and gardens. In his 1933 book* The Garden of Today *he adapted the ideas of the Arts and Crafts gardeners to benefit the small-scale plots belonging to the growing number of suburban gardening enthusiasts.*

As to the variety of schemes, we have, as our basis, all the experience of the past of the ages of both formal and landscape gardens – and we can use what we wish of the one or the other, or of both systems, shaping them in accord with the broad and comprehensive views that mark our present gardening outlook. There seem no limits to the modern Eden that we may imagine in our dreams and even devise. But in practice there is, for most of us, an impassable barrier to wide extent, and that is the purse.

Few, and ever lessening, will be the number who can afford 'grounds' administered by a head gardener with a staff of a dozen or so. To those few this book is not addressed. It aims at being of some assistance to the modest amateur who cultivates his own little Garden of Pleasure.

His name, in our generation, is legion, for we have become a nation of gardeners. The horticultural vogue set in before the War. That checked it, but with the peace it burst out into fuller life. It became on the one hand the country pursuit of many to whom hunting and shooting were extravagances of a past day; on the other hand the outlet for the leisure of the town worker whose garden may be no more than a patch around his suburban dwelling. Thus, as a nation, we have become lovers of the garden in an active sense – not merely casual admirers of professionally conducted gardens, but actual artificers in the making of our own and tillers of it when made.

Such is, indeed, an inborn characteristic of our race. It has had periods of somnolence, but these have been followed by lusty reawakenings.

None, however, has been so lusty as the present one, when we all possess that zest for flower growing and enjoying, which, three centuries ago, animated apothecary Parkinson who, in his Long Acre garden, revelled in 'all sorts of pleasant flowers', and called the newly-come tulip 'the pride of delight'. He is the direct and true ancestor of thousands of ardent amateur gardeners today.

🌺 Even God Would Have to Have a Nose

You might have thought that twentieth-century writers would have abandoned any search for the divine in flowers; and yet 'Red Geranium and Godly Mignonette', by that most sensual of all poets and novelists, D. H. Lawrence, is, in its teasing way, as much a celebration of Eden as anything by Gerard or Parkinson.

Imagine that any mind ever thought a red geranium!
As if the redness of a red geranium could be anything
but a sensual experience
and as if sensual experience could take place
before there were any senses.
We know that even God could not imagine
the redness of a red geranium
nor the smell of mignonette
when geraniums were not, and mignonette neither.
And even when they were,
even God would have to have a nose
to smell at the mignonette.
You can't imagine the Holy Ghost sniffing
at cherry-pie heliotrope.
Or the Most High, during the coal age,
cudgelling his mighty brains
even if he had any brains: straining his mighty mind
to think, among the moss and mud of lizards
and mastodons
to think out, in the abstract,
when all was twilit green and muddy:
'Now there shall be tum-tiddly-um, and tum-tiddly-um,
hey-presto! scarlet geranium!'
We know it couldn't be done.
But imagine, among the mud and the mastodons
God sighing and yearning with tremendous
creative yearning, in that dark green mess
oh for some other beauty, some other beauty
that blossomed at last, red geranium, and mignonette.

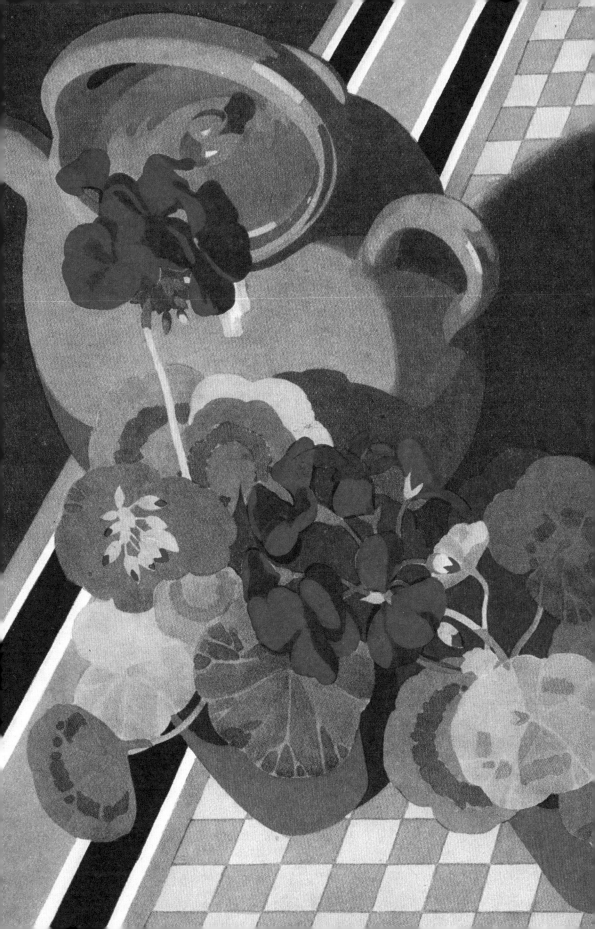

❧ Egoistic Reverie

Unsurprisingly, one of the most popular uses of the garden for literary-minded men and women has always been as a place in which to read and write. I explored many of the books used for this anthology in a shady summerhouse in my own garden, so I felt a natural attraction to writers who enjoy doing the same. Here are three examples of combining literature and gardens. The first is from a letter written by William Cowper; the second is from Edmund Gosse's Gossip in a Library; *and the last is Forbes Sieveking's epilogue to his own splendid gardening anthology* The Praise of Gardens.

WILLIAM COWPER, *LETTER TO MR HILL* (1795)
I write in a nook that I call my boudoir; it is a summerhouse not bigger than a sedan chair; the door of it opens into the garden that is now crowded with pinks, roses, and honey-suckles, and the window into my neighbour's orchard. It formerly served an apothecary as a smoking-room; at present, however, it is dedicated to sublimer uses.

EDMUND GOSSE, *GOSSIP IN A LIBRARY* (1892)
I have heard that the late Mr. Edward Solly, a very pious and worshipful lover of books, under several examples of whose book-plate I have lately reverently placed my own, was so anxious to fly all outward noise that he built himself a library in his garden. I have been told that the books stood there in perfect order, with the rose-spray flapping at the window, and great Japanese vases exhaling such odours as most annoy an insect-nostril. The very bees would come to the window, and sniff, and boom indignantly away again. The silence there was perfect. It must have been in such a secluded library that Christian Mentzelius was at work when he heard the male bookworm flap his wings, and crow like a cock in calling to his mate. I feel sure that even Mentzelius, a very courageous writer, would hardly pretend that he could hear such a 'shadow of all sound' elsewhere. That is the library I should like to have. In my sleep, 'where dreams are multitude,' I sometimes fancy that one day I shall have a library in a garden. The phrase seems to contain the whole felicity of man – 'a library in a garden!' It sounds like having a castle in Spain, or a sheep-walk in Arcadia, and I

suppose that merely to wish for it is to be what indignant journalists call 'a faddling hedonist.'

FORBES SIEVEKING, *THE PRAISE OF GARDENS* (1899)
'And now a last word of egoistic reverie. Where may one indulge in day-dreams, if not in a garden? My dream is of a Library in a Garden! In the very centre of the garden away from house or cottage, but united to it by a pleached alley or pergola of vines or roses, an octagonal book-tower like Montaigne's rises upon arches forming an arbour of scented shade. Between the book-shelves, windows at every angle, as in Pliny's villa library, opening upon a broad gallery supported by pillars of fair carpenter's work, around which cluster flowering creepers, follow the course of the sun in its play upon the landscape. On the last stage of all a glass dome gives gaze upon the stars by night, and the clouds by day... And in this Garden of Books I and my friends would pass the coloured days and the white nights, not in quite blank forgetfulness, but in continuous dreaming, only half-veiled by sleep.'

Envoi: Ferned Grot

T. E. Brown was a Fellow of Oriel College, Oxford and an eminent school-master. A prolific poet, much-enamoured of Manx dialect (he grew up on the Isle of Man), he was also regarded as a notable wit. 'My Garden' appeared in Old John and Other Poems *in 1893.*

A garden is a lovesome thing, God wot!
Rose plot,
Fringed pool,
Ferned grot –
The veriest school of peace: and yet the fool
Contends that God is not –
Not God! In gardens! When the eve is cool?
Nay, but I have a sign:
'Tis very sure God walks in mine.

LIST OF ILLUSTRATIONS

All images are from the collections of the British Library unless otherwise stated.

p. 139 The Gardener, from *The Book of English Trades and Library of Useful Arts*, 1824 (RB.23.a.18153).
p. 140 The Gardener, from *The Child's Coloured Gift Book*, 1867 (12807.ff.15).
p. 145 Children in the garden, from *Sunshine in the Country. A Book of rural poetry embellished with photographs from nature (by Mr Grundy)*, 1861 (1347.f.9).
p. 146 Calendar page for March, from *The Gentlewoman*, March 1897 (Lon 598 NPL).
p. 149 Stripping rough, weedy turf. A. G. Hellyer, *Your New Garden*, 1937 (7029. pp.6).
p. 153 Frontispiece from *Elizabeth and her German Garden*, by Elizabeth von Arnim, illustrated by S. H. Vedder, 1906 (012640.bb.9).
p. 156 Strawberries, from *The Instructive Picture-Book: or Lessons from the Vegetable World* by Charlotte Mary Yonge, 1857 (7028.f.24).
p. 157 from *Hortus Eystettensis* by Basilius Besler, 1613 (10.Tab.29).
p. 159 Mabel, from *At Home* by J. G. Sowerby, illustrated by Thomas Crane, 1881 (12805.k.41).
p. 163 Redcurrants, blackcurrants and gooseberries, from *The Instructive Picture-Book: or Lessons from the Vegetable World* by Charlotte Mary Yonge, 1857 (7028.f.24).
p. 164 Anemone, from *Coloured drawings of plants copied from nature in the Roman States* by Gerardo Cibo, c. 1564–84 (Add. Ms. 22332, f.85).
p. 166 Kazuma Ogawa, *The Hotsuta Garden*, Tokyo, 1880s (Photo 1164.(1)).
p. 169 Krishna and the gopis in the forest, from *Brahmavaivarta Purana*, 1836 (Or.11387, f. 3).
p. 173 Title page to *The Grete Herball*, 1526 (C.27.l.1).
p. 174 from *Coloured drawings of plants copied from nature in the Roman States* by Gerardo Cibo, c. 1564–84 (Add. Ms. 22332, f.85).
p. 176 Title page to *Paradisi in Sole* by John Parkinson, 1629 (C.131.g.18).
p. 180 from *Coloured drawings of plants copied from nature in the Roman States* by Gerardo Cibo, c. 1564–84 (Add. Ms. 22332, f.160).
p. 185 A Snail, from *The Children's Rossetti*, 1914 (11611.de.23).
p. 187 Spring, from the series of prints *Les Quatre Saisons* after Georg Volmar, 1795–1831. British Museum, London.
p. 192 Near Woolwich, drawing by Elizabeth Scharf, 1825 (Add. Ms. 36489A).
p. 197 Title page illustration to *Eugene Aram* by Edward Bulwer-Lytton, 1832 (1208.f.15).
p. 198 Snowdrops and crocuses, from *Temple of Flora* by Robert Thornton, 1799–1807 (10.Tab.40).
p. 207 Peonies, from *The Ladies' flower garden of ornamental perennials* by Mrs Jane Loudon, 1843–4 (722.l.6).
p. 208 Plums, from *Hortus Eystettensis* by Basilius Besler, 1613 (10.Tab.29).
p. 210 Plate from *The Secret Garden* by Frances Hodgson Burnett, illustrated by Charles Robinson, 1911 (0127904.aa.21).
p. 215 Cover illustration to *Metroland*, 1929 edition (W.P.2701).
p. 217 Red geraniums, from *Penrose's Annual*, 1931 (P.P.2495.bd).

INDEX OF AUTHORS

First published in 2014 by
The British Library
96 Euston Road
London NW1 2DB

Cataloguing in Publication Data
A catalogue record for this publication is available from
The British Library

ISBN 978 0 7123 5720 3

Designed and typeset by Briony Hartley, Goldust Design
Printed in Hong Kong by Great Wall Printing Co. Ltd

CREDITS
Page 20: 'On the Way to the Garden' by Robert Bly (trans. from Hafez), from
The Angels Knocking on the Tavern Door by Robert Bly. © Robert Bly. Courtesy of
Archetype, Cambridge. Page 167: Extracts from *Japanese Gardens* by Günter Nitschke
© 2011 TASCHEN GmbH, Hohenzollernring 53, D-50672 Köln, www.taschen.com.
Page 169: Text from *Krsna: The Supreme Personality of Godhead*, courtesy of
The Bhaktivedanta Book Trust International, Inc. www.krishna.com.